Making sense of sport

Sport arouses deep passions. Yet so far, students have lacked an introductory textbook which makes sense of sport by using all the available perspectives. *Making Sense of Sport* fills this gap. Using the disciplines of physiology and anatomy as well as sociology, political science, and history, it offers students an integrated, scientific introduction to sport.

The book defines basic terms in boxed inserts and provides a clear framework for studying key problem areas. Drawing from a whole range of international sports, the analysis helps the reader relate textual discussions with practical settings. Illustrations enable the reader to visualize the theories in the narrative. Further readings and practical assignments make the book the ideal instrument for sport students.

Making sense of sport

Ellis Cashmore

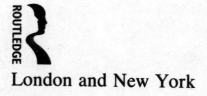

London and New York

First published in 1990
by Routledge
11 New Fetter Lane, London EC4P 4EE

Simultaneously published in the USA and Canada
by Routledge
a division of Routledge, Chapman and Hall, Inc.
29 West 35th Street, New York, NY 10001

© 1990 E. Ellis Cashmore

Typeset by J&L Composition Ltd, Filey, North Yorkshire
Printed and bound in Great Britain by
Biddles Ltd, Guildford and King's Lynn

British Library Cataloguing in Publication Data

Cashmore, Ernest
  Making sense of sport.
  1. Sports
  I. Title
  796

Library of Congress Cataloging in Publication Data also available

ISBN 0–415–02569–9
       0–415–02570–2 (pbk)

Contents

Acknowledgements

Thanks to George Paton and David Podmore, of Aston University, England, for reading and commenting on an early draft of this book, and to Mick Davis for supplying the illustrations.

Introduction

Question: Who would pay to sit for five days watching individuals propel a small leather ball towards three sticks of wood, while another individual defends the sticks with an implement fashioned out of a 3-foot long piece of willow? *Answer:* Billions. Sport is a wondrously puzzling thing; it spellbinds audiences with activities that have no apparent rhyme, less still reason. It reminds us that one of the oldest preoccupations in the world is that of challenge; attempting to surmount obstacles – natural or artificial – has provided people with endless episodes of triumph or folly and, sometimes, disaster. Where the challenges don't exist, we invent them. Sport is a perfect invention because it has challenge, confrontation, and the climactic finality of a result. Someone, or something always wins, loses, or draws.

There's something satisfying, yet oddly discomfiting about this. The idea that someone might play the occasional game of pool or snooker as a mild stimulant, just to get the competitive 'juices' flowing, is understandable enough. But explaining why people will travel great distances, spend small fortunes, and sometimes die in the process not of competing but in watching others compete is confounding. Ask sports' fans why they're prepared to do it and they'll answer, because they enjoy it. That's *their* version; but nothing is what it seems. At least, only until science gets hold of it. After that, the world as it appears masks more than it reveals.

Science goes behind the mask to assess the mechanisms and processes that work to determine and change things, including our thought and behaviour. This in no way denies that people watch football and other sports because they enjoy them. It simply means that this version gives us only a starting point. To make sense of sport, in its its seeming irrationality, and its total lack of logic needs more analysis – and that's precisely what this book provides.

A comprehension of sport needs more than one scientific analysis, so *Making Sense of Sport* has a multidisciplinary approach, combining contributions from behavioural and physical sciences and making bedfellows out of subjects such as biology and sociology, anthropology and history. We need to view sport prismatically: as a kind of splintered structure of perspectives, each of which discloses a different aspect of the same thing. It's not only sport scientists who approach sport like this, of course; fans and performers alike all have their own angles, attach their own meanings, and favour their own interpretations. They're all, in their own ways, fascinated by activities that have little purpose. Why? The next nine chapters contain an answer, or, more accurately, a series of answers.

Chapter one

Naturals

No limits

'A Natural!' We hear the term a lot in sport. Whether it's muttered by a perceptive soccer scout about a schoolboy player, or a tennis coach discerning qualities in the play of an aspiring junior, the meaning is clear: there are some individuals who have properties that suit them ideally for a successful career; properties, in fact, that are wondrous and peculiar, which no amount of training can duplicate in lesser beings. Bernard Malamud's novel, *The Natural*, was a story of one such sports performer, Roy Hobbes, an invincible baseball player.

Actually, we are all 'naturals'; we are all naturally endowed with some capacity for sporting activity. Some, more than others, may possess great mechanical efficiency and skill in performing certain tasks and may even refine these to the point where their expertise appears so effortless as to be the product of a 'gift'. But, on analysis, their mastery is more likely to be the result of painstaking learning than a special inborn ability. All human beings have some natural ability; sport expresses this in exaggerated and often extravagant forms. It provides opportunities to wring from our natural mental and physical equipment behaviour that deviates, frequently quite drastically, from our normal responses. The deviation has, it seems, no limits: runners, rowers, and swimmers cover distances ever faster; gymnasts perform with greater technical perfection; golfers play more accurately.

Those who can't squeeze from their bodies such efforts are often drawn to watch and admire others innovate, sometimes for only seconds. A 100-metre race in Zurich in August 1988 drew television audiences from around the world to watch the two central antagonists, Carl Lewis and Ben Johnson, sprint for exactly 10 seconds (Johnson's losing time). The two rivals reputedly shared $500,000. A Dwight Gooden–Fernando Valenzuela pitching matchup is over in less time than it takes to read a tabloid newspaper, yet American fans clamour to see it; as British fans will to see Ian Rush, whose actual contact with a football is perhaps 15 seconds during the 90 actual minutes of a Liverpool game. No matter what the sport, spectators will go to great lengths and pay money to witness a human performance that may well be over in moments. (A supreme example is Mike Tyson vs Michael Spinks: Tyson wins by KO in the first round; ringside seat price – $500; cost – $5.50 per second!)

The ways in which we watch sporting events, the reasons we watch them, and those whom we watch are shaped by culture, not nature. In other words, we *learn* to appreciate performances, just as competitors learn basic techniques and styles on which they later innovate. The sports fan is like an art critic who acquires a knowledge of what to look for, how to evaluate, the meaning of specific moves. The performer needs not only knowledge, but a physical mastery, a skill. This involves lengthy and, sometimes, complex processes in which he or she is made to call into service devices, ingenuities, and powers that might have gone completely

> **Culture**
> Often used in contrast to *nature*, this refers to the learnt traditions that are socially acquired and appear among mammals, especially primates. Human culture means the lifestyle of a group of people, including their patterned, repetitive ways of thinking, behaving, and even feeling. These ways are picked up through learning experiences rather than through natural inheritance. The classical anthropologist, Edward B. Tylor, in his book *Primitive Culture* (first published in 1871 by J. Murray) proposed a definition of culture that included 'knowledge, belief, art, morals and habits acquired by man as a member of society'. This is a very inclusive definition and others prefer to restrict the use of 'cultural' to refer to *rules* for thought and behaviour and regard the ways in which the rules are put into practice as 'social'.

undiscovered had the performer not been encouraged, influenced or even forced in some way to develop them. During this time, a sports competitor undergoes physical and mental changes and learns to control his or her bodily movements, in many cases synchronizing body movements with inanimate objects, like rackets and balls. In this way, sport is learned.

But, it's also completely natural, for without the basic anatomical and behavioural equipment, one couldn't perform even the simplest operations, let alone the more complicated manoeuvres needed for a sporting performance. There are limiting 'givens' in the physical make-up of humans, just as there are in those of other animals. Humans have succeeded in overcoming all manner of limitations set by nature, basically by creating and employing technologies (though it should be noted that they are not alone in this achievement; many other species use technologies, though not on the scale of humans).

Technology has assisted sporting performance and has been integrated into most spheres of sporting activity. Yet what is technology but an extension of natural human capabilities? Not that we're born with poles to help us vault, or surfboards to ride, or rifles to fire: these are artifacts – manufactured, accumulated and transmitted; their use is communicated from person to person, from one generation to the next. Essential to these processes is a set of physical equipment: a brain large and complex enough to imagine a product, movable limbs and prehensile hands and feet to create and utilize it, and an acute sense of sight to envisage the product and gauge distance. These properties are not unique to humans, but the way in which they are combined in the human

---

Determinism
This is a doctrine that states that internal or external forces impinge on the human will propelling us to think and act in specific ways. To be biologically determined would mean to be under the influence of factors that we inherit rather than learn. It follows that action is never spontaneous but always caused by factors beyond the individual's capacity to influence. Ideas about 'free will' are misguided according to this doctrine.

---

species is very particular and is resembled only in other higher primates, namely monkeys and apes. The question is: what is it about the special combination in *humans* that enables them to develop the potentialities of their animal nature to levels far removed from other species? Sport, as I will argue in detail later, has only been possible because of such advanced developments; other animals engage in activity that looks like sport, but isn't. Pursuing this logic, not only sport, but religion, industry, warfare, education and so on – all conventionally regarded as social institutions – are grounded in our animal origins and biologically determined behaviour. Thus, the entire discipline of physical (or biological) anthropology is dedicated to the task of assessing the relative contributions to social life made by heredity and environment. Sociology may, in a very different way, examine the same things, but finds the former approach too reductionist in its attempt to break down, or reduce, phenomena into their constituent parts to understand them. In a sociological perspective, the human effort to challenge, manipulate or transcend physical and biological facts of life gives rise to distinct patterns of thought and behaviour which cannot necessarily be explained by reference to biological factors alone, but needs some analysis of the interactions between humans and between them and their natural environment. From these interactions, events and processes emerge that defy explanation in purely biological terms.

Between the two disciplinary perspectives, there is a whole range of diverse attempts to describe and analyse human behaviour, each with its own version of causes and theories about the origins of elements of human life. In the course of this book, I will consider several of them and assess what contribution they may make to our understanding of just one element – sport.

Seven keys

Stripped to their bare elements, human beings are mobile, multi-celled organisms that derive their motive force from eating other

---

Reductionism
A method for analysing phenomena based on the philosophy that matter is best understood once divided into its component parts. So, human societies can be approached in terms of individual beings, who in turn may be reduced to genes, which in turn may be reduced further and so on. In other words, complex phenomena can only be fully understood by isolating their parts. Critics argue that the 'sum of the parts' is frequently not the same as the 'whole' and that there are *emergent* qualities produced when all the elements come together, which are distinct and need to be analysed as a whole. ('How can one understand something like fashion by reducing it to its component parts?' they might ask, adding that it becomes meaningful only when everything comes together.) This approach is known as *holism*.

---

organisms. In taxonomic terms, humans are animalia, as distinct from members of the plant kingdom, bacteria, single-celled organisms, and fungi. So, we have a great many characteristics in common with other animals, especially those with whom we share common ancestors, our closest evolutionary relatives being other primates, a taxon that includes monkeys, apes, lemurs, tarsiers, and others. There are seven key characteristics of primates that set them apart from the rest of the living world and afford them special advantages for survival. Humans have extra-special advantages, but, for the moment, we will focus on similarities. The seven features are: an ability to grip and control; relatively great strength of limb; stereoscopic eyes positioned at the front of the head; small numbers of offspring; a high degree of interdependence and a corresponding tendency towards living in groups; a use of reliable, efficient communication systems; and a large brain relative to body size. Now, let us deal with each of these key characteristics in more detail.

All primates have prehensile hands and feet: they can catch, grip, and hold, thanks to relatively long, flexible digits. The ability

---

Taxon
A group in a classification system, usually referring to a genus, species, or subspecies. The science of classifying is called *taxonomy*. The term *Homo sapiens*, meaning literally 'wise man', is taken from the work of the Swedish botanist Linnaeus, who, in 1735, published a vast taxonomic system for classifying all living beings.

---

to grip and control is enhanced by opposable thumbs or big toes which make it possible to lock around objects rigidly and so control an object's movement, as a golfer carefully guides the arc of a club's swing. From an evolutionary point of view, the origins of prehensility are not difficult to trace: distinguishing primates from other mammals was their tree-dwelling capacity. Prehensile hands and feet were useful for climbing up and down and to and from trees in forests, and additionally for plucking fruits and berries and overturning stones to pick up insects to eat.

The ability to grip is complemented by a strong versatile set of fore limbs. Suspending full body weight and swinging needs extremely powerful, long arms and legs. The very specialized functions of arms and legs for primates are reflected not only in the size and heavy muscle of the limbs, but in their range of movement: they can flex (bend), extend, and rotate. Combined with the dexterity of the hands and feet this assists fast, multidirectional travel sometimes over great distances. Gymnasts offer examples of how this ability has not been completely lost despite the human's transition from the trees to the ground.

Related to this mobility is the position of the eyes, which are typically to the front rather than the sides of the head. Two eyes enable stereoscopic vision, which permits reasonably accurate estimates of distances. The sense of vision is highly developed in primates, as opposed to, say, dogs which see the world in monochrome, but have sensitive snouts and use their acute sense of smell as their chief source of information about their environments. It's no accident that no sport is based on smelling or sniffing ability, whereas a great many are organized around the ability to gauge distance and co-ordinate hand movements accordingly, archery and shooting being obvious examples. (It seems feasible to imagine that humans, who are sensitive to smell, might devise a sport in which an acute sense of smell is employed in conjunction with other capacities; a modified form of orienteering perhaps!)

With other primates, humans share a tendency to give birth to one or two infants at a time; larger births are known, of course, but they are deviations from the norm. Mammals that have large litters lose some offspring at, or shortly after, birth. Primates have a smaller number of births, usually after a relatively long pregnancy, and accentuate the role of the mother in caring for and protecting the infant in an environment uncomplicated by the kind of competition that comes from large litters.

One very important consequence of having small families with intense mother–infant contact is that primates learn interdependence. They rely on each other far more than many other species which are abandoned at a young age and learn to adapt and survive individually, or else perish. Primates, by contrast, never learn the skills associated with lone survival. Having a protective mother, the infant has no need of such skills. What an infant does acquire is an ability to co-operate and communicate with others. And this helps explain why primates spend their lives in groups, caring for and co-operating with others. Individual survival for humans as well as other primates is a matter of communicating effectively in groups. Hence all primates are gregarious: they grow and mature socially and not in isolation. Very few sports do not reflect this; most are organized in terms of a club structure with high degrees of interdependence and mutual co-operation needed. Even fabled long-distance runners need coaches to plan their training and other competitors to make their racing meaningful.

A lifetime spent in the company of others on whom one has to depend for survival necessitates a high degree of communication. The process of inculcating communication skills begins with the passing of auditory, visual, and tactile (touch) signals from mother to infant. It continues through life; in fact, group life is contingent on the successful storage and transmission of large volumes of information. At its simplest level, the warning conveys perhaps the single most important communication for survival. The human cry of 'Fire!' imparts much the same effect as a screech of a panicking baboon. In both cases the first communicator supposes the recipients have some facility for recalling the image of impending danger.

It seems that the necessity of communicating and the ability to do so quickly and efficiently has a connection with the large size of the brain of the primate compared to other mammals. Human beings have the largest brains and are clearly the most adept at communicating. They are, as a direct result, most developed socially. A growth in the size of the human brain can be traced back to two periods. The first, between 1.6 and 2 million years ago, witnessed a rapid expansion in cranial capacity, a change which accompanied the origin of what we now call *Homo erectus* (probably in Africa) and the use of new types of primitive tools. Bipedalism emerged as a result of a transference from the trees to the ground; the change in habitat necessitated a behavioural adaptation in posture and, eventually, an anatomical change of great significance, particularly in relation to arms and hands which were no longer employed to suspend the body and could be used for many other purposes.

Anthropological evidence suggests that the size of the typical skull then remained stable for about 1.3 million years, before a second, sudden increase in brain size. The appearance of *Homo sapiens* about 0.2 or 0.3 million years ago was followed by a burst of cultural change in the spheres of manufacture, settlement, and subsistence. This is important as there is much contention about the precise relationship between the growth of what is now the *human* brain and changes in habitat and activity. What is absolutely certain is that there is some form of close relationship, though the direction and way in which it worked is still in dispute.

The idea of a spontaneous expansion is not supportable. More plausible is a scenario in which the actual size of the brain after the advent of *Homo erectus* stayed the same, but the number of brain cells and neural pathways between them continued to increase. This made it possible for *Homo erectus* to become a more effective bipedal hunter and gatherer, operating at the time of day when other predatory creatures (and, therefore, competitors) were sheltering from the intensely hot midday sun. Growing extra brain cells, in this interpretation, was a defence mechanism against the harmful effects of the sun's rays on the brain; that is, the human grew bigger brains, leaving many of the cells redundant, as mere 'fail safe' devices in the tropical heat. This might well have established a neural potential for more sophisticated communication and imaginative thought, which, in turn, stimulated a phase of modifying physical environments rather than adapting to them. The phase marks the beginning of sport as we will see later in chapter 3. One often hears of triathletes who swim, cycle, and run for 13 hours or more, sometimes in hot atmospheres, described as 'mad'. Ironically, they may be demonstrating the extraordinary adaptive brilliance of the human brain in acquiring an ability to function effectively all day in extreme climates. The adaptation dates back to *Homo erectus'* pursuit of game animals.

The human edge: language

The exact causes of the human brain's exponential growth may prompt argument. Beyond this is the fact that this organ is responsible for what many insist is a qualitative difference between *Homo sapiens* and the rest of the animalia. The enlarged neural capacity introduced the possibility of ever-more elaborate forms of communication. The physiology of the human ear and vocal tract meant that audial messages could be sent with a high probability that they would be received with reasonable efficiency. These elements, combined with the enhanced capacity for imaginative thinking, laid the foundations for human language and, by implication, new systems of word-associated thought.

Language assists the accumulation of information to be stored in the brain and confirms the awareness that other humans have similar stores of information. At the blandest level, we might ask how a cricket match would be possible unless the players were cognizant of the rules and aware that all other players had the same knowledge. Any sport has the same prerequisite. Without language or, at least, some derivative communication system, abstract rules would not be possible; nor, therefore, would sport.

Humans are not alone in being able to pass on knowledge from one generation to another and so perpetuate cultures, but they have the special ability to add to, or recreate cultures whereas other primates merely inherit and receive. A verbal language as opposed to sign-based systems of communication makes this possible. Culture, we should note, refers to anything acquired and transmitted by learning and not by physical inheritance. While other animals most certainly maintain recognizable cultures, even higher apes are quite limited in their capacity to communicate and, as a result, do not pass on a vast amount of experience to new generations. The transmission has to be direct and immediate (for example, modelling and imitation); apes lack the linguistic capability to standardize, encode, classify, and concentrate meanings and experience. By contrast, humans can transmit sometimes quite abstract meanings through several generations without any significant loss of informational accuracy. Ancient Greeks (from c.3000 BC) left a largess of information about themselves in the form of inscriptions, mostly on walls or clay tablets. A comprehension of these inscriptions tells us that the Greeks pursued athletics in a recognizable, rule-governed form more than any other ancient culture. Language which articulates this information is such that we can actually use it to project into the future. A future tense permits the communication of imaginative schemes and the transmission of such activities as sport. The unique elements of human language that provide for this type of knowledge of ancient cultures almost certainly arise from our genetic adaptations related to social co-operation and interdependence and changing patterns of subsistence. We have the neural equipment for picking up language; that much is clear. Less clear is the reason for the bewildering diversity of human cultures. Our biological equipment scarcely changes at all over time and space; languages, customs, religions, laws, etc. vary greatly from society to society and from one time period to another.

The suggestion is that, once acquired, the developed language and the new styles of thought it ushers in, launches its users into all manner of trajectories. Humans plan and create complex organizations and institutions of a quite different quality and order than those found among other animals. Obviously these elaborate phenomena are ultimately dependent on biological factors; but their accomplishment can't be exclusively traced to biological equipment and inheritance.

My prehensility and neural circuitry make it possible for me to write this book; but, there are countless other non-physical influences on my ability and disposition to write – and on your willingness to read. The very concept of a book to be produced and used reflects an extremely sophisticated and unique level of communication. Books are needed for records, and records have been vital to the evolution of sport. Any balanced comprehension of sport clearly needs a range of scientific approaches: one '-ology' isn't enough. We must refer to hereditary nature; but equally we must examine environmental life experience, how organisms react to physical conditions surrounding them. Between the gene and the environment, there are all sorts of intervening factors and processes that must be studied if we are to reach an understanding.

The biological characteristics which distinguish humans from other animals – bipedalism, prehensility, large and more complicated brains, and language – are necessary conditions for culture-building. Necessary, but by no means sufficient. Yet in recognizing this, we must at least begin our analysis of sport with a scenario: creative human beings striving to satisfy at least the minimal requirements for subsistence while subjected to the physical constraints imposed by their own biology and the material world around them. Their primary needs are to produce food, shelter, tools, and to reproduce human populations. Unless they can complete these tasks, they will have no opportunity to believe in religions and ethics, create political and economic systems, engage in war, or perform any of the other activities associated with culture. These activities, almost by definition, depend to some extent on genetically predetermined capacities. It follows that an aesthetic, expressive, and intellectual cultural activity such as sport must be a response to physical constraints and conditions. In the next two chapters, I will approach sport as such a response. Beginning with a breakdown of the physical constraints and conditions, I will address the issue of how sporting performance is physically possible. From 'how' I move to 'why', specifically asking the reasons for humans' attraction to sporting endeavours. An answer to this first requires us to look at human efforts to survive and subsist in their material environment and how these efforts have effects on their total life experiences.

Further reading

Culture, People, Nature, *5th edn, by Marvin Harris (Harper & Row, 1988) is an introduction to general anthropology and a model of clarity. Harris favours a materialist approach which complements the one taken in this book. His view is that the shaping of thought and behaviour is the outcome of adaptations to ecological conditions. Taking a Darwinian starting point, Harris argues: 'As a result of natural selection, organisms may be said to become* adapted *to the needs and opportunities present in their environments.' And further: 'All individuals are the products of the interaction of their genes and their environment.' More extreme versions of materialism would insist that thought and behaviour can be understood by studying the constraints to which human existence is subjected; these constraints arise from the need to produce food, shelter, tools, and machines and to reproduce human populations within the limits set by biology and the environment.*

Human Evolution *by Graham Richards (Routledge & Kegan Paul, 1987) provides a clear and thorough introduction to the behavioural sciences, covering aspects of human evolution, including the development of bipedalism, language, and tool use. It has a useful section on 'Throwing and tool-making' in which the author observes 'the ubiquity of aimed-throwing games among human males', a practice which seems to have emerged around 2.5 million years ago.*

Beast and Man: the Roots of Human Nature *by Mary Midgley (Methuen, 1979) considers the various factors contributing to the unique 'human nature' paying attention to the perennial but unanswerable nature vs nurture question.*

Sociobiology: the New Synthesis *by E. O. Wilson (Harvard University Press, 1975) is a hugely ambitious attempt to explain differences and similarities in living forms by reference to the tendency to optimize reproductive success. A central principle states that natural selection favours characteristics that disperse an individual's genes by increasing the number of offspring of close relatives who carry many of the same genes. This is called* inclusive fitness. *Wilson's arguments have been criticized by many who oppose his emphasis on biological factors rather than social, or cultural ones.*

Assignment

'Between the gene and the environment, there are all sorts of intervening factors that must come under consideration' (from page 10). List as exhaustively as possible the factors and processes that contribute to the creation of what we might regard as 'natural' sports performers; in other words, the kinds of factors and processes that show that performers *learn* as much as they inherit.

Chapter two

A performance machine

All systems 'go' – for 48.42 seconds

10 August 1988: the body of 22-year-old Matt Biondi breaks the water of a pool at Austin, Texas. Moments later, Biondi fully surfaces, having travelled a hundred metres through water faster than any other human. In 48.42 seconds, Biondi has set in motion processes and mechanisms of immense complexity: his every muscle has contracted, stretched and twisted; his lungs have filled and emptied repeatedly; his heart has pumped about 30 litres of blood into all areas of the body. All this has been made possible by the intricate organizing and synchronizing capacity of his brain, which has submitted his entire body to one purpose for the duration of the race, the performance.

Question anyone who has witnessed a sports event firsthand, or even on television, and they will be unlikely to disagree that the essence of sport lies in the actual sporting performance. The moment when competitive humans bring to an end their preparations and make visible their self-willed mastery of a particular set of skills is an engaging experience that easily surpasses reading reports, watching interviews, studying form, or any of the other ancillary activities associated with sport. The performance itself occupies centre stage in sport. And while the stage itself – its structure, scenery and props, and the audience – will occupy our attention in the pages to follow, we must provide some analysis of the performance before progressing. Actually, 'performance' is too abstract for present purposes: we should properly focus our sights on the *performer*, whose actions take precedence over all other events, at least for the duration of the contest. When we watch sports, we watch bodies move: the peaks of even a chess game are when the players extend their arms to propel pieces across the board.

So, what makes bodies move? It's an obvious, fundamental question, but one which needs a precise answer and I will at least

13

approach one by offering a portrait. Specifically, I will offer a physical portrait; one in which the structure of the human organism and the functions of its various components will be analysed with a view to understanding how they all interact in the enactment of sporting performance. What constitutes a 'sporting performance'? Let's return to our example.

Imagine Biondi as a series of systems, interacting so as to produce motion. When the starter's gun fires, Biondi's central nervous system receives the signal and very rapidly relays messages to his muscular system which is stimulated to move by electrical impulses. Muscular contractions move his limbs mechanically, this being made possible by the fact that the muscles are attached to the bones of Biondi's skeleton, which is yielding, yet tough enough to withstand the stress of movement without fracturing. Fuel is needed for the performer to be able to repeat the motion and this comes via breathing, circulation, and digestion; once burned up, the waste matter of fuel has to be disposed of.

Viewed as a lump of matter, Biondi's body is a bundle of about 60 billion living units called cells, each of which has the same basic structure, comprising membrane (which holds the unit together), ribosomes (which manufacture proteins), lysosomes (which destroy harmful substances and diseased parts of the cell), golgi complex (which stores endoplasmic substance), reticulum (which transports substances throughout a cell), cytoplasm (which is the liquid in which the other elements float), mitochondria (which are power-houses, where oxygen and food react to produce vital energy to keep the cell alive) and a nucleus (which contains the chromosomes carrying coded instructions for the workings of the cell). Cells often cluster together to form other substances, such as tissue and muscle (which comprises 50 per cent of cells, being a type of tissue) and these tissues can also work in groups to become organs (heart and lungs, for instance). When organs operate together to perform a particular function, like transporting blood around the body, we usually talk in terms of systems. For a swimmer like Biondi to perform at his maximum, all his systems need to be working maximally and synchronously. For our purposes – which are heuristic in this instance – we will probe the body as if it were a series of systems acting interdependently. A logical first step is to ask how a swimmer, or indeed, any living animal is able to move at all and here we're drawn to an examination of the skeletal and muscular systems.

Moving the skeleton

The skeleton isn't just a framework, an elaborate coat hanger on which we drape skin and muscle. It's a rather elaborate, living

> **Heuristic**
> Usually refers to a device or strategy that serves to stimulate investigation. It doesn't attempt to describe reality, but assists in discovery, often by way of analogy or metaphor. Analysing human behaviour by using the metaphors of a vast drama or perhaps a competitive game would be examples of heuristic devices.

structure that serves four important functions: protection, support, storage, and movement. Structurally, it has two aspects: the axial comprises the skull, backbone, ribs and sternum; the appendicular refers to appendages (legs and arms), the pelvic girdle (to which the legs are attached), and the pectoral girdle (to which the arms are connected). In total, there are over 200 bones.

The human brain is disproportionately large compared to those of other mammals and, together with the spinal cord, controls in large part the movements of the whole body. As a complex, yet delicate, piece of equipment, it needs maximum protection: *ergo* the skull (or cranium), a resilient helmet composed of plates of bone fused together to form a hard casing around the brain. The interstices between the bones are called sutures and allow growth in the size of the brain until around the age of 20, after which they weld together. The skull affords sufficient protection for the brain in most activities, although motor sports, hang gliding and other sports in which the risk of direct collision is high (e.g. American football, cricket and cycling) utilize headgear for additional protection.

The other main part of the central nervous system, the spine, also needs the protection of bone; in this case a long, flexible column of vertebrae separated by discs of cartilage. In functional terms, the spine represents a remarkable adaptation, affording protection to a sensitive cable of nerves that runs from the brain to all areas of the body. The spine is articulate so as to permit the movement and flexibility so necessary to survival. This flexibility is bought at a cost, for in certain parts of the back the spine has little or no support. Hence weight lifters strap broad belts around their waists so as to maintain rigidity in and give support to the vulnerable areas of their lower back when it is likely to be exposed to stress. Some other sensitive organs, like the lungs and heart are also given skeletal protection, but, unlike some vertebrates (armadillos and tortoises), humans have discarded external physical protection and rely more on the wit and ingenuity that derives from the large brain, and the fleetness of foot made possible by bipedalism to protect themselves.

The conventional notion of the skeleton as a means of support is true for the majority of bones. But this needs qualification. The bony material itself is not solid, but is a composite of collagen protein fibres and inorganic mineral crystals ordered in a meshwork of cylindrical layers not dissimilar to a 'crunchie' bar. This honeycombed arrangement prevents brittleness and gives bone some degree of elasticity: should stress be applied, bone distributes it to prevent a concentration. Excessive stress will cause cracks or breaks, of course, but bone's yielding capacity, or 'give', reduces the danger of breakage. These qualities make it ideal as a supporting apparatus because it combines tensile strength with the yield needed for a wide range of motions.

As a general principle, the heavier the load a bone must bear, the greater its diameter must be. Human thigh bones, or femur, are large, as are tibia and fibula connecting the knee to the foot; they are responsible for supporting the upper body weight. But, while the femur has some protection from the quadriceps, the tibia and fibula are exposed and may need artificial cushioning from direct knocks in sports like soccer and hockey.

The skeleton can support effectively only if it grows in

16

correspondence with the rest of the body. And bone does grow; it receives food and oxygen from blood vessels. New layers of tissue encircle existing material and form new bone, thus increasing the diameter (growth in length ceases before the age of twenty). Bone grows in response to force, as does muscle. Bend, twist, compress, load, or combine these and, over time, the bone will grow to meet its task and fulfil its function, within limits, of course. It will react to certain pressures or movements by fracturing, breaking, or shearing. (When this happens, cells in the outer layer of the bone – the periosteum – multiply and grow over the break, joining the two parts together.) At the other extreme, bone will lose mass if deprived of function.

Stored inside bone are the minerals calcium and potassium which are delivered to the cells by blood (and which give bone its hardness) and marrow, a soft jelly-like tissue that produces red and white blood cells.

The fourth major function of the skeleton – and the most important for our purposes – is that of providing mechanical levers for movement. Bones are connected to each other at joints which serve as axes for rotation. For instance, the forearm, the upper-arm bone, or the humerus, acts as a fulcrum, and the radius and ulna as a lever. The elbow joint, which is a hinge, makes possible a simple range of movement; flexion (bending) and extension (stretching). Other joints, like the biaxial (between forearm and wrist and at the knee), the pivot (at the wrist), and the ball-and-socket (at the shoulder and hip) are more complicated arrangements and permit multiple movements in different planes and directions. Were the joint a manufactured piece of equipment, the articular surfaces would grind together and need the addition of lubricants. The human body takes care of this by interposing a film of lubricating fluid between opposing bone surfaces (in which case, they are called synovial joints), or by sandwiching a tough pad of gristle between articulating bones (cartilaginous joints). An engineer would love this natural bearing which reduces friction.

Cartilage belongs to a class of connective tissues which, as the name suggests, joins or ties together the various parts of the body and makes movement smooth. Its capacity isn't limitless, however, and cartilage can wear out. Ligaments, which are flexible collagen bands that connect and support joints, are also liable to wear-and-tear, especially amongst sports performers, such as throwers or shot putters, who maximize the intensity or repetition of stresses on shoulder and elbow joints and are therefore prone to sprains (torn ligaments) and dislocations of joints.

Perhaps the most troublesome connective tissue for sports

competitors is tendon, which is basically a collagen cable that joins muscle to bone and so transmits the pull, which makes the bone move. Tendons make it possible to use a muscle to move a bone at a distance. In the case of fingers, which are clearly vital in dextrous activities (e.g. table tennis, darts, and spin-bowling in cricket), we need muscular control of the fine movements without the invasive presence of muscles at the immediate site. Were the necessary muscles attached directly to the finger bones, the size of the digits would be so large that catching, holding, or even forming a fist would be a problem. Without the action permitted at distance by slender tendons, primate prehensility would be severely restricted.

The way the skeleton is framed and its levers fitted together gives the body the potential for a great variety of movement through all planes. But we still need to analyse the source of its motion. Plainly stated, muscle moves our bones; it does so with two actions, contraction and relaxation. Usually, the arrangement features tendons connecting bones to one or more muscles which are stimulated by nerves to contract, causing the tendons to tighten and the bone to move. (Some muscles appear to be attached directly to bone, obviating the need for tendons, but motion is accomplished by basically the same process.)

Muscle use is present in every sporting activity, right from sprinting where muscles are maximally in use, to playing chess where muscles function perhaps only to position eyeballs in their sockets or to move a finger by inches. The various types of muscle present in humans differ in structure and properties, but the striated muscle, which acts as the motor of the skeleton, is our chief concern. Striated muscle is under our control in the sense that we voluntarily induce its contraction and hence movement. Other types of muscles contract in the absence of nerve stimulation: cardiac (heart) muscle, for example, contracts independently of our will and has the property of 'inherent rhythmicity' (we will return to this later).

Skeletal muscle consists of fibres, which are long tubes that run parallel to each other and are encased in sheaths of the ubiquitous collagen. Each fibre is made up of strands called myofibrils, which are themselves composed of two types of interlocking filaments. Thick filaments are made of a protein called myosin and thin ones of actin, and they are grouped in a regular, repeated pattern, so that, under the microscope, they give a striated, or streaky, appearance. The lengths of myosin and actin filaments are divided into units called sarcomeres, the size of which is recognized as the distance between two 'Z-lines' (the structures to which the actin filaments are attached).

Although the filaments can't change length, they can slide past each other to produce the all-important contraction. We will see later how messages from the central nervous system are taken to muscles by nerve impulses. When such an impulse reaches a muscle fibre with the instruction 'Move!' energy is released in mitochondria and the filaments move closer together, shortening the muscle. As they pass, a chemical reaction occurs in which: 1) calcium is released from storage in the tubular bundles; 2) in the calcium's presence, myosin molecules from the thicker filaments form bonds with the actin filaments; 3) the myosin molecule is then thought to undergo a change in shape, yanking the actin filaments closer together; 4) the contraction of the muscle fibre ends when the calcium ions are pumped back into storage so as to prevent the formation of new chemical bonds. The effect of the contraction is a pull on the bones to which the muscles are attached and, as the four phases take no more than a few thousandths of a second, we are capable of mechanical movements at very high speed. The flexion and extension of boxer Henry Cooper's famous left hook, ''Enery's 'ammer', was timed in terms of hundredths of a second. Such a punch, which had a concussing effect, required a great force of movement, so many fibres would have been required to contract together at speed. A golfer's putt, by contrast, would involve fewer fibres.

In both instances, opposing, or antagonistic pairs of muscles would be working to allow free movement. For the hook or the putt, biceps muscle would contract to bend the elbow, which its opposing member, the triceps, would relax. To straighten the arm, the triceps need to contract, while biceps relax. Muscles are equipped with special receptors that let the brain know the extent of contraction and the position in three-dimensional space without having to look constantly to check. We can close our eyes, but know the movement and position of our limbs.

The 206 bones of the adult skeletal system form a protective casing for the brain and the spinal cord, a sturdy internal framework to support the rest of the body, and a set of mechanical levers that can be moved by the action of muscles. All of these make the human body a serviceable locomotive machine for walking, running, and, to a lesser degree, swimming, climbing, and jumping. But, like other machines, the body depends on fuel supply for its power, a method for burning the fuel, and a system for transporting the waste products away. Again, the human body has evolved systems for answering all these needs.

Not by food alone: energy

As a living organism, the human being depends on energy. Plants get by with light and water; animals need food. In particular, humans need protein (built up of chemical units called amino acids), carbohydrates (comprising sugars which provide most of our energy), lipids (or fats for storage and insulation), vitamins (about fifteen types to assist various chemical processes), minerals (like iron and zinc), and water (to replace liquids). These provide raw energy sources that drive the machinery of the body; that is, making the compounds that combine with oxygen to release energy, and ensure the growth and repair of tissues. (The combination with oxygen will be dealt with later.) Obtaining food is of such vital importance to survival that the entire plan of the human body is adapted to its particular mode of procuring food. Sport, as I will argue later, reflects our primitive food-procurement even to this day. For the moment, we need to understand not so much the way in which food is obtained, but how it is used. In their original forms, most of the above substances are unusable to human beings. So we have evolved mechanisms for rendering them usable as energy sources. Processing food is the function of the digestive system, which consists of a long, coiled tube, called the digestive tract, and three types of accessory glands.

Typically, food is introduced to the body through the mouth where it is chewed, pulped, and mixed with saliva in a process of ingestion. After being formed into lumps, it is swallowed and drops into the pharynx (throat) and, then, to the epiglottis, which is a small valve that closes off the windpipe. Water falls under the force of gravity, but food is ushered along by a wave of muscular contractions called peristalsis. Fibres in the wall of the oesophagus tube (gullet) push the food downwards to the stomach (which explains why cosmonauts can still eat in the absence of gravity).

From here, the food passes into the stomach, a sausage-shaped organ which can expand to hold about two pints' capacity. At this stage, a churning process starts in which the food is mixed with mucus, hydrochloric acid, and enzymes (chemical substances that speed up processes, in this instance, the breaking up of protein). The effect of this is to liquefy the food, so that, after between three and four hours the churned-up mass (called chyme), which now resembles a cream soup, gets transferred, via peristaltic waves, to the stomach's exit point and then to the duodenum which is the first chamber of the small intestine. Contrary to popular belief, it is here rather than the stomach, where most of the chemical digestion gets done: bile from the liver and enzymes from the pancreas are released. (An exception is alcohol, which is readily absorbed in the stomach and doesn't pass through.)

A note here about the role of the brain in regulating the discharge of naturally-secreted juices that aid digestion: seeing, smelling, tasting, or even thinking about food can stimulate the brain to send messages to the glands in the mouth and stomach to release a hormone called gastrin that is quickly absorbed into the blood and then to glands where it triggers the release of gastric juice. Hence sports competitors who chew gum to enhance their concentration are usually doing a disservice to their stomachs by producing gastric juices when there is no food. Gastric juices have enough acidity and protein-splitting capacity to burn human flesh. The stomach has natural protection against this, although resistances can be lowered by alcohol or aspirin and by over-producing the juices when no food is available. A possible result is an open sore in the wall of the stomach, or a duodenal ulcer.

Lymph

A body fluid derived from the blood and tissue and returned to the circulatory system in *lymphatic* vessels. At intervals along the vessels there are *lymph glands* which manufacture anti-bodies and lymphocytes that destroy bacteria. The lymph system has no pump like the blood system and the movement of lymph is brought about largely by pressure from contracting skeletal muscles, backflow being prevented by valves.

The lymph system doubles as the body's immune system in that it produces proteins called antibodies, lying at the surface of certain white blood cells (lymphocytes). When needed, antibodies and cells rush into the blood stream and 'round up' the harmful bacteria and viruses. While the lymph system can make thousands of antibodies, its vital adversaries are constantly mutating so as to find ways of defeating it, as the Aids pandemic indicates.

Basically, the idea is to reduce the parts of the food that can be profitably used by the body (the nutrients) to molecular form and allow them to seep through the cells lining the long digestive tube, through the minuscule blood or lymph vessels in the stomach wall and into the blood or lymph. All the cells of the body are bathed in a fluid called lymph. Exchanges between blood and cells take place in lymph. Lymph is derived from blood, though it has a kind of circulatory system of its own, filtering through the walls of capillaries, then moving along channels of its own (lymphatics), which join one another and steer eventually to the veins, in the process surrendering their contents to the general circulatory system. Food is absorbed through the wall of the intestine which is covered in villi, tiny absorbant 'fingers' that give the tube a vast surface area. Not all food passes directly into blood vessels: the lymphatics are responsible for collecting digested fats and transporting them to the thoracic duct which empties into one of the large veins near the heart.

Once absorbed the nutrients are carried in the blood and lymph to each individual cell in the body where they are used up, that is, metabolized. The residue of indigestible or unabsorbed food is eliminated from the body by way of the large intestine. En route, bacteria in the large intestine feed on vestiges and, in return produce certain vitamins which are absorbed and used. Some of the unwanted water is converted to urea and passed out via the bladder. The body has precise control over what it needs for nutrition, growth, and repair. One of the many functions of the liver is to store surplus nutrients and release them together to meet immediate requirements. This large abdominal organ receives digested food from the blood and reassembles its molecules in such a way as to make them usable to humans. Different cells need different nutrients, so the liver works as a kind of chef preparing a buffet for the blood to carry around the rest of the body.

A supply of glucose is needed by all body and especially brain cells, especially as they have no means of storage. If, after a sugar-rich meal, the body has too much glucose in the blood, the liver cells remove it and store it, later pushing it back into the blood when the glucose level drops. After a carbohydrate-rich meal, the level may increase briefly, but the liver will take out the surplus for later use. Muscle cells are also able to store large amounts of glucose molecules, packaged as glycogen, which is why endurance event competitors, like marathon runners, try to pack muscle and liver cells with stored glycogen prior to competition in the expectation that it will be released into the blood when levels fall. After the glucose is used up, liver cells start converting amino acids and portions of fat into glucose and the body shifts to fat as a source of fuel.

Metabolism refers to all the body's processes that make food usable as a source of energy. The success of these depends on how effectively the body can get the nutrients and oxygen it requires to the relevant parts of the body and, at the same time, clear out the unwanted leftovers, like carbon dioxide. The substance employed for this purpose is blood, but it's actually more than just a convenient liquid for sweeping materials from place to place. Cells, cell fragments (platelets), proteins, and small molecules

Muscle-packing or -loading
Carbohydrates (carbs) provide most of our energy and can be ingested in many forms, after which they are reduced to simple sugars before being absorbed into the bloodstream. Carbs are an economical source of fuel. Liver and muscles store carbo-hydrates in the form of glycogen, which converts rapidly to glucose when extra energy is needed. Mindful of this, endurance performers sometimes seek to 'pack' or 'load-up' their muscles with glycogen by consuming large amounts of carbohydrate foods, such as bread, cereals, grains, and starchy products for about 72 hours preceding an event. The idea is to store as much glycogen as possible, making more glucose available when energy supplies become depleted.

float in a liquid plasma, which is mainly water (and makes up about 60 per cent of the blood's composition). The plasma contains red and white blood cells; the latter are capable of engulfing bacteria and combating infections with antibodies. Red cells are more numerous and contain haemoglobin, a chemical compound with a strong affinity for oxygen. Haemoglobin allows blood to increase its oxygen-carrying capacity exponentially. Long- and middle-distance runners have exploited the advantage of having more haemoglobin in their blood by training at high altitudes, where there is less oxygen naturally available in the air. Their bodies respond to the scarcity by producing a chemical that triggers the release of larger numbers of red cells in the blood. After descending to sea level (or thereabouts), the body will take time to readjust and will retain a high haemoglobin count for some weeks, during which an athlete may compete and make profitable use of a generous supply of oxygen to the muscles (blood doping, as we will see in chapter 6, involves extracting haemoglobin-packed blood during altitude training, saving it, and administering a transfusion to the athlete immediately prior to a race). At the other extreme, excessive bleeding or a iron-deficient diet can lead to anaemia, a condition resulting from too little haemoglobin.

So, how do we manage to circulate this urgently-required mixture throughout the body? The internal apparatus comprises the heart, blood vessels, lymph, lymph vessels, and some associ-ated organs, like the liver. These form a closed system, meaning that the blood that carries the vital substances all over the body is confined to definite channels and moves in only one direction, rather than being left to swim about. It travels in three types of vessels. The thickest are *arteries* in which blood moves at high pressure from the heart *to* the body's tissues. These arteries split over and over again to form microscopic vessels called *capillaries* that spread to every part of the body. A single capillary is only about half a millimetre long and a single cubic metre of skeletal muscle is interlaced with 1,400 to 4,000 of them. Laid end-to-end the length of all the body's capillaries would be about 96,500 kilometres. While coursing around, oxygen and nutrient-rich liquid, plasma, seep through the ultra-thin walls of the capillary. At the same time, capillaries, like vacuum cleaners, suck up waste products from cells. Gradually, capillaries merge together to form larger vessels that turn out to be *veins*; these keep blood at a lower pressure as they deliver it back to the heart.

A fist-sized muscle weighing less than a pound, the heart is a four-chambered pump that pushes blood into the arteries, gets it back from all parts of the body (except the lungs), pumps it out of the lungs, takes it back from the lungs, then returns it to the body. The chambers of the right side of the heart consist of one atrium and one ventricle. Connected to the right atrium are two large veins, one of which brings blood from the upper body and one from the lower. Blood flows from the right atrium into the right ventricle via a one-way valve; it leaves this chamber through a pulmonary artery that branches and services the lungs. Another valve stops any backflow. Blood returns from the lungs via pulmonary veins which drain into a left atrium and, then, to a left ventricle. From here, the blood is squeezed into the aorta, the single largest artery of the body, which runs into several other arteries connected to head, arms, and the upper chest, and, later, to abdominal organs and body wall. In the pelvis, the aorta branches and sends arteries into the legs. Blood returns to the right atrium of the heart through veins. The direction of the blood is ensured by a series of valves (blood, controlled by the valves, moves in one direction only). We call the movement away from ventricles systole and its opposite diastole. At any one time, there are about 1.5 gallons of blood in the mature human body. It takes less than a minute for the resting heart to pump out this amount and considerably less for the exerting sports performer, who can push out as much as 6.6 gallons per minute when active.

As mentioned before, the heart muscle has inherent rhythmicity and the pump acts independently of our volition. It will (given a suitable atmosphere) pump even outside the body, and with no stimulation; this makes heart transplants possible. Not that the heart is indifferent to outside influences; a sudden shock, for example, can cause sufficient stimulation to slow down, or 'skip', the heartbeat. During exercise or competition the action may accelerate to over 200 beats per minute. The heart muscle itself would stretch and automatically increase its strength of contraction and flow of blood. Athletes work at increasing blood flow without the corresponding heartbeat. The extra blood flow results in a heightening of the pressure of blood in the arteries of the chest and neck, which are detected by special sensory cells embedded in their walls. Nerve impulses are sent to the brain, resulting in impulses being relayed back to the heart, slowing its beat rate and lowering potentially harmful blood pressure levels. So, the brain has to monitor or feed back what is going on during intense physical activity.

The rate of heart action is also affected by hormones, the most familiar in sport being adrenaline which causes an immediate quickening of the heart in response to stressful situations. The reaction is widespread; amongst other things, blood vessels in the brain and limbs open up, and glycogen is released from the liver. In this type of situation, the skeletal muscles might receive up to 70 per cent of the cardiac output, or the total blood pumped from the heart. Under resting conditions, the liver, kidneys, and brain take 27, 27, and 14 per cent respectively. Immediately after eating, the digestive organs command great percentages (to carry food away), thus reducing the supply to the muscles. So, activity after a meal tends to be self-defeating; you can't get as much blood to the muscles as you would if you waited for three hours or so.

Mitochondrion
This is the power station of a cell where glucose and oxygen react together to create energy which converts the chemical adenosine diphosphate (ADP), which is like a flat battery, to charged-up adenosine triphosphate (ATP). This then supplies the rest of the cell with power. As its energy is used up, the ATP reverts back to ADP and returns to the mitochondria for recharging. ATP is most likely the supplier of energy for every activity in animals and plants. Energy, of course, is needed for muscular movements, but also for nerve conduction and other functions.

I mentioned before that food alone does not give the body energy, but needs the addition of oxygen, which is, of course, inhaled from the surrounding air, taken to the lungs, and then transferred to all parts of the body via the blood. Once it arrives at cells, the oxygen reacts with glucose, supplied by courtesy of digested carbohydrates, and produces energy at the mitochondria sites. During this process of respiration, unwanted carbon dioxide and water are formed in the cells. Exhaling gets rid of them.

Lungs and windpipe make up the respiratory system, though the actual process of breathing is controlled by the contractions of muscles in the chest, in particular the diaphragm muscle beneath the lungs and the muscles between the ribs. Space in the lungs is created by the diaphragm moving down and the ribs expanding. Air rushes in mainly through the nostrils where it is filtered, warmed, and moistened, and then into the lungs via the windpipe, or trachea. To reach the lungs, the air travels along tubes called bronchi which, when inside the lungs, divide into smaller and smaller tubes, ending in small bunches of air sacs called alveoli. Oxygen seeps out of the alveoli and into surounding capillaries which carry haemoglobin, a compound which, as we noted, readily picks up oxygen. While oxygen leaves alveoli, carbon dioxide, produced by the body cells, enters ready to be exhaled, a motion initiated by a muscular relaxation of the diaphragm and ribs. Air rushes out when we sigh 'Phew!' to denote relief and relaxation; the ribs close in and diaphragm lifts up.

The motions are more pronounced during continuous, physical

Hyperventilation

Carbon dioxide (CO_2) is a waste product and needs to be flushed out of the blood. Even a small increase in CO_2 content of the blood stimulates deep and, later, more rapid breathing to reduce the CO_2. The action is brought about involuntarily, usually during physical activity because of the fast breakdown of carbohydrates to release energy (impulses are sent to the medulla, resulting in increased breathing). Occasionally, this can lead to an over-reduction and a loss of consciousness. When this happens, hyperventilation is said to occur.

exertion; the body makes a steady demand for more oxygen and to meet this we breathe more deeply and more fully. The heart responds by pumping the oxygen-rich blood around the body faster. The process involves sustained use of oxygen in the breakdown of carbohydrates and, eventually, fats to release in the mitochondria of cells where the raw fuel ADP is energy charged up as ATP. This is why the name aerobic (meaning 'with air') is applied to continuous activities, such as cycling, swimming, and running over distances. In contrast, weight lifting, high jumping, and other sports requiring only short bursts of energy are *anaerobic*. In this case, food is not broken down completely to carbon dioxide and water, but to compounds such as alcohol or lactic acid. An incomplete breakdown means that less energy is released, but what is released can be used immediately. 'Oxygen debt' affects many sports competitors, particularly ones whose event requires explosive bursts, but over a reasonably sustained period. Four-hundred-metre runners often 'tie up' in the home straight; they can't get the oxygen and glucose round their bodies fast enough, so their muscles use their own glycogen stores for releasing ATP anaerobically (without oxygen). The product of this process is lactic acid, which needs oxygen to be converted into carbohydrate to get carried away. As runners need all the oxygen they can process for the release of energy so they 'borrow' it temporarily, allowing the lactic acid to accumulate in the muscles and cause fatigue. After the event, the debt has to be repaid, so rapid breathing invariably carries on. Shorter distance sprinters also incur oxygen debts, but the buildup of lactic acid in their muscles is not usually great enough to hinder contraction. Longer distance performers tend to get 'second winds': an increase in heart beat rate and breathing enables the runner to take in enough oxygen to convert and dissipate the lactic acid without over extending the oxygen debt.

Communications and control

Let us return to Matt Biondi for a moment. We now have an idea of how his movements are possible: how the supporting scaffold of his skeleton is urged into motion by the contraction of muscles; how those muscles are fed a supply of fuel to turn into energy; and how that fuel, in the form of food and oxygen, is pushed to its destination by blood which, at the same time, picks up waste products to dispatch. Although we have examined these processes separately, this is a device; in actual performance, all the processes are closely connected and dependent on each other. The digestion of food, for instance, would be no value without a blood stream to absorb it and to distribute the products; release of energy in a contracting muscle would cease if the lungs failed to supply oxygen via the circulatory system; a contracting muscle has to be connected to articulated bone to get a movement. The workings together of these is no haphazard affair. During strenuous activity, when muscles need to lose excess carbon dioxide and take in more glucose and oxygen, the rate of breathing increases automatically and the heart beats faster, so sending a greater amount of oxygen-rich blood to the muscles.

Crudely stated, the information we receive about the environment arrives by way of cells called *receptors*, which respond to changes in, for example, light and sound. They produce pulses of electricity which travel along nerves to the brain, which quickly interprets the meaning of the changes and issues instructions to the relevant other parts of the body (e.g. 'loud noise – cover ears'). Some of the information received by the brain is stored for future use, a facility of crucial importance in the acquisition of skill, which involves the capacity to react in precisely the same way to similar stimuli time after time.

The two components of the whole nervous system are: 1) the central nervous system (CNS), comprising the control centre of the brain and its message conduit, the spinal cord; and 2) the peripheral nervous system (PNS), which is the network of nerves originating in the brain and spinal cord and which is responsible for picking up messages from the skin and sense organs (sensory nerve cells) and carrying messages from the CNS to the muscles (motor nerve cells). Nerves are spread throughout the entire body; each one consists of a bundle of minute nerve fibres and each fibre is part of a nerve cell, or *neuron*, of which there are about 100 billion woven into each body in such a way as to bypass the packed body cells. To do this, the network needs a shuttle service provided by connector neurons which carry signals back and forth. Further physical facts about signals are, first, that the nerve fibres that pick up sensations from receptors and deliver them to the CNS, do so with electrical impulses that are chemically charged; changes in the balance of the minerals sodium and potassium in the cells cause the impulse. Second, the speed of the impulse varies from fibre to fibre and with environmental conditions. And third, fibres covered in sheaths of myelin (a fatty substance) conduct impulses faster than naked fibres.

Perhaps the clearest way of depicting the role of the nervous system is by tracing its stages. Suppose you are a gun marksman; you must use primarily the senses of sight and touch when focusing on the target and aligning the gun and make adjustments to these environmental factors. A first step is made by bringing the target into focus: the eyes are, of course, sense organs (i.e. an assembly of receptors) and their surface, known as the retina, will react to rays of light by changing its chemical structure; this triggers off an electrical impulse that travels along nerve cells, or neurons, to the brain. There are no direct connections between neurons, so the impulse may have to travel a circuitous route. The tiny gaps between neurons are *synapses* and these are bridged by a chemical *neurotransmitter* that takes the impulse across the synapse to the next neuron. The points of connection with the next neuron are called *dendrites*, which are in effect short, message-carrying fibres. One long fibre, called an *axon*, carries messages away from one neuron to the dendrites of the next. It takes only fractions of a second for the impulse to make its way through the synapses and neurons to the brain.

The fine web of nerves running through most of the body pale beside the densely complex mesh of neurons in the brain. Senses gleaned from our contact with the environment provide inputs which are sent to the brain; this processes the information before sending out instructions to muscles and glands. Most of our behaviour in and out of sport is controlled in this way. A fast bowler in a game of cricket may choose to do many different things on the basis of his sense impressions, mostly picked up by his vision and touch. He may notice a shuffle in the batsman's gait; he may feel moisture rising to the surface of the wicket. His brain sends messages to his muscles so that he deliberately bowls a short, rising delivery. But not all of our behaviour is produced by such a process: the receiving batsman may not expect the short delivery which kicks sharply towards his head, prompting him to jerk his head away almost immediately to protect it from damage – as we would withdraw a hand inadvertently placed on a hot iron. This type of reflex action is controlled by the spinal cord section of the CNS. The nervous impulse defines an arc that short-circuits the brain, so that the message never actually reaches it. The behaviour resulting from the reflex arc is sudden and often uncoordinated because all the muscle fibres contract together to avoid the danger. A boxer drawing away from a punch, a goalkeeper leaping to save a short-range shot, a volleyball player blocking an attempted spike; all these suggest automatic responses that need not involve conscious will for their successful completion. We hear much about reflex movements in sport and, clearly, sports in which fast reaction is crucial do exhibit such responses. But most sports action is governed by the brain and, for this reason, we need to look in more detail at the structure and functions of this most vital of organs.

While the brain itself is an integrated unit which, like any other living organ, needs a continuous supply of food and oxygen to produce energy, it can be seen in its component parts, each of which has specific functions. The medulla, for instance, controls involuntary activities that we can't control consciously, but which are essential for survival (such as breathing and heartrate). Also of interest for sporting performance is the cerebellum which receives messages from the muscles, ears, eyes, and other parts and then helps co-ordinate movement and maintain balance, so that motion is smooth and accurate. Injury to this component does not cause paralysis, but impairs delicate control of muscle and balance; for instance, the ability to surf or skate would be lost. All voluntary and learned behaviour is directed by the cortex, the largest portion of the brain; this forms the outer layer of the area known as the cerebrum lying at the fore of the brain. The cerebrum is divided into two halves, or hemispheres, each of which is responsible for movement and senses on its opposite side. Nerves on the two sides of the body cross each other as they enter the brain, so that the left hemisphere is associated with the functions of the right-hand side of the body. In most right-handed people, the left half of the cerebrum directs speech, reading, and writing while the right half directs emotions; for left-handers, the opposite is true. So, John McEnroe's service would be controlled by the right side of his brain, while his emotional outbursts against umpires would be associated with the left. Physical movement is controlled by the motor area: motor neurons send impulses from this area to muscles in different parts of the body. The more precise the muscle movements, the more of the motor area is involved; so a shot putter's actions would not use up much space while a dart player's would, as he or she would be utilizing fine movements of the fingers.

The only other zone of the brain I want to note at present is the thalamus, which is where pain is felt. Pain, of course, is principally a defensive phenomenon designed to warn us of bodily danger both inside and outside the body. Impulses originating in the thalamus travel to the sensation area so that a localization of danger can be made. This is a mechanistic account of our reactions to pain: it is actually affected by all manner of intervening factors, including self-belief. In other words, if people do not believe they will feel pain, they probably won't – at least under certain conditions. There are also cultural definitions of pain: we learn to interpret pain and react to it and the thresholds may differ from culture to culture. Such is the nature of competitive sports nowadays that few concessions to pain are allowed. Ways of 'tricking' the brain have been developed. Some drugs, for example, cause nerve cells to block or release a neurotransmitter (the chemical that carries nerve impulses across synapses to the dendrite of the adjacent neuron), the idea being to break the chemical chains linking brain to cell. We will look at the use of drugs more closely later. The point to bear in mind for now is that the CNS generally, and the brain in particular, play a central role, not only in the process of movement, but in the delicate sensory adjustments that have to be made in the operation of all sports, even those such as power lifting, which seem to require pure 'brawn'. The lifter's cerebellum enables him or her to control the consequences of the lift; without this, initiation might be possible, but corrective feedback co-ordination would be absent. In short, there would be no balance and no instruction to the opposing (antagonistic) muscles to make a braking contraction on the lift's completion. The whole operation would collapse.

While we exert a large degree of control over our bodies through the CNS, many of vital activities, such as heartbeat, peristalsis, and functioning of the kidneys simply can't be controlled voluntarily. Handling these is a secondary system of nerves called the autonomic nervous system (ANS). Many of the cell bodies of the ANS lie outside the brain and spinal cord and are massed together in bunches, each bunch being a *ganglion*. These ganglia receive information from receptors in the various organs of the body and then send out the appropriate instructions to muscles, such as the heart, and glands, such as salivary glands. The instructions are interesting in that they are two-fold and antagonistic. Unlike skeletal muscle which is either stimulated to contract or not (it needs no nerve impulse to relay), cardiac muscle and the smooth (as opposed to striated) muscle of other organs must be stimulated either to contract more than usual or to relax more than usual. To achieve this the ANS is divided into two substrata: the sympathetic system (more centrally located) and the parasympathetic system (more dispersed). The parasympathetic system constricts the pupil of the eyes, increases the flow of saliva, expands the small intestine, and shrinks the large intestine; the sympathetic system has the opposite effect. Impulses are propagated continuously in both systems, the consequences of which are known as *tone* – a readiness to respond quickly to stimulation in either direction. Tone is rather important in certain sports: for instance, a panic-inducing visual stimulus will cause an increase in sympathetic impulses and a decrease in parasympathetic impulses to the heart, eliciting a greater response than just a sympathetic stimulation. Impulses from the two systems always have antagonistic effects on organs. The name *autonomic* nervous system implies that it is independent and self-regulated, whereas, in fact, the centres that control ANS activity are in the lower centres of the brain and usually below the threshold of conscious control. The appeal of bringing ANS functions under conscious control is fascinating, yogi have for centuries been able to slow heartbeat quite voluntarily, with corresponding changes to the entire body. The potential for this in sport, particularly in the areas of recovery and recuperation, is huge.

In sport, responses to change in the environment have usually got to be swift and definite. Consequently, our treatment of the nervous system has focused on its ability to direct changes and issue instructions to the relevant parts of the body in order that they react quickly. The quickest communication system is based, as we have seen, on electrical impulses. But the body's response to an *internal* change is likely to occur over a period of time and be brought about by chemical adjustments. The substances involved are hormone molecules and they are manufactured by a group of cells called endocrine glands, the most important of which is the pituitary attached to the hypothalamus on the underside of the brain. This produces a growth hormone by regulating the amount of nutrients taken into the cells. Hormones themselves are messengers, secreted into the blood in which they travel to all body parts, interacting with other cells and effecting a type of finetuning.

Because some hormones have very specific effects – many of them local rather than body-wide – they have been of service to sports performers seeking to enhance performance (as we will discover in later chapters). The male testes secrete the hormone testosterone, which regulates the production of sperm cells and stimulates sex drive. Testosterone has been produced chemically and the synthetic hormone introduced into the body of competitors. Among the alleged effects are an increase in muscle bulk and strength and a more aggressive attitude. Adrenaline is another example: as we have seen, it pours into the blood, stimulating the release of glycogen from the liver, expansion of blood vessels in the heart, brain, and limbs, and contraction of vessels in the abdomen. Fatigue diminishes and blood coagulates more rapidly (which is why boxers' seconds apply an adrenaline solution to facial cuts). Competitors 'pumped-up' with adrenaline will usually have a pale complexion, on account of their blood being diverted from skin and intestine, and dilated pupils; hearts will be pounding and the breathing will be fast. The muscles will have the capacity to contract quickly and effectively either for, as the expression goes, *fight* or *flight*. This is an unusually fast hormonal change and most influences are long-term concerning such features as growth and sexual maturity. When they pass through the liver, the hormones are converted to relatively inactive compounds which are excreted as waste product, or urea, by the kidneys; this is why urinalysis is the principal method of detecting proscribed substances – it determines hormonal products in urine.

The chemical finetuning of the body is extensive and, in the healthy body, works continuously to modify us internally. Sweat glands are largely responsible for our adjustment to heat and, as many sports activate these, we should recognize their importance. The glands' secretions cover the skin with millions of molecules of water and they begin rising to the surface (epidermis) when external temperatures exceed about 25°C, depending on weight of clothing or the rigour of the activity performed. When blood reaching the hypothalamus is 0.5–1°C above normal, nerve impulses conveyed by the ANS stimulate sweat glands into activity. Fluid from the blood is filtered into the glands and passes through their ducts so that a larger amount of moisture is produced on the skin surface. As it evaporates, the heat in the molecules escapes, leaving coolness. The internal temperature of the body is kept within acceptable limits, as long as the sweat continues to take away the heat. (When temperatures drop, a reflex action is to shiver, which is a spasmodic muscular contraction that produces internal heat.) Most, but not all, sweating results from the eccrine glands; secretions around the armpits and nipples of both sexes and the pubic area of females come from apocrine glands, which discharge not only salt and water, but odourless organic molecules that are degraded by skin bacteria and give off distinct smells. In mammals, the smell has a sexual function, though the lengths to which humans go in trying to suppress or disguise the smell suggests that the function has been discarded in our species.

A general point here is that sweat is not just water but a concentration of several materials and profuse sweating may deprive the body of too much salt. Heat prostration and sunstroke are curses to marathon runners and triathletes and their efforts to conquer them include swallowing salt tablets before the race, drinking pure water at stages during the race, and taking solutions of electrolytes (salt and other compounds that separate into ions in water and can therefore help in the conduction of nerve impulses and muscle contraction). Problems for these athletes multiply in humid climates where the air contains so much vapour that the sweat can't evaporate quickly enough to produce a cooling effect, instead, it lies on the skin's surface forming a kind of seal; the result is known as heat stagnation. Even more dangerous is the situation when, after prolonged sweating due to activity in hot atmospheres, sweat production ceases and body temperatures soar to lethal levels. Sweat glands perform a vital compensatory function in minimizing the effects of heat during physical activity and, under instruction of the brain, try to stabilize body temp-erature at around 37°C. But their thermostatic powers have clear limitations when tested by athletes, for whom 26 miles is but the first station of the advance towards the boundaries of human endurance.

The journalist who coined the now-clichéd term 'well-oiled machine' to describe some highly efficient football team actually and, perhaps, unwittingly advanced a rather accurate description of the collection of trained and healthy individuals in question. Machines in the plural would have been more correct because, when examined in one perspective, that's what human beings are: a functioning series of systems made of cells and based on principles that any engineer, biologist, or chemist would find sound. But this is a partial and inadequate description and this chapter has merely set up a model; now it must be set in context and seen to work. We now have a grasp of the basic equipment and capabilities of the body; we still know little of its properties and motivations. Sport as an activity, derives from natural facul-ties, but the particular form or shape it has taken and the way it has been perpetuated and mutated over the centuries is not understandable in purely biological terms. It needs explanation all the same and this will be the task of the following chapters.

Further reading

The Human Side of Biology *by W. H. Mason and N. L. Marshall (Harper & Row, 1983) introduces its subject matter to its readers as 'about being alive' – which sets its scope very widely! Not specifi-cally a textbook, it is organized systematically, beginning with a chapter on 'Origin of life' and ending with 'Populations, environ-ment and humans'.*

Biology: Its Principles and Implications, *3rd edn, by G. Hardin and C. Bejema (W. H. Freeman, 1978) and* Biology, *7th edn, by C. A. Villee (W. B. Saunders, 1977) are both comprehensive tomes analysing the two central concepts of matter and energy, their sources and relationships in all living forms.*

The Dialectical Biologist *by R. Levins and R. Lewontin (Harvard University Press, 1985) refers to a 'new approach to the organism-environment relationship based on their interpenetration' and contains a Marxist challenge to the idea that living organisms are in any analytical way separable from their surroundings.*

Biomechanics *by R. McNeill Alexander (Chapman and Hall, 1975) is a standard textbook for this field of study which concerns the application of mechanics to the study of organisms and is therefore of great service to those interested in analysing the performer as an elaborate machine. Sebastian Coe's training schedules were based on strict mechanical principles.*

Assignment

In the seventeenth century, the French philosopher René Descartes tried to explain living processes like digestion, growth, and reproduction in terms of a mechanical model, i.e. the human as a machine. Repeat the exercise: break the human body down into its component parts and analyse the relations between them as if you were studying a machine, then do a specification sheet (rather as car manufacturers do). Finally, create some copy for a possible advertisement, for example: 'Beneath the sleek contours of its outer shell is an engine incorporating all the latest technological advances – from electronic microchip management systems controlling fuel injection and timing through to the latest 16-valve system with turbo charger and intercooler together with 170 brake horse power. With an acceleration of 0–60 mph in 7 seconds and a top speed of 140 mph the machine runs well without adjustment on unleaded or leaded fuel. The fully independent multi-link suspension, disc brakes on all wheels, power steering, and electronically controlled 4-wheel antilock brake system combine to offer precise handling.'

Chapter three

Genesis and history

The mystery of ancestry

It's possible, given the right conceptual approach and historical direction, to trace the origins of modern sport back to primitive matters of survival. The methods we once used for getting nutrition have been reshaped and refined, but are still vaguely discernible. Track and field events such as running and throwing are virtually direct descendants of our ancestors' chase of prey and their attempts to stun or kill them with missiles; some events still consciously model themselves on the disciplines and aptitudes associated with hunting, modern pentathlon (riding, fencing, shooting, swimming, and running) being the clearest example. More advanced tool use, which enhanced the ability to survive and improved nutrition, also generated a new adaptation that we see reflected in current sport. Tools that were once used for killing or butchery have been transformed into symbolic instruments like bats, rackets, and clubs and used in a fashion which disguises the functions of their predecessors. The origins of others, such as épées, are more transparent.

The purpose of this chapter is to provide an account of the beginning of sport and its subsequent development up to the last century. In the perspective I choose to view sport, the entire phenomenon has human foundations that were established several thousand years ago. It follows that any chronicle must track its way back through history to discover the reasons for the human pursuit of what are, on analysis, mock hunts and battles and the purposes they serve at both individual and social levels. The latter point will be answered in the next chapter, but the immediate task is to unravel the mystery of ancestry: how did sport begin? It's a question that requires an ambitious answer, one which takes us deep into history for a starting point.

Between 1.5 to 2 million years ago, *Homo erectus* arrived on the scene in East Africa and, later, spread to Asia and Europe. A highly successful creature in evolutionary terms, *Homo erectus* survived up to about 100,000 years ago and instituted some significant adaptations. According to some theories of evolution, *Homo erectus* evolved into the earliest members of our species *Homo sapiens*, who were succeeded in Africa by the anatomically modern *Homo sapiens sapiens* and in Europe by *Homo sapiens neandertalensis*, or Neanderthals. *Homo erectus* was a respectful and cautious scavenger, though much evidence points to males banding together in predatory squads and becoming proficient hunters of large animals like bears, bison, and elephants and using equipment such as clubs and nets. Layers of charcoal and carbonized bone in Europe and China have also suggested that *Homo erectus* may have used fire. Physically, the male of the species might have stood as tall as 5 feet 11 inches (1.8 metres) and, while the brain was smaller than our own, the animal had enough intelligence to make primitive tools and hunting devices.

Neanderthals, who were well-established in Europe by 70,000 BC, certainly had sufficient intellect to use fire on a regular basis and utilized a crude technology in making weapons which, as predatory creatures, they needed. As their prey were the large and mobile bison, mammoth, and reindeer, they made good use not only of physical weapons but also of tact, or stealth. They would hunt in packs and allocate assignments to different members. Other hints of social life are found amongst Neanderthals. Evidence of burials, for example, indicates an awareness of the significance of death; ritual burials are not conducted by species other than humans. There is also something uniquely human about the rapport with other species: the relationships humans form with other animals is an unusual one and Neanderthals may have been the first to forge this special link. It's possible that Neanderthals attempted to domesticate as well as hurt other species. The cartoon depiction of Fred Flintstone adorned in bearskins is actually more accurate than it seems: it's quite probable that the wearing of skins was thought to invest the wearer with some of the animal's qualities (such as strength of the mammoth or speed of the deer). The close association between many sports and animals is undoubtedly connected to this type of belief.

Some see Neanderthals as distinct from and having no breeding with *Homo sapiens*, while others see them gradually replaced by *Homo sapiens* after long periods of genetic mixing. Whether or not they were replaced or just became extinct, two facts are clear: one is technological, the other social. Neanderthals exploited raw materials for tool manufacture and use; they also displayed collective behaviour in the division of labour they used to organize and co-ordinate their hunts. Related to these two activities is the fact that the reciprocal obligations systems used in hunting were carried over into domestic life. Neanderthals were cave dwellers and so used a home-base arrangement; this leads to the suggestion that they most probably constructed a stable pattern of life, possibly based on role allocation.

Homo sapiens shared these features: they used tools, hunted in groups, and had division of labour, at the home base and especially in the hunting parties. Accepting responsibility for specific duties had obvious advantages for survival: co-ordinating tasks as a team would have brought more success than pell-mell approaches. Signals, symbols, markers, and cues would have been important to elementary strategies. Complementing this was the sharing of food at the central home base. Maybe this awakened humans to the advantages of pair-bonding and the joint provisioning of offspring: the mutual giving and receiving, or reciprocity, remaining the keystone of all human societies.

The hunter-gatherer mode of life is central to our understanding of the origin of sport. It began with foraging and scavenging as much as 3 million years ago; hunting as a regular activity followed a period of feeding off carcasses or spontaneous picking. Including more meat in the diet brought about nutritional changes, but also precipitated the invention of more efficient means of acquiring food. The response was to hunt for it – and this had widespread behavioural repercussions, not only in terms of social organization, but in physical development. Covering ground in pursuit of quarry required the kind of speed that could only be achieved by an efficient locomotion machine. The skeleton became a sturdier structure able to support the weight of bigger muscles and able quickly to transmit the force produced by the thrust of limbs against the ground. Lower limbs came to be more directly under the upper body, so that support was more efficient in motion; leg bones lengthened and the muscles elongated, enabling a greater stride and an ability to travel further with each step. The human evolved into a mobile and fast runner, and, though obviously not as fast as some other predators, the human's bipedalism left upper limbs free for carrying.

Where quarry was near enough to be approached, but also near enough to be disturbed, hunters would need short bursts of explosive speed, an ability to contract muscles and release energy anaerobically. In short, they needed the kind of power which modern sprinters possess. Hunts might take up an entire day and would demand of the hunter stamina, endurance, and the capacity to distribute output over long periods – precisely the type of aerobic work performed by middle-distance and marathon runners, not to mention triathletes. Effective synthesis of ATP from ADP and the removal of waste lactic acid was enhanced by respiratory evolution. Ribs expanded and the muscles between them developed to allow the growth of lungs, which permitted deeper breathing to take in more and more air. Since the sustained release of energy depends on a supply of glucose and other foods, the hunter's diet was clearly important. While we can't be certain exactly what proportion of the diet was taken up by meat, we can surmise that this protein-rich food source played a role in balancing the daily expenditure of energy and providing enough fats and proteins for tissue repair.

Habitual meat-eating was not unqualified in its advantages; it introduced the very severe disadvantage of bringing humans into open competition with the large mammalian carnivores and scavengers like hogs, panthers, and tigers which roamed the savannahs looking for food. Ground speed was, in this instance, a requisite quality for survival, the clawless, weak-jawed biped being ill-equipped to confront the specialist predators. In time, evolution yielded a capacity to make and use not only tools but also weapons like clubs and stones, which at least evened up the odds. The physical clash with other animals continues to fascinate elements of the human population, a fact witnessed in such activities as bear baiting, boxing kangaroos, and the type of man vs horse races in which Jesse Owens performed during the undignified twilight of his career (see chapter 5).

A momentous change in the period, as we have noted, was the increase in human's most important asset. The larger brain, with its larger neurons and denser, more complex circuitry of dendrite branches, may well have been related to the long days spent beneath the hot sun, hunting in comparative safety while the bigger predators sought shade and rest. Obscure as the relationship between brain growth and behavioural change may remain, we should at least recognize that neither are independent of the environment in which the processes take place. For instance, survival success would have depended on the ability to identify in the surrounding environment things that were needed: rocks for tools and weapons, tracks of game and competitive predators, sources of vegetable. The need to discriminate perceptually encouraged larger brains and better communication skills, which in turn occasioned bigger and better brains; these more complicated organs needed nourishment in terms both of food and social stimulation, and this would have been reflected in subsistence methods and social arrangements. The process had no 'result' as such, for the brain constantly developed in response to behavioural change but at the same time triggered new thoughts that were translated into action: a continuous feedback motion.

Hunting, gathering, and to a decreasing degree, scavenging were the main human adaptations. Among their correlates were division of labour, basic social organization, increases in communication, and, of course, increase in brain size. Slowly and steadily the species evolved ways of satisfying basic biological drives and needs: food supply, shelter against the elements and predators, sex and reproduction. In the process a prototype emerged: 'man the hunter' (and I choose the phrase with care, as evidence suggests that the more robust males assumed most responsibility in catching prey). The species' greater brain capacity gave them the advantage of intellect, an ability to devise methods of tracking and capture, to utilize cunning and stealth as well as force. Concentration became important; intelligence enabled our ancestors to ignore distractions and fix attention on the sought-after game. Hunts, especially for large animals, would be more effectively performed in squads and these required a level of co-ordination, synchronization, and communication. Co-operation and reciprocity were qualities of great utility in hunting and at the home base, where the spoils would be shared.

The accumulated experience of the hunt itself would impart qualities, like courage in the face of dangerous carnivores who would compete for food. Risks were essential to reproductive success; if they were not taken, the species would still be picking fruit! Among the specific skills refined in this period would have been an ability to aim and accurately deliver missiles, a capacity to judge pace in movement, and to overwhelm and conquer prey when close combat was necessary. We might also take note of the fact that humans became impressively good swimmers and divers, evolving equipment and functions that aided deep diving and fast swimming; this aquatic adaptation may have been linked to hunting for fish.

All these features are responses to the manner in which the species procured its food: this is essential to life and so has a strong, if not determining effect on every aspect of both lifestyle and personality. If an existing method of obtaining food does not yield enough nutrition, then bodies suffer and the species either perishes or makes new adaptations, perhaps formulating alternative methods. In the event, what seems to have happened in the case of *Homo sapiens* is that they hit upon a novel way of guaranteeing a food supply which eliminated the need for many of the activities that had persisted for the previous 2 million years or more, and had carved deeply the features of human character and capacities. As recently as 10,000 years ago, *Homo sapiens* devised a way of exploiting the food supply which was to remove the necessity of hunting and release humans to concentrate on building what is now popularly known as 'civilization'.

Instead of exploiting natural resources around them, the species began to exploit its own ability. In short, the ability to create a food supply. This was accomplished by gathering animals and crops together, containing them in circumstances that permitted their growth and reproduction, then picking crops or slaughtering animals as necessary, without ever destroying the entire stock. In this way, supply was rendered a problem only by disease or inclement weather. The practice of cultivating land for use, rather than for mere existence, gave rise to farming.

Recreating the hunt

Although now open to debate, the beginnings of agriculture are seen in orthodox teaching to coincide with the end of what is called the paleolithic age. The transition was seen by some as swift and dramatic, though the view has been challenged by others who accentuate the uneven process of development over periods of time. For example, in Europe, following the recession of the ice age, there appears to have been an interlude in which certain animals, especially dogs, were domesticated, some cereals were harvested, and forms of stock management were deployed, but without the systematic approach of later agriculturalists. Obviously, regions differed considerably ecologically, and the period characterized by the transition from hunter-gatherer to farmer was neither smooth nor uniform. But it was sudden – in evolutionary terms, that is. Only as recently as 10,000 years ago do we see the systematic domestication of animals – a process central to agriculture. It may have taken the form of controlled breeding or just providing fodder to attract wild herds, but the insight was basically the same: that enclosing and nourishing livestock was a far more effective and reliable way of ensuring food than hunting for it.

Complementing this discovery was the realization that planting and nurturing plants and harvesting only enough to meet needs so that regrowth was possible was an efficient exploitation of natural resources compared to the cumbersome and less predictable gathering method. The breakthroughs spawned all manner of toolmaking and other technologies that added momentum to the agricultural transformation that is loosely referred to as the neolithic age (from the Greek *neo* meaning new and *lithos* meaning stone: a period when ground and polished tools and weapons were introduced).

What we need to remind ourselves is that hunting and gathering had been dominant for more than 2.5 million years before. During that period the lifestyle and mentality it demanded became components of our character. Chasing, capturing, and killing with their attendant dangers were practised features of everyday life. The qualities of courage, skill, and the inclination to risk, perhaps even to sacrifice on occasion, were not heraldic but simply human: necessary for survival. What we would now regard as epic moments were in all probability quite 'ordinary'. The coming of farming made most of these qualities and features redundant. The hunting parties that honed their skills, devised strategies and traded on courage were no longer needed. Instead, the successful farmer needed to be diligent, patient, responsible, regular, and steadfast. A farmer was more interested in breeding animals rather than hunting them. The switch was bound to introduce strains.

Hunting and gathering affected us not only socially but perhaps even genetically, so long and sweeping was its reign. No organism is a product purely of hereditary nature or of environmental experience. Humans are no different in being products of the interaction between genes and the environment. But the kind of evolutionary change we are interested in proceeded at different levels: the human way of living changed, but not in such a way as to incur an automatic switch in human beings themselves. After all, even rough arithmetic tells us that the 10,000 years in which agriculture has developed represents 0.4 per cent of the period spent hunting and gathering. Sport, in this scenario, is the evidence that we are still catching up with the changes. It is as if cultural evolution sped ahead of biological evolution: we did not completely change from one type of organism into another as quickly as the cultural pace required. There was still too much of the hunter-gatherer in us to permit an easy settling down to breeding animals and sowing crops.

One response to this strain was to re-enact the hunt: imitate the chase, mimic the prey, copy the struggle, simulate the kill, and recreate the conditions under which such properties as bravery and resolution would be rewarded. It was a fairly minor but important adaptation in which the customary skills, techniques, and habits were retained even when their original purpose had disappeared. It made far more sense to enclose, feed, and domesticate animals than to hunt them, as it did to sow crops rather than gather wild fruits and grains. It was perfectly possible to acknowledge this, while craving the *frisson* the hunts used to bring. How could the spirit of the hunt be recaptured? The answer was: let it continue. Hunt for its own sake rather than for food. No matter that hunting served no obvious purpose any longer, let people engage in it for the sheer pleasure or excitement it generated. In this way, people played at hunting: they did not direct their efforts to meeting the immediate material needs of life, or acquiring necessities. Hunting became instead an *autotelic* activity, having no purpose apart from its own existence.

Autotelic
From the Greek *auto*, meaning by or for itself, and *telos*, meaning end. An autotelic activity is one which has an end or purpose in itself and is engaged in for no external purpose.

Once it became detached from the food supply, the activity took on a life of its own. When survival no longer depended on killing game, the killing became an end; what was once an evolutionary means to an end became an end in itself. The new hunt no longer had as its motive the pursuit of food but rather the pursuit of new challenges. Although in behavioural terms much the same activity as hunting, the new version was an embryonic sport or at least an expression of the drive or impulse underlying sport right to the present day. Stripped of its original purpose, the processual aspects of the activity came to prominence. Team co-ordination,

Years
(millions)   2–5   1,000   5,000

stealth, intelligence, daring, physical prowess, and courage in the face of danger were valued more than the end product and, over time, these became integrated into a series of activities, each in some way mimicking the original activities.

It sounds trite to say that the roots of sport lie in our primeval past when so much of modern sport operates not in response to survival but as an adjunct to commercial interests. At the same time, we should recognize that the impulses that make sport attractive enough to be commercially exploited are part of our evolutionary make-up. Sport was the result of the attempt to reintroduce the excitement and thrill of the hunt into lives that were threatened with mundane routines in unchallenging environments. As such it was and remains both precious and profound. It may owe nothing to the hunt nowadays; but it still owes a good deal to the attempts at replacing the hunt with something comparably as exciting. So, there is perfect sense in Gerhard Lukas' claim that 'the first sport was spear throwing' (or *speer worfen*) (Lukas 1969). Darts, blowguns, and bows and arrows were modifications of the basic projectile and unquestionably featured in mock as well as genuine hunts. The use of the bow is interesting in that it stimulated the construction of an artifact, the target, the bull's eye, which, as its name implies, represented the part of the animal to be aimed at. Archery, as a purely autotelic behaviour, actually had the quality of compressing a symbolic hunt into a finite area and allowing a precise way of assessing the results. As such, it had potential as an activity that could be watched and evaluated by others, who would not participate except in a vicarious way (that is, they might experience it imaginatively through the participants – which is what most sports spectators do, even today).

This vicariousness was, as we now realize, absolutely crucial to the emergence and development of sport. The facility for bringing the rationality and emotion of a hunt to a home base made it possible to include dozens, or hundreds, of people in the whole experience. Just witnessing an event offered some continuity, however tenuous, within change: spectators could 'feel' the drama and tension of a supposed hunt from another age, through the efforts of the participants.

The obvious acknowledgement of this came with the custom-built stadia. These came with the clustering together of human populations and the creation of city-states. Irrigation was crucial to farming, of course, so most of the earliest known civilizations had their urban centres near rivers, as in China, India, and the Near and Middle East. Richard Mandell, in his *Sport: a Cultural History*

(1984) urges caution in gleaning evidence of what we now call spectator sport in ancient civilizations. But he does show that the Mesopotamians, for example, left traces of evidence that suggest physical competitions. These might have been tests of strength and skill; though they may also have been more military training regimes than amusements for the masses. The seminal Egyptian civilization of some 5,000 years ago left much material in the form of documents, frescos, tombs, and bric-a-brac. In these we find depicted one of the most essential, enduring, and unchanging activities, and one which we will consider in the next section – *combat*.

State
An organized administrative apparatus in which a single government is empowered to rule. Governments may change, but the bureaucracy stays essentially intact, giving a stability and continuity to the state and its main institutions. See chapter 8 for an analysis of the modern state's intrusion in sport.

In pursuit of *agōn*

At some stage in ancient history, the idea of rivalry seems to have struck chords. The straightforward drive of the hunt, in which packs pursued game, acquired a provision. The object was not merely the climax of a kill, but in administering the kill faster or more effectively than others. Competition between individuals or groups added a new and apparently appealing dimension to an already perilous activity, turning it into a *game* with some semblance of organization and a clear understanding of what constituted an achievement. The amusement value, it seems, was boosted by the introduction of a human challenge and by spectatorship.

It is probable, though undocumented, that physical combat activities between humans and perhaps animals co-existed with the autotelic hunts. We need not invoke the Cain and Abel fable to support the argument that intra-species fighting, for both instrumental and playful purposes, existed throughout history. It is one of the least changeable aspects of *Homo sapiens*. Combat has many different forms, ranging from wrestling to fencing; stripped to its basics, it expresses the rawest type of competition. As such, it seems to have held a wide appeal both for participants seeking a means to express their strength and resilience and for audiences who to this day are enraptured by the sight of humans disputing each other's physical superiority.

The hunt, or at least the mimetic activity that replaced it, would have satisfied a certain need for those closely involved, but the actual behaviour would have been so fluid and dispersed that it would not have been closely observed, certainly not as a complete and integrated action. Spectators would have been much more easily accommodated at a home base where fighting could be staged in much the same way and with a similar purpose to mock hunts: to break up tedious routines and raise emotions with brief but thrilling and relatively unpredictable episodes of violent action. The emphasis may well have fallen on animal fighting, unarmed human combat and, possibly, armed humans pitched against large animals such as bears or tigers. Given the purpose of this type of combat, some loose structure or framework governing the fight was likely; combatants fighting to kill or disable an opponent in order to save themselves in any way possible would be warring rather than engaging in a sport.

A fresco excavated from the tomb of an Egyptian prince and dated to about 4,000 years ago looks similar to a modern wall chart and shows wrestlers demonstrating over 100 different positions and holds. Mandell suggests that there may have been professional wrestlers in the Egyptian civilization. Artwork shows fighters also using sticks of about one metre's length; even today, stick fighting persists in parts of Egypt, though in a more ritualized form. It is quite possible that the proximity to the Nile encouraged competitive swimming and rowing. In the plains of the Upper Nile region, hunting of large game, including elephants, was commonplace, the chariot being an effective vehicle for this purpose. Pharaoh Tutankhamun (14th century BC) is shown on one fresco hunting lions from his chariot. Amphibian Nile dwellers like crocodiles and hippopotamuses were also hunted. Crete had trade contacts with Egypt and some kind of cultural cross-fertilization is possible. Certainly, Cretans were avid hunters and their relics suggest they were combat enthusiasts also, though the form of fighting they favoured seems more akin to boxing than wrestling. We also have evidence of a version of bull fighting, and a type of cattle wrestling that resembles the modern rodeo in the United States.

The mythical and the mundane are intertwined in our knowledge of Greek civilization, popularly and justifiably regarded as the first culture to incorporate sport or, more specifically, competition, into civic life. The compulsion to pursue public recognition of one's supremacy through open contest with others was known by the Greeks as *agōn*. Athletic excellence achieved in competition was an accomplishment of, literally, heroic proportions. Myths of

Hercules sending discuses into oblivion and Odysseus heaving boulders are important signifiers of the high value Greeks placed on physical feats, but the less spectacular evidence shows that they approached, organized, and assessed the outcomes of activities in a way which is quite familiar.

Their approach was to win, and here we find the almost obsessional drive for success that characterizes much of modern sport: winning was quite often at any cost and scant respect was paid to such things as 'fairness'. Some may argue that the search for supremacy is a primordial competitive instinct. It is more likely that particular social arrangements in which inequality and distinct strata are key components encourage individuals to strive hard and 'better themselves' by whatever means they can. Athletic prowess was one such means in the ancient civil society of Greece – the *polis*. Victors could acquire *arete* (excellence), the ultimate attainment.

In terms of organization, Greeks created events which exist today without major modification. They are credited with being the first organizers of sport on a systematic basis, the Olympic games, which began in 776 BC, being the clearest expression of this. This event integrated sport into a wider festival, drawing disparate competitors and spectators together at one site every four years in an effort to convince themselves they were in some sense united. Greeks were also influential in their attempts to determine outcomes. Despite aphorisms about competing being more important than winning, victory was crucial and systems were designed to ensure accurate assessment of performance. Exact distances were measured and staggers were introduced on racing circuits. Tallies of points were kept in multi-discipline events like the pentathlon. Records of performances were kept (each Olympiad took the name of the victorious sprinter at the previous festival). The games may have been less important as a spectacle than they were as a focal point around which to organize training. Physical fitness, strength, and the general toughness that derives from competition were important military attributes, and so the process was tuned to producing warriors as much as sports performers. Sparta is the best-known city-state in this context: it was a site of phalanx training in which youths would be taken from their families and reared in an austere garrison where they would be honed for combat. There was also a religious element to competition, for the Greeks believed that athletic victory indicated that the victor would be favoured by the capricious gods in whom they believed.

Whatever the motivation in striving to achieve, we can be sure

47

that the Greeks went to great lengths in their preparations and so provided something of a prototype for what we now call training. Spartans in particular used a cyclical pattern of increasing and decreasing the intensity of preparations which is used in most modern sports. The very concept of preparation is important: recognizing that excellence does not spring spontaneously, but is the product of periods of heavy labour and disciplined regimes prompted the Greeks to provide facilities. So, in the sixth century BC, we see a new type of building called a *gymnasium* (meaning, literally, an exercise for which one strips).

By the time of the Greeks' refinements, sport had undergone changes in purpose and, indeed, nature. While the content showed clear lines of descent connecting it with more basic hunting and combat, the functions it served were quite novel: it was seen as a military training activity, as a vehicle for status-gaining, or what we might now refer to as social mobility, and as a way of securing divine favour. This does not deny that the impulses associated with hunting and gathering were present, but it does highlight the autonomy of sport once separated from its original conditions of creation and growth. The Greek adaptation was a response to new material and psychic requirements. Powerful Greek city-states needed defence against outside attacks and they ensured this by encouraging and rewarding warriors. Accompanying the development of the *polis* was the growth of the state's control over human expressions of violence; sophisticated social organization and internal security were impossible without some regulation of violence. The state's response was to obtain a legitimate monopoly over violence and establish norms of behaviour which discouraged the open expression of violence by citizens and encouraged saving violence for the possible repulsion of attacks from outside powers. Contests, challenges, and rivalries were ways in which the impulse could reassert itself, but in socially acceptable forms.

The value of sport earned it a central place in Greek civilization and the importance of this is reinforced by writers such as Huizinga and Elias, who stress that the process of becoming civilized itself implicates a culture in controlling violence while at the same time carving out 'enclaves' for the 'ritualized expression of physical violence'. We will return to the theory later, but should note the basic observation that sport serves as a legitimate means through which primitive, violence-related impulses and emotions can simultaneously be engendered *and* contained. Much of what the ancients would have regarded as expressions of civilization would be seen as barbarous from the standpoint of the late twentieth century. Gouging, biting, breaking, and the use of spiked fist thongs were all permissible in Greek combat. But these were occasions for the exhibition of warrior-like qualities and mercy was not such a quality. While victory was a symbolic 'kill' it was also, at times, a quite literal kill.

For Romans, part of the appeal of sport lay in the climax of killing. One of their innovations of Greek sport was in establishing preparatory schools exclusively for gladiators, who would sooner or later be publicly feted or slaughtered. The actual events would be staged in hippodromes, cavernous stadia where spectators would joyously witness the death of one human being by either another or a beast. Influenced in large part by Greek activities, Romans held foot races, chariot races, and many types of one-to-one combat in the centuries either side of the start of the Christian era. They were also aware of the immense military advantages of having a fit, disciplined, and tempered population. It was expensive to train gladiators, especially if they were all to be killed, so convicted prisoners and slaves were virtually sacrificed. Adding to the extravagance was the cost of importing animals: wild beasts from throughout the world were captured, transported, and nourished. For five or more centuries, hundreds of thousands of beasts were brought into the colosseum and other stadia and, watched by massed audiences, pitched against each other or against humans. Death seems to have been an accepted part of this activity. There was nothing curious about the Romans' apparent lack of interest when it came to hunting (no artifacts to suggest much interest). They had no need to leave their cities: the hunts were effectively transferred to the stadia where audiences could satisfy their appetites for violence, or their 'blood lusts', as some might say. Gladiatorial conflicts featuring wild animals were comparable to the primitive hunts; the comparisons between human combat and modern fighting sports are clear.

There are few deaths to observe in modern combat, and when tragedy does strike it leads to a period of earnest self-reflection as well as attacks from medical authorities on the 'barbaric' nature of such activities. The fact remains: audiences are amused and excited by the prospect of human combat, as they are by animal conflict – about which there is much less restraint, as the slaughter in bull fighting, cock fighting, and hare coursing suggests. The threshold of tolerance has dropped, but this is largely a function of the cultural forces that emanate from civilization: the human proclivity to watch, enjoy, and appreciate the infliction of damage during combat does not seem to waver. Perhaps we are not so dissimilar to our Roman ancestors who wallowed in the blood-letting and cheerfully pointed their thumbs to the floor to answer the question, life or death? The gladiatorial schools finally closed after Christian opposition in 399 AD. In the following century, the combat grew less deadly and was superseded as an entertainment by less expensive chariot racing, which was arguably the first *mass* spectator event, drawing crowds of up to 250,000 to the Circus Maximus. Chariot racing required teams, each team wearing different-coloured uniforms and the winners receiving prize money.

It has been argued that Roman sport assumed a political character in this period. With no genuinely democratic means of representation, the populations may well have grown restive and demanded change were it not for the diversionary effect of the combat and racing. The entertainment that drew crowds in their hundreds of thousands diverted their attention, if only temporarily, from their grievances and so served the function of maintaining the *status quo*. Masses were distracted and amused, if not by bread by circuses. The theme was updated in the movie *The Running Man* set in a totalitarian future in which 'have nots' are kept docile by a competition in which convicted criminals are pursued through a maze by 'stalkers' – athletes trained to kill. 'The public wants sport and violence,' observes the competition's MC. 'We give them what they want.' We will consider the scholarly attempts to portray modern sport in a similar way later.

Sport and spectacle

Beside the civilizations of Egypt, Greece, and Rome, other cultures emerging in the pre-Christian era had activities resembling sport, though in this historical context, we should observe Mandell's caveat that 'the boundaries that we moderns use to separate "sport" from other areas of human endeavour have been indistinct or not worth noticing in other cultures' (1984: 93). So, we can't be certain that the swimming, diving, and combat, armed and unarmed, practised by inhabitants of South Asia around 2,500 years ago approached what we would recognize as sport; they may have had a more specific traditional significance, possible bound up in the caste system. Similarly, the equestrian pursuits of the Chinese, together with their competitive archery may have been based less on recreation or amusement and more on military training. Yet, as with Greeks and Romans, the activities themselves have been adapted to suit changing circumstances. For example, the sport we call polo almost certainly started life as a Chinese method of target practice. Many of China's martial exercises, which could be used competitively, were functional and were used to maintain a high level of fitness amongst the working population. Japanese industries have successfully adopted this ancient policy, holding exercise sessions before work in modern factories.

The Chinese were probably the first to employ a ball effectively, though there is evidence that the Egyptians experimented. In northern China there was a primitive kicking game. The Chinese invented a projectile that was the forerunner of the shuttlecock and, presumably, propelled it by means of some sort of racket or bat.

The military importance of the horse, especially fast and manoeuvrable breeds, is obvious and the Japanese perhaps more than any other population recognized this in their sporting traditions. Their competitive shows of speed and intricacy have clear counterparts in today's horse-oriented events, including dressage. Japan's legacy of martial arts is large and well-known; combat in the feudal age of the *samurai* was based on several ancient disciplines and included the mastery of horses, weapons, and unarmed conflict. Many of the skills survive, though with modifications. The pattern that emerges in Japan as elsewhere is the use of sport as a military exercise as well as a pursuit to retain interest and capture enthusiasm while preparing its participants for the more practical discipline of defence. Wherever we find a cavalry, we almost invariably discover some form of competitive endeavour involving the horse. Typically, the competitors would be something of an elite, with resources and possibly patronage enough to compete and serve; they may well have been lionized as Greek heroes were. Certainly in medieval Europe, armed knights were the basis of the continent's supremacy and glory. The knights would be served by peasants and would enjoy status, though in material terms they may not have been much better off.

Practice fights between mounted knights gave rise to a form of combat known as jousting and, as modern fans are drawn by sparring sessions or 'friendly' games, spectators stood in line as the combatants galloped towards each other, lances extended. The object was to tilt the lance at the adversary in an attempt to unseat him. As the jousts gained popularity they were surrounded by pomp and ritual, and formal tournaments were lavish affairs attended and heavily patronized by nobility. Jousting became an expensive pursuit quite beyond the reach of the peasantry, and indeed all, apart from the wealthy landowners whom the jousters served. Peasants would merely look on as the often huge and elaborate tournaments unfolded. The combat was frequently along territorial lines, as in a 1520 tournament in northern France between King Henry VII of England and King Francis I of France.

A truly 'international' event, it was spread over three weeks and attended by dozens of thousands.

Jousting, as with the many other forms of combat, had the military purpose of keeping knights in good fighting shape, but may have been transformed into an alternative to warring. Disputes could be settled less expensively and more enjoyably by tournaments than by costly internecine battles. Between the twelfth to sixteenth centuries, tournaments became more organized and orderly, as did European society as a whole. Accommodation was made for spectators, scaffolds and stands being built as the jousts grew more popular and attracted large crowds. After the sixteenth century, the grand tournaments faded and rural events emerged, though tilts were often at targets, not humans. The tournaments gradually changed character from being hard-edged and competitive; 'from sport to spectacle' is how Allen Guttmann describes the change in his book *Sports Spectators* (1986). The process is familiar to anyone who has witnessed the transmutation of wrestling after it became a popular spectator 'sport'.

Hunting and archery coexisted with jousting and outlasted it, though never attracting comparable numbers of spectators. Archery survived virtually intact and is today an Olympic event; the old longbows have been considerably modified, of course. Civic festivals were organized around competitions and were grand occasions, drawing vast crowds to pageants all over Europe. The stag and fox hunts were direct predecessors of the modern fox hunts, with the rich amusing themselves by setting free their hounds and giving pursuit; the poor would amuse themselves by pursuing them all.

Cock fighting

This probably has origins in ancient China and Persia. Greeks may have become aware of it after their victory over Persia at Salamis in 480 BC and, in turn, introduced it to the Romans. For Greeks, the courage of fighting birds was regarded as exemplary: youths were encouraged to watch and emulate the birds' tenacity and valour in combat. Later, it became a mere source of entertainment, especially for gamblers. It first appeared in England in the twelfth century, though its popularity waxed and waned until the sixteenth century when Henry VIII built a royal cockpit at his palace. In the eighteenth and nineteenth centuries, cocks were bought and sold, bred and trained in a more organized way, one trainer, Joseph Gulliver, acquiring quite a reputation. Cock fighting was banned in 1835 but, as recently as 1985, pits, tackle, and dead birds were discovered in Shropshire and northern England.

Hunts and other 'blood sports' continued to enjoy popularity among lower classes, whose penchant for watching tethered bears prodded with sticks and then set upon by fierce dogs is similar to that of the spectators who gathered at the Roman colosseum centuries before. Cock fights, which have almost universal appeal, were held in England from about the twelfth century and attracted audiences from the various classes. Although condemned systematically from the eighteenth century, blood sports persist to this day, most famously in the Spanish bull rings and in the streets of Pamplona. England's bull ring, in Birmingham, reminds us that such events were not always confined to Spain; bull running ceased in England in 1825, a year after the founding of the Royal Society for the Prevention of Cruelty to Animals (RSPCA). The same organization brought pressure against cock fighting, which was banned in 1835, only to 'go underground' as an illicit, predominantly working-class pursuit. The practice persists in the west to this day.

Mimetic
This describes an activity that imitates or resembles another, and which is carried out especially for amusement. A child may mimetically play cowboys-and-indians, or adult members of Round Table organizations may imitate battles, albeit in a mock way.

Blood sports in general and fox hunting in particular are seen as having central importance by Norbert Elias and his collaborator Eric Dunning. The 'civilizing' of society demanded greater personal self-control and a stricter constraint on violence, but the process of hunting or just observing allowed 'all the pleasures and the excitement of the chase, as it were, mimetically in the form of wild play' (1986: 48). While the passion and exhilaration associated with hunting would be aroused, the actual risks would be absent in the imagined version (except for the animals, of course) and the effects of watching would be, according to Elias and Dunning, 'liberating, cathartic'.

The comments could be applied without alteration to all of the activities considered so far. They are products of a human imagination ingenious enough to create artificial situations that human evolution has rendered irrelevant. But, once created, they have seemed to exert a control and power of their own, eliciting in both participants and audience a pleasurable excitement that encapsulates the thrill or 'buzz' of a hunt, yet carries none of the attendant risks.

History shows that activities which at least resemble sport are rarely purely autotelic and can be augmented with other purposes. From ancient to medieval ages, the tendency was to imbue supposed sporting activities with a military purpose, often encouraging qualities within participants that were of obvious utility in serious combat. We also find a subtheme in sports history in which many of the main roles were occupied by privileged or elite groups who performed, while most of the supporting roles were played by peasantry or plebeians who watched. The public provision of entertainment by the powerful had a latent political function in diverting attention away from *realpolitik* and animating sentiments and emotions that were not challenging to the established order of things.

Realpolitik
This refers to political realities based on material needs rather than on, for example, the ambitions and ideals to which sport appeals.

Human relationships with other animals have been peculiarly ambivalent. Dogs, for instance, have been domesticated and cared for, and used to hunt other more vulnerable creatures and to retrieve birds which have been killed. Many other animals have simply been used as expendable prey, an observation that gives credence to the view that, while the hunt as a survival mechanism has receded, the violent impulses that it once fostered remain. Animal abuses very gradually declined in the long period under review and, though they have been under pressure this century, they certainly have not disappeared in the modern era. Animal uses, as opposed to abuses (though the distinction may not be acceptably clear-cut for everyone), are still very much with us, as dog racing, horse racing, etc. remind us.

The close relationship with animals suggests a continuity in sport and one which, if traced back, has its origins in the transition from hunter-gatherer to farmer. While the connecting thread appears at times to be only tenuous, we can infer that there is surely some human property that elicits a desire for a form of autotelic enterprise based on competition. The way in which it manifests itself differs from culture to culture, and in this chapter I have pulled out only fragments from history to illustrate the general argument. The impression is still clear enough to draw a plausible scenario and one in which a basic impulse continues to operate in widely different contexts. In most of these contexts, some spectacle was made of violence. Despite the ostensibly civilizing forces at work, physical cruelty and the infliction of damage on others continued to attract and entertain people. But, in the nineteenth century, very sharp and dramatic changes took place, particularly in Europe, that were to affect the sensitivity to, and public acceptance of, violence, and this was to have an impact on the entire shape and focus of sport. It was also to establish the framework of what would now legitimately pass for modern sport.

Further reading

Sports Spectators *by Allen Guttmann (Columbia University Press, 1986) is a successor to the author's previous* From Ritual to Record *(Columbia University Press, 1978) and is densely packed with historical detail on the emergence of sport. Guttmann's focus is far wider than that implied by the title and actually provides a basis for understanding sport. 'We are what we watch,' writes Guttmann towards the end of a book that captures how sport can be used as a barometer of historical change and one which should be read by any serious student of sport.*

Combat Sports in the Ancient World *by Michael Poliakoff (Yale University Press, 1987) describes in fine detail the early forms of combat, such as the Greeks'* pankration *('total fight') and Egyptian wrestling. 'The will to win is a basic human instinct, but different societies give varying amounts of encouragement (or discouragement) to the individual's attempt to measure himself against others,' observes Poliakoff in his chapter entitled 'The nature and purpose of combat sport'.*

Barbarians, Gentlemen and Players *by E. Dunning and K. Sheard (Martin Robertson, 1979) traces the origins of rugby football in England to the 'folk games' of pre-industrial society, noting the social changes than accompanied and often precipitated its transformation into a modern sport.*

Die Körperkultur in frühen Epochen der Menschenentwicklung *by Gerhard Lukas (Sportverlag, 1969) is a Marxist attempt to see sport as both a reflection and reinforcement of the economy; its title means 'Physical culture in early stages of civilization'.*

Sport and the British *by Richard Holt (Oxford University Press, 1989) examines what now seem to be crude forms of sport and reveals the links between these and modern versions. Older activities gradually faded as industrialization encroached and cultural patterns changed, but Holt emphasizes the continuities and 'survivals' from old to new.*

Assignment

Cock fighting and boxing: these are two sports that have deep historical roots, but which have aroused controversy. Cock fighting is illegal; and both American and British Medical Associations lobby for a ban on boxing. Despite its illegality, cock fighting persists 'underground'. Would a ban on boxing lead to a similar consequence? Develop your answer by taking note of the patterns of change both in social conditions and popular attitudes over the past 150 years.

Chapter four

Functions of sport

Tenor of life, tempo of work

One of the fashionable haunts of the nobility and upper classes in the early eighteenth century was James Figg's amphitheatre, in London. Figg, himself a swordsman and all-round fighter, opened the venue in 1719 and attracted large crowds to watch displays of animal baiting as well as human contests, featuring swords, fists, and staffs. No sexism, here: Figg held contests between and amongst men and women. Figg's cachet brought him appointments as a tutor to the gentry, instructing in the 'art of self-defence', which was regarded in those days as very much a gentleman's pursuit. There was very little gentlemanly restraint in the actual contests, which were bare knuckle affairs without either specified number of rounds or a points-scoring system. A match was won when one fighter was simply unable to continue. Three- and four-hour contests were commonplace, with wrestling throws, kicks, and punches all permissible. Such types of combat were rife in England in Figg's time (he died in 1734) and drew on what was ancient tradition, as we have noted. (Homer's *Iliad* makes reference to competitive bouts.) No doubt similar forms of combat took place in other parts of the world in the eighteenth century though, in England, fighting was to undergo a special transformation.

At about the same time as Figg's venture, another combat activity was gaining popularity, at least in parts of Great Britain. Ball games, such as Cornwall's 'hurling' and Wales' 'knappan' were local exercises, very loosely organized according to customs, rather than central rules and were played with an inflated animal bladder. Ancient Greeks and Romans also used pig or ox bladders, though they tended to fill them with hair and feathers, more suited to throwing than the fast kicking games that became popular much later. In the intervening centuries ball games were always peripheral to activities such as combat, racing, or archery, but, in the nineteenth century they seemed to 'take off'.

I describe ball games as different to 'combat activity' although it seems that at least some variants of what was to evolve into football allowed participants to complement their delicate ball-playing skills with cudgels and other instruments that Mr Figg and his associates would have been adept at using. Meetings would have resembled an all-out struggle much more than a practised, rule-bound game with clearly-defined goals and final results.

But violence was popular and the rough and wild 'folk games', as Dunning and Sheard call them in *Barbarians, Gentlemen and Players* (1979), were 'closer to "real" fighting than modern sports'. The authors suggest that football's antecedents reflected the 'violent tenor of life in society at large' and also the low threshold of repugnance 'with regard to witnessing and engaging in violent acts'. Sometimes, the distinction between witnessing and engaging became blurred and spectators would join in the action.

It's rather artificial to link these pursuits of the eighteenth century with modern boxing or wrestling and soccer or rugby football, first, because of the regional variations and, second, because of combinations of rules and characteristics that made any systematic differentiation of games impossible. Yet, somehow, the essentials of both activities have dropped into the stream of history and arrived in the 1990s as well-ordered, highly-structured, and elaborately-organized sports. I use the two examples because they embody currents and changes that have affected the entire assortment of activities that have become modern sport. The decline in spontaneity and open brutality in sports mirrored trends in society generally.

The new rules of prize fighting, instituted in 1838, introduced some measure of regulation, including a 'scratch' line which was a mark in the centre of a 24-foot square ring which competitors had to reach unassisted at the start of each round, or else be judged the loser (that is, 'not coming up to scratch'). It was a small but significant modification that removed the necessity of a beating into submission or a knockout to terminate a bout. In 1886, Queensberry rules were devised to reduce the degree of bodily damage possible and to increase the importance of skill as a decisive factor in the 'noble art'.

The same forces affecting combat helped reshape football, taking out some of its ferocity and establishing sets of rules in what was previously a maelstrom. In 1863, the Football Association was formed to regulate the kicking form of the sport. The version that stressed handling was brought under the control of the Rugby Union, which was created in 1871. The Union split into distinct amateur and professional organizations in 1895, the latter being known as Rugby League (which remained confined to the northern counties of England).

In both cases, the organizations were responses to demands for orderliness and standardization. England had metamorphosed into an industrial society where the valued qualities were discipline, precision, and control. Sport not only absorbed these qualities, but promoted them, gradually influencing perceptions and expectations in such a way as to deepen people's familiarity with the industrial regimen.

Industrialization drew populations to urban centres in search of work; not work quite as we know it today, but uncomfortable, energy-draining activities performed for long hours often in squalid and dangerous conditions. This type of work needed a new mentality. People were expected to arrive at work punctually and toil for measured periods of time. Their labours were planned for them and their efforts were often highly specialized according to the division of labour. Behaviour at work was subject to rules and conditions of service. Usually, all the work took place in a physically bounded space, the factory. There was also a need for absoluteness: tools and machines were made to fine tolerances. Underlying all this was a class structure, or hierarchy, in which some strata had attributes suited to ruling and others to being ruled. The latter's shortcomings were so apparent that no detailed investigation of the causes was thought necessary: their poverty, or even destitution was their own fault.

All these had counterparts in the developing sports scene. Time periods for contests were established and measured accurately thanks to newer, sophisticated timepieces. Division of labour in team games yielded role-specific positions and particular, as opposed to general, skills. Constitutions were drawn up to instil more structure into activities and regulate events according to rules. They took place on pitches, in rings and halls – in finite spaces. Winners and losers were unambiguously clear, outright, and absolute. And hierarchies reflecting the class structure were integrated into many activities. Captains of teams, for example, were 'gentlemen' from the upper echelons. The sense of order, discipline, location, and period which sport acquired helped it both complement and support working life. As the form and pace of sport imitated that of industry, so it gained momentum amongst the emergent working class seeking some sporadic diversion from its toil, something more impulsive and daring than the routine labours that dominated industry. While sport was assuming a symmetry with work, it still afforded the working class an outlet, or release from labour; it was pursued voluntarily, at leisure.

Yet there were trends to offset this. Despite the popular beliefs that public schools in the nineteenth century were upholders of the virtues of sport, they actually echoed many of the sentiments of the Puritans, who disapproved utterly of any activity that seemed frivolous, including dancing, blood sports, and wagering (betting). Such entertainments were seen by Puritans as the mindless pleasure of idlers and, of course, idlers were ripe for the devil's work. In the thirteenth and fourteenth centuries, Puritans suppressed any activity resembling a contest in their attempts to create an atmosphere of strict moral discipline. In the sixteenth century, the universities of Oxford and Cambridge banned football.

Public school masters initially tried to prevent the development of football in particular, believing it to be disruptive of order and morally debilitating. There was also the feeling that it was demeaning for the sons of the upper classes to practise activities that were, as one headmaster of the day described them, 'fit only for butcher boys ... farm boys and labourers' (quoted in Dunning and Sheard 1979: 47). Intellectual trends in Germany and France were influenced by the philosopher J. J. Rousseau whose treatise *Emile* (first published in 1762) argued that physical training and competitive sport would yield positive results in the overall education of a child. Ideas drifted across to English public schools, so that, by the 1850s, two main revisions were made to the original ideas on sport. Expressed by Peter McIntosh in his *Fair Play*: 'The first was that competitive sport, especially team games, had an ethical basis, and the second was that training in moral behaviour on the playing field was transferable to the world beyond' (1980: 27). Together, the ideas formed the core of 'muscular Christianity'. Unselfishness, justice, health: these were the type of ideals that were manifest in sport, but also in any proper Christian society. Public schools, influenced by the doctrine, began to integrate a programme of sport into their curricula. Team games were important in subordinating the individual to the collective unit and teaching the virtues of alliances. It was often thought that England's many military victories were attributable to the finely-honed teamwork encouraged by public schools. Again, we glimpse the notion of sport as a preparation for military duty: the playing fields of public schools were equated with battle grounds (Eton and Waterloo, for example). Thomas Hughes' classic, *Tom Brown's Schooldays* is full of allusions to the role of public schools in producing populations suited to rule over an Empire.

Muscular Christianity
A doctrine about the positive moral influence of physical exercise and sport, which had its intellectual roots in the philosophy of J. J. Rousseau in France and Gutsmuths in Germany and which was approvingly adopted by the public schools of England in the late nineteenth century.

The physically tough and toughening version of football, as practised by Rugby School under the headship of Thomas Arnold and his assistant G. E. L. Cotton, gained acceptance in many public schools. Its toughness was useful in sorting out those fit enough to survive and perhaps later prosper in positions of power. The frail would either strengthen or perish. Its appeal to the prestigious public schools bent on turning out 'great men' was soon apparent as the sport of rugby spread through the network and in time, to a number of 'open' clubs in the north of England (which admitted *nouveaux riches* and working-class members).

Muscular Christianity was also instrumental in carrying the other principal variant of football to the working class. 'Socker' was encouraged by churches. A quarter of today's Football League clubs were founded and, for a while, sustained by churches eager to proselytize in urban centres which by the 1880s were humming with the sound of heavy machinery. Industry itself wasn't slow to realize the advantages of possessing a football team comprising members of its workforce. Places like Coventry, Stoke, and Manchester can boast enduring Football League clubs that were originally works outfits. Arsenal was based at Woolwich Arsenal, a London munitions factory. Matches which were only held on designated holy days and other festive occasions became more and more regular, routine, and organized. We might stretch the point and describe the early works teams as 'para-industrial': organized much as an industrial force and intended to supplement the strictly industrial. It was a very deliberate policy pursued by factory owners in much the same way as their European counterparts of the day and contemporary Japanese industries. In some ways, sport was a foil for industrial order; a potent instrument for instilling order in the workforce.

If sport was an instrument, it had two cutting edges for, as well as carving out new patterns of order, it was also responsible for outbreaks of disorder. Work and leisure were cut in two to the imperatives of industry. The more fluid way of life in which the manner in which one earned a living blended imperceptibly with the rest of one's life disappeared as the factory system issued its demands, which were a workforce ready to labour for a set amount of time at a specific site. During that time workers operated under virtual compulsion; outside that time they were free to pursue whatever they wished (and could afford). Sport was a way of filling leisure time with brief, but exhilarating periods of uncertainty: the questions of who or which team would win a more-or-less equal competition was bound to prompt interest and speculation, as, it seems, it always has. The spell of physically competitive activity, far from being broken, was strengthened by the need for momentary release from a colourless world dominated by the monotonous thuds and grinds of machinery. Competitions, whether individual combats, ball games, or animal baits, drew crowds; but public gatherings always carried the potential for disruption.

Public gatherings and festivals and other staged events attracted a working class which was in the process of becoming industrialized but which had not yet done so by the mid- to late nineteenth century. It was still adjusting to what John Hargreaves in *Sport, Power and Culture* (1986) calls the changes in 'tempo and quality of industrial work'. Hargreaves argues that the churches' efforts in building football clubs had the effect of controlling the working class so that it would be more pliant for ruling groups. In fact, Hargreaves' entire thesis revolves around the intriguing idea that sport has helped integrate the working class into respectable 'bourgeois culture' rather than struggle against it. But the integration was never smooth and police or militia were regularly called to suppress riots and uprisings at football matches, prize fights, footraces, cock fights, and so on, as large groups spontaneously grew agitated and unruly. Boxing events to this day employ 'whips' who are promoters' *chargés d'affaires* responsible for most of the minor business. But as the etymology suggests, the original whips were employed to encircle the ring, cracking their whips or lashing at troublesome members of the audience. Local laws were enacted, prohibiting meetings in all but tightly-policed surroundings, sometimes banning sports completely. The rise of the governing bodies within individual sports represents an attempt to absorb working-class energies within a formal structure, thereby containing what might otherwise have become disruptive tendencies.

As the nineteenth century drew to an end, most sports took on a much more orderly character: both participants and spectators came to recognize the legitimacy of governing organizations, the standards of conduct they laid down and the structures of rules they observed. The whole direction and rhythm of sport reflected the growing significance of industrial society. 'Sport, like manufacturing and trade, became ever more directed to attaining efficiency and its emphatic evidence, statistically provable and stateable accomplishments,' Richard Mandell sums up, adding: 'like concurrent movements in law and government, which led to codifications, and rationalization, sport became codified, and civilized by written rules which were enforced by supervising officials (the equivalent of judges and jurors)' (1984: 151).

The reasons for concentrating on nineteenth-century England are: 1) it is here we find something like a factory's smelter shop where organized sport appears as an extract from the molten historical trends; 2) the English experience radiated out amongst the imperial colonies, with sport, as well as trade 'following the flag'; and 3) it is this period of history that has excited many writers sufficiently to produce grand theories of the purposes or functions of sport in the modern world. We'll now consider three of the major functions.

The 'civilizing spurt': Elias

'Sportization' is how Norbert Elias refers to the process in which precise and explicit rules governing contests came into being, with a strict application to ensure equal chances for competitors and supervision to observe fairness. He acknowledges that this took place in the nineteenth century and accompanied the English industrial revolution. Yet, he is wary of theories that explain one in terms of the other. 'Both industrialization and sportization were symptomatic of a deeper-lying transformation of European societies which demanded of their individual members greater 'regularity and differentiation of conduct', he writes in 'An essay on sport and violence' (1986b: 151).

The 'transformation' had roots as far back as the fifteenth century and involved the gradual introduction of rules and norms to govern human behaviour and designate what was appropriate conduct in a given situation; it also involved the rise of impersonal organizations to maintain rules. These reflected a general tendency in Europe towards interdependence: people began to orient their activities to each other, to rely less on their own subsistence efforts and more on those of others, whose tasks would be specialized and geared towards narrow objectives. In time, chains of interdependence were formed: a division of labour ensured that each individual, or group of individuals, was geared to the accomplishment of tasks that would be vital to countless others. They in turn would perform important activities, so that every member of a society depended on others, and no one was an 'island'. The pattern of relationships that emerged is called figuration. For this kind of system to operate with reasonable efficiency, people would have to be discouraged from pursuing their own interests and whims in an unrestrained way. There had to be a method of control over emotions and behaviour, particularly violent behaviour. The need for control grew more acute in eighteenth-century England, where in the aftermath of civil strife, many people feared a recurrence (Elias and Dunning 1986: 171). The state was the central authority responsible for internal orderliness and overall organization and planning. With the formation of state control came what Elias calls a 'civilizing spurt'.

Here we come across Elias' more general historical account, *The Civilizing Process* (1982), which describes a sweeping trend, or even evolution, in which human societies have controlled the use

---

Figuration
While, in a general sense, this refers to the form, shape, or outline of something, Elias has applied it to interdependent relations between people and used it to represent 'chains of functions' between them. Some have found in the concept a new approach to study, while others, like Bauman (in *Sociology*, vol. 13, 1979) have found it reminiscent of more orthodox notions, like 'pattern' or 'situation', and question the value and originality of the concept.

of violence and encouraged an observance of manners. The two aspects are part of one general tendency. So, for example, the decline of dispute settlements through violence and the rise of social prohibitions on such things as spitting and breaking wind are not unconnected in Elias' scheme. They both represent new standards of conduct in changing figurations. The level of acceptable violence drops as the emergent state takes over the settling of disputes and monopolizes the legitimate use of violence. As rules and conventions develop, they spread to all areas, so that standards are imposed, both externally and internally as well as being controlled by the state; individuals control *themselves* according to accepted or 'correct' codes of conduct.

Since the days of the ancient Greeks, which is Elias' starting point, civilization has progressed with the state's power and therefore control over violence within the family and between neighbours, clans, and fiefdoms, increasing at a pace roughly equivalent to our internal controls over emotions and behaviour; in other words, self-restraint. (The similarity to Freud's conception of society taming our more primitive urges through the super-ego is quite pronounced here.)

The civilizing process is a vast world trend, but not a completely linear one: there are phases in history when a figuration may 'decivilize' and regress to barbarism, tolerating a higher level of violence and ungoverned behaviour. This is described by Elias as a 'reverse gear'. Equally, there is allowance for sharp accelerated movements 'forward', such as in the civilizing spurt Elias believes is so crucial to our understanding of modern sport.

While it would caricature the civilizing process to equate it with changes in self control this particular aspect of the wider development acted as an agent in generating 'stress-tensions' which, in turn, agitated the need for organized sport. How does Elias see this happening? First, an abstract observation: 'In societies where fairly high civilizing standards all round are safeguarded and maintained by a highly effective state-internal control of physical violence, personal tensions of people resulting from conflicts of this kind, in a word, stress-tensions are widespread' (1986a: 41). Next, most human societies develop some countermeasures against stress-tensions they themselves generate and 'these activities must conform to the comparative sensitivity to physical violence which is characteristic of people's social habits (customs and dispositions) at the later stages of a civilizing process' (1986a: 41–2).

So, the ways in which people 'let off steam' mustn't violate the standards that have become accepted by society at large. Watching humans mauled by wild animals might have provided stimulating and enjoyable release for the ancient Romans, as might burning live cats or baiting bulls for the English in the last century. But, the civilizing process, according to Elias, changes our threshold of revulsion for enacting and witnessing violence, so that, nowadays, some cultures in the west find a sport like boxing – relatively mild in historical terms – intolerably violent. The methods we choose to discharge tension closely reflect general standards and sensitivities.

Fox hunting is Elias' favourite example. Once synonymous with the word 'sport', fox hunting is now an anachronism and pressure against it would have no doubt prompted its demise were it not a pursuit practised exclusively by England's landowning elite. Developing in the late eighteenth century, this peculiarly English sport was quite unlike the simpler, less regulated, and more spontaneous forms of hunting of other countries and earlier ages where people were the main hunters and foxes were one amongst many prey (boar, red deer, and wolves being others). Fox hunting (itself an example of a figuration) was bound by a strict code of etiquette and idiosyncratic rules, such as that which forbade killing other animals during the hunt. Hounds were trained to follow only the fox's scent, and only they could kill, while humans watched. The fox itself had little utility apart from its pelt; its meat wasn't considered edible (not by its pursuers, anyway) and, while it was considered a pest, the fields and forests were full of others which threatened farmers' livestock and crops. The chances of anyone getting hurt in the hunt were minimized, but each course in the wall of security presented a problem of how to retain the immediacy and physical risk that were so important in early times. Elias believes that the elaboration of the rules of hunting were solutions. The rules served to postpone the outcome, or finale of the hunt and so artificially prolong the process of hunting. 'The excitement of the hunt itself had increasingly become the main source of enjoyment for the human participants' (Elias and Dunning 1986: 166). What had once been foreplay to the act of killing became the main pleasure. So the fox hunt was a virtual 'pure type' of autotelic hunt: the thrill for participants came in the pace and exhilaration of the chasing and the pleasure of watching violence done without actually doing the killing.

But, the influence of the civilizing spurt is apparent in the restraint imposed and exercised by the participants. The overall trend was to make violence more repugnant to people, which effectively encouraged them to control or restrain themselves. Elias stresses that this should be seen not as a repression, but as a product of greater sensitivity. The fox hunters didn't secretly feel an urge to kill with their own hands; they genuinely found such an act disagreeable, but could still find pleasure in viewing it from their horses; what Elias calls 'killing by proxy'.

Despite all attempts to abolish them, hunts persist to this day, probably guided by appetites similar to those whetted by the sight of humans being masticated by sharks. Hundreds of millions of *Jaws* fans can attest to the enjoyable tension provided by the latter, albeit through the medium of film. While Elias doesn't cover the modern hunts, we should add that their longevity reveals something contradictory about the civilizing trend and the impulse to condone or even promote wanton cruelty. To ensure a long and satisfying chase, and to be certain that foxes are found in the open, 'earth stoppers' are employed to close up earths (fox holes) and badger sets in which foxes may take refuge. Many hunts maintain earths to ensure a suficient supply of foxes through the season (foxes used to be imported from the continent). The hunt does not start until after 11 a.m. to allow the fox time to digest its food and ensure that it is capable of a long run. During the course of a hunt, a fox may run to ground and will either survive or be dug out by the pursuant dogs, a virtual baiting from which even the dogs emerge with damage. New hounds are prepared by killing cubs before the new season, a practice observed and presumably enjoyed by members of the hunt and their guests.

In Elias' theory, fox hunting was a solution to the problems created by the accelerating trend towards civilization and the internal controls on violence it implied. The closing up of areas of excitement, which in former ages had been sources of pleasurable gratification (as well as immense suffering), set humans on a search for substitute activities and one which didn't carry the risks, dangers, or outright disorder that society as a whole would find unacceptable – what Elias, in the title of one of his books calls the *Quest for Excitement*. The English form of fox hunting was only one example of a possible solution, but Elias feels it is an 'empirical model', containing all the original distinguishing characteristics of modern sport. Other forms of sport, such as boxing, soccer, cricket, and rugby showed how the problem was solved without the use and abuse of animals; the first two of these were appropriated by the working class. All evolved in a relatively orderly manner, well matched to the needs of modern, bureaucratic society with its accent on organization and efficiency and ultimately in line with the general civilizing process.

The explanation of sport is but one facet of Elias' grand project which is to understand the very nature and consequences of the civilizing process. It follows that critics who are not convinced by his general model are certainly not by his specific one. The actual idea of a civilizing process has the tinge of a theory of progress in which history is set to proceed through predetermined stages which can't be altered. Elias' mention of the irregularity of the process and the 'reverse gear' are rather peripheral to the main thesis which suggests that, as Paul Hoggett puts it, 'civilization seems to march onwards fairly straightforwardly without any collapsing back into barbarity' (1986: 36).

Many modern observers of sport might want to argue that 'collapses' are quite commonplace and point fingers in the direction of soccer stadia, often the sites of open, almost ritualistic violence between rival fans. Elias and his devotees would recommend a more detailed examination of history to appreciate that violence has for long been related to soccer; only the media's amplification of it has changed. Presumably the same could be said about fox hunting which continues unabated today. However, this response is only partially satisfactory, as many other sports have developed violent penumbra quite recently and it is hard to establish any historical connections with, say, boxing, cricket, and rugby, all of which have experienced major crowd disorder over the past two decades.

It is interesting that the nucleus of Elias' model has not been attacked. A basic proposition is that 'pleasurable excitement ... appears to be one of the most elementary needs of human beings' (1986: 174). Elias never documents the sources of such 'needs' and, considering that the entire theoretical edifice rests on them, one might expect some expansion. This is mysteriously absent. Is it a biological drive? Part of a survival instinct? A deep psychological trait? Elias' treatment seems to suggest that the 'need for pleasurable excitement' is of a similar order to the need for food, shelter, sex, and other such basic needs. I agree that it *appears* as basic as these, but, for reasons outlined in chapter 3, I would want to look closely at the changing contexts, social and ecological, in which such 'needs' manifest themselves. This may seem a small quibble with what is after all a hugely ambitious attempt to illuminate the nature and purpose of modern sport by connecting its changing character to the civilizing transformation of the past several centuries. Far from being an autonomous realm separated from other institutions, sport is totally wrapped up with culture, psyche, and the state. Human 'stress-tensions' are linked to large-scale social changes. Yet the analysis still seems caught in a timewarp; as Vera Zolberg concludes, it does 'not devote adequate attention to one of the most striking features of sport in modern society, that of the *business* of sport' (1987: 573). The way in which sport has been seized upon by commercial organizations in recent years has tended to show Elias' theory as adequate at a certain level, but unable to cope with the developments imposed on sport by the pressures of professionalism in recent years. The state may once have played a key role in precipitating organized efforts to satisfy basic needs for excitement, but private business has become a powerful force. Alternative theories have tried to link the two.

Capitalism and class: Marxian theories

Sport is a remarkably ironic thing, its chief characteristic being that it provides an entertaining relief from work while at the same time preparing people for more work. This is the central insight of a group of theorists who have, in one way or another, been influenced by the work of Karl Marx. Although Marx himself didn't write about sport, his theories have great relevance. The focus of his work was the development of modern capitalism, an economic system based on a split of the ownership of the means of production (factories, land, equipment, etc.). Owners of the means of production are bosses, or bourgeoisie, in whose interests capitalism works and who are prepared to milk the system to its limits in order to stay in control. The working class, or proletariat, are forced to work for them in order to subsist. As the system doesn't work in their interests, they have to be persuaded that it *could* if only they were luckier, or had better breaks, or worked harder. In other words, the system itself is fine; it's actually the workers who need to change for the good. As long as workers are convinced of the legitimacy of economic arrangements, then capitalism is not under threat. So the system has evolved methods of ensuring its own survival. And this is where sport fits in.

John Hargreaves identifies four main areas. First, organized sport helps train a 'docile labour force': it encourages in the working class an acceptance of the kind of work discipline demanded in modern production; hard work is urged in both sport and work. We've noted before how the organization and tempo of industry became reflected in sport and Hargreaves sees the symmetry as almost perfect. Compare the features of sport and industry: 'a high degree of specialisation and standardisation, bureaucratised and hierarchical administration, long-term planning, increased reliance on science and technology, a drive for maximum productivity, a quantification of performance and, above all, the alienation of both producer and consumer' (1982: 41). Major events, like the Olympics and SuperBowl are given as examples of the final point. Second, sport has become so thoroughly commercialized and dominated by market forces that events and performers are treated as or perhaps just *are* commodities that are used by capitalist enterprises: 'Sport is produced, packaged and sold like any other commodity on the market for mass consumption at enormous profits' (1982: 41). The transferring or trading of players typifies the 'commodification'. The third area in which sport fits in is in 'expressing the quintessential ideology in capitalist society'. What Marxian theorists have proposed here is that sport works in subtle ways at indicating qualities or imperatives in people; all these qualities have counterparts in society at large. Aggressive individualism, ruthless competitiveness, equal opportunities, elitism, chauvinism, sexism, nationalism: all these are regarded as admirable. Their desirability isn't questioned in sport and the uncritical approach to them is carried over to society. Fourth, there is the area of the state: this bureaucratic administration represents capitalist interests in the west and the state-capitalist societies of the Soviet bloc. It follows that every intrusion into sport by the state must be seen as some sort of attempt to link sports participation with the requirements of the capitalist system.

Four areas, then, but hardly a theory; they are really only lowest common denominators for all those favouring a Marxian conception of sport. Beyond these, there are a variety of interpretations all taking their lead from Marx in the sense that they see the split over the means of production as central. In other words, sport has to be analysed in terms of class relations. Paul Hoch has advanced one of the most acerbic Marxian critiques of sport, which he likens to the mainstream religions about which Marx himself wrote much. Religion was regarded as little more than a capitalist convenience, absorbing workers' energies and emotions and supplying a salve after the week's labours. Sport has much the same significance. Both religion and sport work as an opiate that temporarily dulls pain and gives a false sense of well-being, but which is also a dangerous and debilitating narcotic that can reduce its users to a helpless state of dependence. The attraction of sport is as compelling as that of religion and its effects are comparable: it siphons off potential that might otherwise be put to political use in challenging the capitalist system.

Jean-Marie Brohm has added to this approach a book of equal astringency whose title describes sport as 'a prison of measured time'. By this, Brohm means that the institutional, rule-governed, highly-organized structure of modern sport has been shaped by capitalist interest groups in such a way as to represent a constraint rather than a freedom. Sport is in no sense an alternative to work, less still an escape from it 'since it removes all bodily freedom, all creative spontaneity, every aesthetic dimension and every playful impulse' (1978: 175). The competitor is merely a prisoner, whose performances are controlled, evaluated, and recorded, preferably in quantitative terms. Capitalism as a system stifles the human imagination and compresses the human body into mindless production work; and as sport is but one part of that system, it can do little more than reproduce its effects. It just obeys the 'logic' of the system. As Richard Gruneau writes: 'For Brohm, capitalism has shaped sport in its own image' (1983: 38). Others, like Gerhard Vinnai and Bruno Rigauer agree with the basic assumptions and emphasize how corporations have penetrated, or completely taken over sport. It is as if sport has been appropriated by one class and used to bolster its already commanding position in the overall class structure. For Rigauer, sport has aided the economic system by improving the health of workers and so minimizing the time lost at work through illness (we presume he would interpret the British Sport Council's 'Sport for all' campaign in such terms).

Like Brohm, he sees a 'technocratic' takeover of sport, with performances being subject to rationalization and planning and training becoming more time-absorbing and important than performance itself. Initiative and creativity are stifled, rendering the human performer as the 'one-dimensional man', so called by the Marxian philosopher Herbert Marcuse (from whom Brohm and Rigauer draw insights). In all accounts, the human beings are depicted as passive dopes, pushed around by factors beyond their control. But are humans just like hockey pucks? Do they really respond so readily and easily? Those who think not find the work of Hoch and Brohm rather too deterministic – all thoughts and behaviour are determined by outside forces emanating from the capitalist system. Sport is but one instrument for maintaining the domination and exploitation of the working class. In contrast, other writers prefer to see the working class playing a more active role. Certainly, there is a complementarity between the way in which modern sport is organized and the functions it fulfils on the one hand, and the requirements of capitalism on the other. But this doesn't deny that different groups (classes) are involved in different sports *and* at different levels at different stages in history.

Sport is not, as Hargreaves puts it, 'universally evil'. It's meaning and significance have to be investigated more closely. Other Marxian writers, including Richard Gruneau, John Hoberman, and Hargreaves himself, have attempted to do this. All would go along with the more orthodox Marxian approach, but only so far. Sport is much more multifaceted than the others acknowledge. It may give substance to wider ideologies and slough off working-class energies, but it can also be useful as a builder of solidarity within working-class groups which are brought together with a common purpose. 'It is precisely this type of solidarity that historically has formed the basis for a trenchant opposition to employers,' observes Hargreaves (1986: 110).

Public gatherings at sports events have always generated a potential for disorder and have attracted the state's agents of control. Some writers have even inferred a form of political resistance from the exploits of soccer hooligans. So, involvement in sport can actually facilitate, or even encourage challenge rather than accommodation. Far from being a means of controlling the masses, sport, on occasion, has needed controlling itself. On the issue of sport as a preparation for work, Hargreaves reminds us that not all sports resemble the rhythms and rationality of work. Fishing and bowling provide relaxation and relief in very stark contrast to work.

Soccer hooligans

The term 'hooligan' is thought to derive from the name of a riotous and rowdy Irish family which lived in nineteenth-century London. It now refers to those involved in violent activity on a regular basis at or near British soccer stadia. Violence has been a feature of soccer crowds since the last century, but it has become increasingly organized so that some supporters, like West Ham United's 'InterCity Firm' and Chelsea's 'Headhunters', are run almost as exclusive clubs with their own hierarchies. Some researchers (Marsh *et al.* 1978) deny the seriousness of the violence and emphasize its ritualistic or symbolic qualities. Others (Dunning *et al.* 1988) take a figurational approach, seeing violence as an integral part of working-class life and a way of attaining a certain status or prestige. It has merely transferred to football stadia and been amplified by the mass media, which, in their own way, sustain the violence by providing models for future imitation.

Hargreaves (1986) argues against a firmly negative view of sport as providing only 'surrogate satisfactions for an alienated mass order . . . perpetuating its alienation' and instead argues for a more flexible, spontaneous interpretation. Sport may perform many services in the interests of the status quo, amongst them a belief in the ultimate triumph of ability ('if you're good you'll make it' – in sport or life generally). It also helps fragment the working class by splintering loyalties into localities, regions, etc. But, it can also provide a basis for unity and therefore resistance to dominant interest groups: 'Part mass therapy, part resistance, part mirror image of the dominant political economy,' as David Robins puts it (1982: 145).

The idea that sport provides a politically safe channel, or an outlet for energies that might otherwise be disruptive to capitalism has been given a different slant by ethologists (scientists of animal behaviour). Unlike Marxian writers who see the dissatisfaction resulting from capitalism as having potential until it is diverted into sport, ethologists see the dissatisfaction, or more correctly, frustration, as having *natural* sources. Whereas Marxian writers would see that frustration possibly transformed into political protest should sport disappear, ethologists would insist that it would lead to humans fighting each other. Sport is a vent; a system through which we release violent behaviour. We will now examine one ethological approach.

An ethological approach: Morris

While he dismisses most of the Marxian approaches to sport as 'political claptrap', Desmond Morris discerns a 'small grain of truth' in the idea that events that fascinate, excite, and entertain people also distract them from 'political terrorism and bloody rebellion'. But, on examination, this aspect of sport 'is not political after all, but rather has to do with human nature' (1981: 20). Morris, as a student of animal behaviour and who affords humans pride of place in his perspective, has turned his sights to sport in his book *The Soccer Tribe*. He begins from an observation of the 1978 World Cup Final between Argentina and Holland, an event comprising twenty two brightly clad figures 'kicking a ball about in a frenzy of effort and concentration' on a small patch of grass, and watched by something like one-quarter of the entire world's population. 'If this occurrence was monitored by aliens on a cruising UFO, how would they explain it?' asks Morris. His book is a kind of answer.

Morris adopts the role of the puzzled, detached observer, recording notes in the ship's log in an effort to discover 'the function of this strange activity' and, while his sights are fixed on soccer, his records have relevance for all sports. His rejection of the Marxian 'social drug' approach is understandable, for Morris' ethology follows that of Konrad Lorenz, who believed that aggression is instinctive in all animals, including humans. Sport is truly a 'safe' diversion from violent behaviour. But were political systems to change, the aggression would still exist and would still need an outlet. Political frustrations may aggravate aggressive tendencies, but they do not cause them. This removes the need for any detailed social or psychological theory: sport in general and soccer in particular are grand occasions for venting instinctively violent urges. But Morris goes on to expose several interesting facets, the first being the *ritual hunt*. Morris' initial premiss is much the same as the one offered in this book: that the predecessors of sport were activities that 'filled the gap left by the decline of the more obvious hunting activities' (Morris 1981). The activities passed through a series of phases, the final one being symbolic in which players represent hunters, the ball is their weapon and the goal the prey. Footballers 'attack' goals and 'shoot' balls. Sport is a disguised hunt, a ritual enactment.

Morris calls modern players 'pseudo-hunters' whose task of killing the inanimate prey is deliberately complicated by introducing opponents to obstruct them, making it a 'reciprocal hunt'. Goalkeepers of a football team resemble 'claws' of a cornered prey 'lashing out to protect its vulnerable surface'. Its parallels with hunting have given soccer global appeal. Some sports, such as archery, darts, bowling, billiards, snooker, skeet, skittles, curling, croquet, and golf, all concentrate on the climax of a hunt in the sense that they all involve aiming at a target. They lack the physical risks and exertions of a headlong chase and the necessary co-operation between members of the hunting pack. Tennis and squash are more physical, but, unless played in doubles, lack teamwork. Some sports, especially motor racing, capture the chase aspect of hunting and also retain dangers. Basketball, netball, volleyball, hockey, cricket, baseball, lacrosse, and rugby football have plenty of fast flowing movement and a climactic aiming at targets. Yet the risk of physical injury isn't too high. Morris believes that, apart from soccer, only Australian rules football and ice hockey approach what he calls the 'magic mixture'. The former has been isolated geographically and the latter suffers because the small puck (the 'weapon') makes it difficult for spectators to follow the play. Soccer seems to capture all the right elements in its ritual and has the potential for involving spectators to an intense degree, which makes watching all the more satisfying.

For all its ritual, soccer and, for that matter many other sports, have a tendency to degenerate into what Morris calls a *stylized battle*. At the end of play, there is usually a winner and loser and this is not a feature of hunts. Soccer caricatures many other sports in arousing its spectators; fans seethe and fight, they are outraged at bad play or decisions, and euphoric at good results. Other sports engender similar reactions, but at a milder level. At least one piece of research has put this to the test, focusing on hooliganism at football grounds as 'ritualized aggression' in that it is not typically violent in a destructive way, but conforms to an 'order' with unwritten rules and codes of behaviour. As befits an ethological approach, comparisons are made with nonhuman species which use ritual displays of aggression for various purposes, but do so without transgressing boundaries. The stylized war for Peter Marsh *et al.* is bounded by *The Rules of Disorder*.

In a similar vein, Morris argues that sport serves as a safety valve through which people vent their spleen in a way which would be unacceptable in many other contexts. But attending an emotional event, as well as providing an outlet for anger and frustrations built up during the week's work may add a new frustration if the result isn't satisfactory and so make the spectators and players feel worse than before. So, the fan (who happens to be male in Morris' example) 'goes home feeling furious. Back at work on Monday, he sees his boss again and all the pent-up anger he felt against the soccer opponents wells up inside him' (1981: 20). So, every match is therapeutic and inflammatory 'in roughly equal proportions'.

Another ambiguous function of sport is its capacity to act *as a status display*. Again, Morris writes about soccer, but in terms that can be adapted to fit other sports: 'If the home team wins a match, the victorious local supporters can boast an important psychological improvement, namely an increased sense of local status' (1981: 20). Soccer, like most other organized sports, developed in a period of industrialization; as we have noted, many British clubs began life as factory teams. A successful side conferred status not only on the team, but on the firm and even the area. Winning teams and individuals are still held in esteem locally because a victory for them means a victory for the community or region.

The conferment of status is quite independent of objective material positions. Since the publication of Morris' book, this aspect of his argument has become more relevant, as depressed areas in which local manufacturing industries have collapsed or in which communities have been destroyed, have yearned for success through sport. The troubled West Midlands city of Coventry was boosted by the local football club's first-ever English Football Association (FA) cup win in 1987. Northern Ireland gained respite from destruction and bloodshed on Barry McGuigan fight nights when the fight occupied centre stage in the sports world.

Morris' fourth function of sport *as a religious ceremony* is arguably the most underdeveloped in his assessment, but others before him have expanded on this concept. Like a religious gathering, a sporting event draws large groups of people together in a visible crowd; it temporarily unites them with a commonly and, often, fervently held belief not in a deity but in an individual sports performer, or a team. Sport is a great developer of social solidarity: it makes people feel they belong to a strong homogeneous collectivity which has a presence far greater than any single person. Morris equates the rise of sport with secularization: 'As the churches . . . emptied with the weakening of religious faith, the communities of large towns and cities have lost an important social occasion' (1981: 23). The function has been taken over by sport.

This argument has been expressed by a number of writers, perhaps most famously by Michael Novak whose book *The Joy of Sport* (1976) is a reverent acknowledgement of the ecstatic elements of sport. Certainly, the general view that sport has assumed the position of a new religion is a persuasive one and is supported by the mass idolatry that abounds in modern sport. We need look no further than Olympic games opening or closing ceremonies, or half-time at the SuperBowl, to see the most stupendous, elaborate displays of ritual and liturgy. These are precisely the type of rituals that have been integral to mass religious worship in the past. The purposes they serve would be similar. In measurable terms, one could suggest that sport is more popular than religion: *far* more people watch sport than go to church; sport gets *far* more media attention than religion. Sports performers are better-known than religious leaders. In all probability, people discuss sport more than they do religion. So, it seems feasible to say that sport occupies a bigger part of people's lives than does religion.

But religion is intended to provide transcendental reference points beyond everyday experience; it gives moral guidelines; it instructs, informs, and enlightens. Some fanatics may believe sport does all these things. Realistically, it doesn't, though this isn't the thrust of the argument. Do religious believers follow the guidelines or learn from the enlightenment? Some might respond that sports fans do. Otherwise, why ask Daley Thompson to tell people to drink Lucozade, or any number of American sports stars to drink Coca-Cola? People *follow* sports with much the same zeal and commitment as active church-goers follow religion and, although it might seem insulting to religious adherents, sports fans do pursue a faith, albeit in their own way.

The comparison between sport and religion extends beyond superficial resemblances when we recognize that sport has become a functional substitute, supplying for the follower a meaningful cause, an emblematic focus, and a source of allegiance, even belonging. But there is still another way in which sport fills a vacuum left by religion and here we move on to the concept of sport *as a social drug*. Morris, who is dismissive of Marxian theories of sport, fails to make the connection between the two functions. The 'opiate thesis' we encountered earlier, when applied to sport shows how sport can function to keep workers' minds off political revolt and so preserve the status quo – which is, according to Marx, what religion was supposed to do. Morris, in rebutting this, states the argument rather crudely, making sport seem a 'bourgeois-capitalist plot', a conspiracy orchestrated by the bosses. As we saw in the previous section, this isn't quite the intention of Marxian writers.

There are two residual functions, both of which Morris concedes are exaggerations. *As big business* sport is commercialized and run effectively as if making money was the sole organizing principle. This is partly true, but misses the reason for the involvement of the 'vast majority' which is because they 'love' sport. 'Money is a secondary factor', according to Morris. *As theatrical performance* showbusiness influences are very evident in sport nowadays and the suggestion is that sport has become a mass entertainment. This is true for football, boxing, baseball, and other sports, but not for bowls, netball, judo, and many other minority sports. Even then, sport, by definition, can never be pure entertainment for as soon as the unpredictable element of competition is gone, it ceases. It then becomes pure theatre.

Morris' treatment is not a formal theory, but a catalogue of functions which soccer serves, as indeed do all sports at various levels, from the psychological to the political. There is no attempt to link the functions together, nor much evaluation of which functions are most effective. Its minor strengths lie in drawing our attention to the many ways in which sport has embedded itself in modern culture and the modern psyche. Try thinking of something that can simultaneously function as a stylized battle, a religious ceremony, and a status display. Morris offers what is really no more than a preamble to his 'dissection' (as he calls it) of soccer, but even in this he dismantles the notion that sport is 'only a game' and indicates that a match is 'a symbolic event of some complexity'.

So much for attempts to make sense of sport through grand theories, all of which have merits yet none of which is without problems. At least they provide frames of reference within which we can operate when investigating some of the more specific issues concerning sport. In the next three chapters we will do exactly that, in each case looking at popular ideas that circulate in sport and exposing some of their shortcomings.

Further reading

Class, Sports and Social Development *by Richard Gruneau (University of Massachusetts Press, 1983) considers some Marxist contributions to the study of sport before offering his own 'developmental' model which is influenced by the work of the sociologist Anthony Giddens.*

Rip Off the Big Game *by Paul Hoch (Anchor Doubleday, 1972) has been criticized as a rather too crude Marxist account, but still packs a punch as a powerful critique of modern sport. At the time of its publication, it was a landmark that influenced other aproaches to the study of sport.*

Sport, Power and Culture *by John Hargreaves (Polity Press, 1986) examines sport in relations to the roles it has played in 'reproducing power relations': in some historical periods, sport has stimulated resistance and rebellions, while at others it has helped bring the working class under the control of ruling groups by 'integrating' it into the bourgeois dominated order of things.*

Quest for Excitement *edited by N. Elias and E. Dunning (Blackwell, 1986) is subtitled 'Sport and leisure in the civilizing process' – which indicates its main theme. A collection of linked essays, this is a guide to the figurational approach, which itself is evaluated in a special edition of* Theory Culture and Society *(vol. 4, 1987), though only one of the articles in this journal is mildly critical (see D. Jary's review of the above title).*

The Soccer Tribe *by Desmond Morris (Cape, 1981) has been largely neglected by serious students of sport, possibly because of Morris' reputation as a 'coffee table book' author. Yet there are ingenious and stimulating perspectives in this title which make it worthy of consideration.*

Assignment

Consider ways in which sport reflects almost perfectly changes in technology, patterns of work, and people's values and attitudes in a manner *not* suggested by any of the theories covered in this chapter.

Chapter five

Myths about minorities

Meaningless dreams

By the time he was approaching school-leaving age, Maurice Hope had but two options as he saw them: 'To buckle under, or be determined and ambitious.' He settled for the latter and, eventually, became a world boxing champion. In the process, he distinguished himself as a competitor of great resolve and resilience, properties that he had acquired during his youth, when he was spat at, physically abused, and habitually called a 'black bastard'. Being black could have been an impediment to his progress, but, instead, Hope transformed it into a stimulus. It hardened him and hardness proved to be a valuable asset in the ring.

Hope was born in Antigua, but migrated to the UK with his family when he was nine and completed his formal education in the London area of Hackney. In this sense, he was no different from tens of thousands of other young Afro-Caribbeans who grew up in British inner cities in the 1960s. His first-hand experience of racism was by no means unique, nor, for that matter, was his attraction to sport as a possible career. The mundane possibilities of working in industry or being unemployed seemed poor alternatives to the seemingly broad horizons of sport, where a person's skin colour was far less important than it was in other areas, or so it seemed, at least. Hope was drawn to boxing not as a hobby or even just a leisure pursuit; sport was to be his prime interest and career. Countless other young blacks have done much the same, sensing the limits imposed on them because of their race and trying to escape them through sport. Small wonder that sport has been regarded as 'the way out' for blacks on both sides of the Atlantic. What's more, there is plenty of empirical support for the belief that sport does offer blacks a better-than-even chance: Mike Tyson's colossal earnings, Florence Griffith Joyner's stardom, and John Barnes' international reputation are some proof of this.

But appearances are often deceptive and these highly unrepresentative superstars unwittingly create an illusion. As American sports writer Jack Olsen observed in his 1968 book, *The Black Athlete*: 'At most, sport has led a few thousand Negroes out of the ghetto. But for hundreds of thousands of other Negroes it has substituted a meaningless dream.' While the time and effort demanded in trying to become another Tyson or Griffith Joyner is so great that it may ruin a young person's prospects of doing anything else, the actual chances of emulating them are infinitesimally small. Failed sports performers have quite frequently destroyed any other career possibilities they might have had. No sports performer can avoid making sacrifices; the black performers' sacrifices are just greater than most.

Why? This is one of the many questions we must address in this chapter. Others that arise are: why do so many blacks achieve *success* relative to the number of blacks in the total population? This isn't quite as contradictory as it sounds for it's a fact that many blacks do reach levels of excellence; it's also a fact that far more leave sport in failure and disappointment. In the course of this chapter, we'll uncover some of the processes at work beneath these facts.

There are also questions to be asked about women, not a minority group in a numerical sense, but certainly a minority in terms of top jobs, wealth, income, and political influence. The position of women in sport is, generally speaking, quite unlike that of black people, for they have been discouraged from participating, often by means of convenient fallacies about their being physically incapable of withstanding the pressures of competition and naturally unsuited to the demands of sport. Their results have – certainly up to quite recently – shown this to be so. Women do not, by and large, compete head-to-head with men (and when they do, they are invariably beaten) and where performance can be measured, women are some way behind their male counterparts. Again, this is deceptive for there have been concealed processes at work for many decades and these have served to suppress women's success in sport.

Cast in a different light, women's experience is comparable with blacks'. Being minorities, both have marginal positions, meaning that they are largely excluded from many of the key areas of society. Neither features prominently in politics, the professions, or other areas of society where important decisions are made that affect people's lives. Their exclusion is usually the product of an '-ism': as blacks are discriminated against and their accomplishments diminished through racism, so women are prohibited from competing on equal terms with men through sexism. Both remain on the underside of a lopsided structure of inequality and this has affected the involvement of both in sport – in quite different ways, as we will see.

Racism
A set of beliefs or ideas based on the assumption that the world's population can be divided into different human biological groups designated 'races'. Following on from this is the proposition that the 'races' are ordered hierarchically, so that some stand in a position of superordinacy, or superiority, to others. This is a classic type of racism; nowadays, ideas of superiority are often veiled in arguments concerning culture, nationalism, and ethnic identity. Quite often, these contain connotations of racism that are not specific, but only inferred. When ideas, or beliefs, about racial superiority are translated into action, we speak in terms of racial discrimination, or simply *racialism*. Racism is the idea; racialism is the practice.

Sport as an escape attempt

There is quite a story to blacks' involvement with organized sport in the west. It begins in the late eighteenth century during the American War of Independence, when General Percy of the British forces captured the town of Richmond. Impressed by the fighting prowess of a slave who worked on the plantations there, Percy took Bill Richmond – as he named him – under his tutelage and groomed him for prize fighting. While it couldn't have been an easy life, prize fighting had its perks (like extensive travel in Europe) and must have seemed far preferable to plantation work. Richmond was something of a prototype, his modest success encouraging slave owners and merchants to scour for potential fighters whom they might patronize.

The celebrated Tom Molyneaux was one such fighter. Once a slave, he was taken to England and trained by Richmond, eventually winning his freedom. Molyneaux built on his predecessor's success, hobnobbing with the nobility and generally mixing with the London beau monde. It was in his classic fight with English heavyweight champion Tom Cribb, in 1810, that he created his niche in sport history. Peter Jackson was born on the West Indies island of St Croix and travelled to Sydney and San Francisco before settling in England in the late nineteenth century. He, more than any pugilist of his day, embraced fame, though world champion John L. Sullivan's refusal to fight him denied him the ultimate title. Yet his decline was abrupt and he became a habitual drinker and was made to play in a stage version of Stowe's *Uncle Tom's Cabin*.

Some slaves continued to leave America to campaign as prize fighters in Europe, but the majority were pitted against each other locally. The years on either side of emancipation in 1865 saw blacks filtering into other sports; they were most successful at horse riding and baseball. In the latter, they were not permitted to play with or against whites. Ninety-eight years after the first Molyneaux-Cribb clash, a black man ascended to the apogee of sporting achievement. John Arthur Johnson in 1908 challenged and beat Tommy Burns, a white man, to become the heavyweight champion of the world. Fighting as 'Jack Johnson', he broke the 'colour line' which segregated blacks from whites in all areas, including sport. In fact, after Johnson eventually lost the title in 1916, the line was redrawn and no black man was allowed to fight for the world title until 1937 when Joe Louis started a succession of black champions interrupted only by Rocky Marciano (1952–5), Ingemar Johannson (1959–60), and Gerry Cooney (1983–4). It's puzzling to wonder why Jack Dempsey is often acknowledged as one of the 'greats' when he either refused or was prevented from defending his title against blacks.

Johnson and, in an entirely different way, Louis were black sports' symbols, Johnson especially cultivating a reputation as a 'bad nigger', a moral hard man who, as Lawrence Levine puts it, 'had the strength and courage and ability to flout the limitations imposed by white society' (1977: 420). Johnson's imagery was based as much on his penchant for the company of white women as his boxing. This was a time when the Ku Klux Klan was in its ascendancy and blacks were lynched for far lesser deeds than consorting with white females. Far from being 'bad', Louis was a virtual Uncle Tom character, obsequious, apolitical and exploitable – as his poverty, despite vast ring earnings, demonstrates. Yet, he too was a potent symbol for black Americans who were short of heroes or role models on whom to style their own lives. Both were anomalies: conspicuously successful black men in a society where success was virtually monopolized by whites.

The other outstanding black sportsman of this period was Jesse Owens who, like Louis, was 'a credit to his race' – which meant he was self-effacing and compliant to the demands of white officials. Well, not totally compliant: after returning a performance of theatrical proportions at the 1936 'Nazi Olympics' in Berlin, where he won four gold medals and shamed Hitler into a walk-out, he was expelled from the American Athletics Union for refusing to compete in a Swedish tour. Owens was eventually reduced to freak show racing against horses and motorcycles. Other black sportsmen were similarly brought to reduced circumstances. Johnson suffered the indignity of imprisonment, of fighting bulls in Barcelona, of performing stunts in circuses, of comically playing Othello, and of boxing all-comers in exhibitions at the age of 68. Louis ended his days ignominiously in a wheelchair, welcoming visitors at a Las Vegas hotel. The careers of all three followed a comet's elliptical path, radiating brilliance in their orbit, yet fading into invisibility. Plenty of other blacks have followed the same route. Sports history is full of dreams turning to nightmares. But black sportsmen seem particularly afflicted. Not even 'The Greatest' (Muhammad Ali) himself could maintain his dignity in later years.

While boxing was the first sport in which blacks were able to cross the colour line and compete with whites, others followed the form. In 1946, when Joe Louis was nearing the end of his reign as heavyweight king (and the year in which Jack Johnson died), Jackie Robinson became the first black person to play major league baseball. He was sent death threats and his teams, Montreal and the Brooklyn Dodgers, were sometimes boycotted by opponents. The hostility of his reception may have initially daunted administrators from recruiting black players, but by the 1950s, the numbers entering major league were multiplying.

Nowadays, US basketball is dominated by black players. The trend began in 1951 when Chuck Hooper signed for Boston Celtics and precipitated a rush: within sixteen years, over half the National Basketball Association players were black. The spectre of freak show that had hung over Owens and the others visited basketball in the shape of the Harlem Globetrotters whose goals were more in making audiences laugh than scoring hoops. The comic Globetrotters' popularity with whites was probably because of the players' conformity to the image of blacks as physically adept, but too limited intellectually to harness skill to firm objectives. James Michener in *Sports in America*, wrote of the Globetrotters: 'They deepened the stereotype of "the loveable [sic], irresponsible Negro"' (1976: 145).

Civil rights legislation in the 1960s erased the colour line, in a *de jure*, or legal, sense at least. As the segregationist barriers in education tumbled down, so black youngsters began to mix and play competitively with whites. College football came within reach of more blacks and this, in turn, translated into more black professional players. By 1972, black footballers comprised 40 per cent of the NFL.

In Britain, the historical developments were similar, though compressed into a shorter timespan and with considerably fewer numbers, of course (the UK's black population is less than 2 per cent of its total compared with 12 per cent in the USA). Richmond and Molyneaux were followed by a succession of prize fighters, one notable being Andrew Jeptha, who migrated from Cape Town in 1902 and became the first ever black boxer to hold a British title in 1907 (this was before the formation of the British Boxing Board of Control). On the track, sprinters from the British West Indies, like Arthur Wharton, Jack London, McDonald Bailey, and Arthur Wint established reputations from the end of the nineteenth century to the 1950s. Wharton transferred to professional soccer with Preston North End, thus becoming the first-ever black player, though the person popularly credited with that distinction is Lloyd Lindbergh Delaphena, who played for Middlesbrough and Portsmouth in the 1950s. This period was one of mass migration from the Caribbean and, as a consequence, many migrants, such as Trinidad's Yolande Pompey and Guyana's Cliff Anderson, were active in British rings. Hogan 'Kid' Bassey, originally from Nigeria but based in Liverpool, won the world featherweight title in 1957.

But one boxer embodied all the elements of the black sportsman in this period. Born in the Midlands town of Leamington Spa in 1928, Randolph Turpin had a Guyanese migrant father and an English mother. Inspired by the example of his older brother Dick, who, in 1948, won the British middleweight title, Randolph had a shimmering boxing career that came to a climax in 1951 when he upset Sugar Ray Robinson to become the world middleweight champion. Lacking any financial acumen, he ran into trouble with the Inland Revenue which filed a bankruptcy petition against him for unpaid tax on his considerable ring earnings. His career plunged to humiliating depths when he engaged in 'boxer vs wrestler' bouts and even consented to a fully-fledged comeback in an unlicensed boxing promotion at the age of 35. On 16 May 1966, he committed suicide by shooting himself, though rumours of a gangland murder were rife, according to his biographer Jack Birtley (1976: 140–53). His fall resembled that of other black champions.

Marilyn Fay Neufville broke the world's 400-metre record in 1970 when she was 18. Born in Jamaica, she ran for Cambridge Harriers, a London club, and became the first black female to make an impact on British sport. Sprint events were later virtually dominated by black women, but less conspicuously, judo and volleyball also benefited from the growing participation of black women.

Unlike the USA, Britain has never had formal segregation, so black school children have competed in sport with peers from a variety of ethnic backgrounds. Soccer, as the nation's most popular game, has been practised in schools throughout the country so it was not unexpected when, in the late 1970s and early 1980s, black players began appearing in football league teams. First, the trickle: Albert Johanneson, a Leeds United player in the 1960s; Clyde Best, who played for West Ham United in the 1970s. Then the flood: dozens of professional players, including Viv Anderson, who in 1979 became the first black footballer to represent England, began to appear, prompting reactions from the racist fans, who frequently pelted them with bananas and targeted them for abusive chants. Through the 1980s, black footballers continued to make their mark on British soccer often to the ambiguous rejoicing of newspapers whose 'Black Magic' and 'Black Power' headlines were more than faintly reminiscent of a London paper's banner after a promotion in June 1946 when five black boxers posted wins: 'Black Night for British Boxing' (quoted in Henderson 1949: 340).

At the close of the 1980s, a 'second generation' of British-born blacks was established in British sport. Over half the British boxing champions were black as were more than 40 per cent of the

Olympic squad of 1988 and virtually every football league club had two or three black players on its books. It is no coincidence that the major sports in which blacks have excelled – boxing, track and field, football, and basketball – are ones which demand little in the way of equipment. They can be practised away from any formal organization and with minimal resources. A strong pair of legs, fast hands, sharp reflexes, and a desire to compete are basics. Much more than this is needed to progress in the club-oriented sports, like cricket, golf, and tennis, which tend to be accessible only to the middle class. It might be argued that cricket has some possibilities for players of working-class backgrounds – and blacks in the main come from such backgrounds – but the very structure of the sport and the educational institutions in which it is encouraged make it more available to the middle class. The same argument applies to Rugby Union. In the more accessible sports, blacks have grown to a prominence that belies their numerical minority status in both the USA and Britain. Their sometimes overwhelming success in certain sports is quite disproportionate to their numbers within the total population. The ratio is most pronounced in boxing, track and field, and basketball. But in sports in which blacks have either been allowed to compete or have been attracted to, they seem to approach a mastery that is difficult to match. Black's apparent predilection for sport and the high orders of success they have achieved has been the subject of bar room discussion and academic controversy. Why so many in sport and why so many champions? The answers are intertwined.

One of the simplest and influential explanations has been supplied by Martin Kane in an article in the magazine *Sports Illustrated*; the article is entitled 'An assessment of black is best' (18 January 1971). At the centre of Kane's argument is the 'insight' that blacks are endowed with a natural ability that gives them an advantage in certain sports. Around this lie a number of other related points, many culled from Kane's interviews with medical scientists, coaches, and sports performers. An important, though oddly dated, point is that there are race-linked physical characteristics. Blacks as a 'race' have proportionately longer legs to whites, narrower hips, wider calf bones, greater arm circumference, greater ratio of tendon to muscle, denser skeletal structure, and a more elongated body. Typically, they have power and an efficient body heat dissipation system. Kane inferred these features from a small sample of successful black sportsmen, that is, a minority with proven excellence rather than a random sample from the total population. And he concludes that blacks are innately different and the differences, being genetic in origin, can be passed on from one generation to the next. So, cold climates are said to affect all blacks badly, even ones who are born and brought up in places like Toronto. Weak ankle bones would account for the relative absence of black ice hockey players. The disadvantages are transmitted genetically; as are natural advantages which equip blacks to do well in particular sports where speed and power are essential. Kane argues that blacks are not suited to endurance events. Since the publication of the article, hundreds of African distance runners have undermined this point, though Kane tries to cover himself by claiming Kenyans have black skin, but a number of white features.

Kane's arguments border on the absurd, especially when we consider anthropologists' dismissal of the concept of race itself as having any analytical value at all. Black people are descended from African populations, but, over the centuries, their genetic heritage has become diversified and complicated by various permutations of mating. There is no 'pure' race. Kane ignores this when he examines the area of psychology, emerging with a set of personality traits that are supposed to be determined by race. Blacks have the kind of yielding personality that puts them, as one coach told Kane, 'far ahead of whites ... relaxation under pressure' (1971: 76). This has a common-sense authenticity about it, for coaches and spectators seem to associate black sports performers with a 'laid-back' approach to competition, never stressing-out, or growing tense. But competitors themselves actually work at portraying this: they consciously try to convey an image that reflects coolness. That's all it is – image. Beneath the surface, black performers are as tense and concerned as anyone else. Possibly more so: sport for many blacks is not a casual recreation (as it may be for white youths), but a career path and every failure represents a possible sinking to obscurity. Every event has to be approached as if it were the most demanding of one's life; defeat is not easily assimilated as a result. Kane mistook impression management for deep psychological profiles.

Slavery is the key to the third part of Kane's argument. 'Of all the physical and psychological theories about the American black's excellence in sport, none has proved more controversial than one of the least discussed: that slavery weeded out the weak' (1971: 80). Here Kane introduces some homespun Darwinism, his view being that, as only the fittest survived the rigours of slavery, those best suited to what must have been terribly harsh environments passed on their genes to successive populations, who used them to great effect in sport. There are two drawbacks to this. First, it's preposterous to suggest that blacks bred for generations in such a controlled way as to retain a gene pool in which specific genes related to, for instance, speed, strength, and agility, became dominant. Second, these properties were probably of less significance in matters of survival than intelligence, ingenuity, and anticipation and Kane considers none of these as essentially black features.

All three categories of Kane's theory gel into a formulation that states that blacks' achievements in sport are linked to their so-called race. Sport is seen as 'second nature' to a black person. This implausible suggestion belongs in the realms of racist folklore and not scientific inquiry. Unfortunately, its simplicity and comprehensiveness have made it appealing to many who want to explain the success of blacks in sport as due to race. US writer Harry Edwards has even suggested that the explanation itself has effects for white competitors who, believing blacks to be innately superior, start off at a psychological disadvantage. 'The "white race" thus becomes the chief victim of its own myth' (1973: 197). But its appeal disguises something more sinister because, if we accept as proof of the natural ability argument the outstanding results recorded by blacks sports performers then what are we to infer from the 'underachievement' of blacks in formal education? That they are naturally limited intellectually? If so, it could be argued that they should be encouraged to develop their gifts and possibly neglect areas in which they haven't much aptitude. Sadly, this is what has happened in the past and it gives us the first clue in answering the question of blacks' sporting success all over again, this time with an entirely different approach.

Losers and still champions

History alone tells us that sport has been one of the two channels through which blacks have been able to escape the imprisonment of slavery and the impoverishment that followed its dissolution; the other being entertainment. In both spheres, blacks performed largely for the amusement of patrician whites. This holds true to this day: the season ticket holder or cable television subscriber, no less than old time slave masters, have decisive effects on the destinies of sports performers. For this reason, slaves were encouraged; the incentive might be freedom or at least a temporary respite from daily labours. The old Yorkshire adage that, during the 1930s depression one could shout down any coalpit and expect a half-dozen fast bowlers to emerge suggests broadly the same theme: that material deprivation is an ideal starting point for sporting prowess. 'Hungry fighters' are invariably the most effective. As we have seen, many fight their way out, only to return to indigence; but they're not to know that as they're striving for improvement. Blacks' supposed predilection for sport is more a product of material circumstances than natural talent.

Whether or not sport is a viable avenue from despair is not the issue: it has been seen as such by people who lacked alternatives. And the perception has stuck and, probably, will continue to stick as long as obstacles to progress in other avenues remain. The argument here is that the early slave prize fighters began a tradition by setting themselves up – quite unwittingly – as icons, or images to be revered and copied; in modern parlance, role models. The stupendous success of blacks in such sports as boxing and athletics has clearly been inspirational to countless young blacks over the decades. Racism and racial discrimination have worked to exclude blacks from many areas of employment, restrict their opportunities and, generally, push them towards the 'marginal' or least important areas of the labour market. Experiencing this first hand or anticipating it through the stories of others has set young people thinking about alternative sources of employment. 'There aren't too many successful black tycoons, professionals, or politicians, so where should I look for an example?' black youths might ask themselves. Answers spring to mind readily: Sugar Ray Leonard (estimated ring earnings: $60 million), Florence Griffith Joyner (enjoys a status on par with a movie star), Eric Dickerson (the greatest running back in NFL history); the list goes on. Blacks *can* make it, but only in certain areas. Evaporating into insignificance are the millions of other aspirants whose fortune never materialized and whose career ended shabbily. No matter how remote the chances of success may be, the tiny number of elite black sports stars supply tangible and irrefutable evidence that it can be achieved.

Encouraged, even cajoled, by physical education teachers at school who might subscribe to the popular if mistaken view that blacks have 'natural talent', young persons might, while running or fighting, discover new dimensions of themselves. Many even find comfort in the view that they do possess natural advantages. The fact that such views are based on stereotypes not realities doesn't enter into it: beliefs often have a self-fulfilling quality, so that if you believe in your own ability strongly enough, you eventually acquire that ability.

Some years ago, I wrote a book *Black Sportsmen*, in which I challenged the view that blacks have natural qualities suited to sport. The book's argument was that this myth has actually worked to deny black people opportunities in other areas of life. But, the response from some areas of the black community in Britain was that the book destroyed vestiges of pride. 'Sport is one of the few areas where blacks can feel superior and gifted; now the book has taken even that away from us', was how one sprinter put it, suggesting that at least some blacks were comfortable with an idea that has, on analysis, done the vast majority a disservice over the years.

Actually, it's not the myth itself that has performed the disservice so much as the environment in which it has stayed credible; that being one in which blacks have been regarded as unsuited to or just unwanted for work that demands intellect and imagination – cerebral rather than physical skills. Study after study in the USA and UK has chronicled the extent and intensity of racism in modern society. We need not dwell on specific examples; suffice it to say that in the post-war years in Britain and for many more years before that in the USA, blacks have been systematically squeezed out of education and employment opportunities for reasons that derive from, in its rawest form, racist hostility. The origins of this hostility lie in the European colonial expansion of the seventeenth century, the settlement of the West Indies, and the expansion of trade in slaves, gold, and sugar between Africa, the Americas, and Britain. Slavery meant that whites maintained their domination over blacks and so kept a rigid inequality. The inequality has been modified and lessened in the decades following emancipation, but blacks have never quite shed the remnants of their shackles and whites have passed on their 'colonial mentality'. Seeing blacks as great sports performers might seem a compliment, but, as Harry Edwards observes, 'the only difference between the black man shining shoes in the ghetto and the champion black sprinter is that the shoe shine man is a nigger, while the sprinter is a fast nigger' (1970: 20).

Historically, sport, along with entertainment, was one of the areas in which blacks were allowed to maximize their prowess and circumstances haven't changed sufficiently to permit a significant departure. Blacks still approach sport with vigour and commitment at least partly because persistent racism effectively closes off other channels. Even if those other channels have become freer in recent years, black youths have become accustomed to anticipating obstacles to their progress. So that, by the time they prepare to make the transition from school to work, many have made sport as a career their first priority.

With sights set on a future filled with championships, black youths fight their way into sport determined that, slim though their chances may be, they will succeed. And they usually do, though

---

Colonialism and sport
British colonial domination was not only political and commercial in nature; there was a cultural component in the sense that ideas, beliefs, conventions, and customs were carried throughout the empire by such servants as administrators, military officers, industrialists, farmers, traders, financiers, settlers, educators, and advisors. Sport was practised by these groups. In some cases, new sports were invented in the colonies, billiards being first developed in India during the Raj. Most popular sports in the world today had their origins in nineteenth-century Britain and were disseminated during that time. Even the USA's national game, baseball, didn't spring fully-formed from the American imagination, but had its roots in England. In fact, Jane Austen refers to 'baseball' in *Northanger Abbey* (published in 1818). Brian Stoddart's article (1988) examines sport as a facet of 'cultural imperialism'.

---

mostly in an altogether more modest way than they envisaged. Few attain the heights they wanted to conquer and even fewer surpass them. An unstoppable motivation and unbreakable commitment are valuable, perhaps essential, assets to success in sport and this is why so many possessors of these achieve some level of distinction. But titles are, by definition, reserved for only a very small elite and, while blacks are always well-represented among the elite of all sports in which they compete, there are never enough championships to go round. The majority inevitably fail. Blacks' success in sport may look impressive, but, compared to the numbers of youths entering sport, their interest primed, their success is not so great, even when their chances are affected by 'stacking' and other racialist manoeuvres.

Some American writers, like Jack Olsen and Nathan Hare, have looked at the underside of this 'shameful story' (as Olsen calls it) which begins with visions of wealth and glamour but frequently ends in poverty, crime and, sometimes, insanity. Their conclusions concur with those of Edwards in the sense that they believe that young blacks are seduced into sport and, in the process, ignore their formal academic and vocational studies. They invest so much energy in sport that little is left for other pursuits. So, by the time when fine dreams fade, they are left with few if any career alternatives. In the unlikely event that they have amassed enough capital they retire securely. If not, they join the gallery of 'also-rans'.

The attempts of young blacks to make their way to the top are directly due to nothing more mysterious than social deprivation.

Stacking
This refers to the disproportionate concentration of ethnic minorities in certain positions in a sports team. In American football, black players have been allocated to running back and wide receiver positions; in baseball, they have been stacked in outfield positions. This tends to exclude them from, for instance, quarterback and starting pitching positions – which are the most prestigious – and compels them to compete against other blacks for their team position. It could be argued that stacking is based on stereotypes and that such stereotypes are in the process of being dismantled by quarterbacks such as Doug Williams, who shows intelligence and judgement rather than power and speed in his play. Equally, recent evidence from baseball (Jiobu 1988) suggests that the stereotypes still operate. (Eitzen has studied stacking in depth, both with Sanford 1975, and with Yetman 1977; see also Curtis and Loy 1978.)

There are always a small number of outstanding performers with naturally endowed faculties, but there's no reason to suppose that the black population has a monopoly or even a majority of them. Success in sport is due much more to non-physical qualities such as drive, determination, and an ability to concentrate. Given that blacks see the job market as a maze of cul-de-sacs, they may well accrue more than their fair share of these qualities. Failure potentially has direr consequences for them than for their white, working-class counterparts who, while still having limited opportunities, at least escape racialism.

Black youths are never short of assistance when they move towards sport: teachers, coaches, and any number of others are willing to lend their services. Their motives may be mixed, but their perceptions are usually based on stereotypes. Time after time when researching my book on the subject, I was told that teachers in particular supplied the initial push into sport. Now a successful pro footballer, Vince Hilaire reflected: 'I was pushed into certain sports at school, like athletics. The teachers naturally thought because you're black you must have some sort of athletic ability in you' (Cashmore 1982: 98).

Add to the inner motivation and the 'push' of outsiders the magnetizing influence of black role models and you have a heady mixture – one which sends young blacks into sport year after year. If and when this slows, it's been suggested that this would reflect a quickening of the rate at which opportunities arise in the job market. In other words, if racialism disappeared completely, there'd be only a few black sports stars. That's not the case at present and, while discrimination persists, sport is bound to prosper from the contributions of blacks. This shouldn't disguise the practices and processes which effectively produce the black sports star, who is both a champion and loser – a symbol of failure. From the 1770s and Bill Richmond to the 1990s and Mike Tyson, sport has been a route to fame and material fortune for thousands of blacks and will continue to be that in the future. For tens of thousands of others, it will be only a route to nowhere. Sport conceals deep inequalities and, for all the positive benefits it yields, it remains a source of hope and ambition for blacks only as long as those inequalities remain.

Not cut out for sport

We can take the questions we asked about blacks' involvement in sport, invert them, and apply them to women. Why so few and why so little success compared to men? Both may draw objections on the grounds that women, nowadays, enter sport in considerable numbers and their achievements are many. But sportswomen are still a numerical minority and in measurable terms at least, their performances do not match those of men. Pressed to offer an immediate explanation, we might take the simple, but misleading natural ability argument, suggesting that women are just not equipped to handle sport and are always carrying a physical handicap. But the argument has much the same failings as the 'black is best' theory; it exaggerates physical factors and ignores social and psychological processes that either facilitate entry into or halt progress within sport. It replaces fact with myth, in this case a myth about women's inferiority.

In this sense, beliefs about women in sport have virtually exact parallels with those about women generally: they're not as capable intellectually or physically as men, their natural predisposition is to be passive and not active and their relationship to men is one of dependence. All three beliefs have been strongly challenged since the late 1960s, of course, but their effect on sport is still evident.

Hunting has historically been a predominantly male pursuit, the early sexual division of labour ensuring that women, as bearers of children, had necessarily to spend more time at base camp while men sought food. This didn't prevent women's active involvement in sport and, as societies transformed, women took active roles. In ancient Greek and Roman times, they would hunt, ride, swim, and run, but not (usually) engage in combat. The medieval period saw some women, certainly noble women in parts of Europe, jousting. It's also probable that women competed in a forerunner of the modern game of darts which involved throwing 18-inch hand weapons at a barrel. Certainly, many women were adept archers.

Sexism
Like racism, a set of beliefs or ideas about the purported inferiority of some members of the population, in this case, women. The inferiority is thought to be based on biological differences between the sexes: women are naturally equipped for specific types of activities and roles and these don't usually include ones which carry prestige and influence.

As I've stated before, activities before the nineteenth century, while resembling sport in content, were not strictly sports in the modern sense of the word. By the time of the emergence of organized, rule-bound activities we now recognize as sports, women were effectively pushed out of the picture. The 'age of chivalry' had made sure women were seen not as active agents, but as objects to be placed on a pedestal, protected and revered. Frail of body and mind, women could not be expected to engage in any manner of physically exerting activity, save perhaps for dancing, horse riding, bowling, and the occasional game of lacrosse. By the eighteenth century, the image of women as the 'weaker sex' was well-established: their hair was to be worn up and their skirts to their ankles. Even if quite recent pictures of women playing tennis remind us that long skirts were *de rigueur*.

Tennis was actually one of the few areas where women were allowed to compete, though only those of means could afford to. As well as full skirts, they wore tight corsets, long-sleeved blouses, and boaters. Not until 1931 did a woman break tradition: Lili de Alvarez, of Spain, caused a rumpus when she appeared in shorts at Wimbledon. The tradition she broke was one based on the Victorian ideal of women as gentle, delicate, and submissive. Women might let perspiration appear on their alabaster complexions, 'glow' during exercise, but should never succeed in sport which was customarily associated with ruggedness, resilience, assertiveness, and a willingness to expend 'blood, sweat, and tears'. Women weren't capable of such feats and, even if they were, shouldn't attempt them on account of the harm they would inflict on themselves. Among the problems thought to result from physical exertion were an inability to conceive and 'masculinization' of body features.

Pierre de Coubertin, to whom so much is owed for his vision of the modern Olympics, embodied Victorian sentiments when he urged the prohibition of women's participation in sport. The sight of the 'body of a woman being smashed' was, he recorded, 'indecent'. 'No matter how toughened a sportswoman may be, her organism is not cut out to sustain certain shocks' (quoted in Snyder and Spreitzer 1983: 155–6). Despite his reservations, women were included in the 1900 Olympics, four years after the inauguration, though in a restricted number of events and not in competition with men. Even as recently as 1980, Kari Fasting notes how women were not allowed to run a 3,000-metre event, the reason being that 'it was too strenuous for women' (1987: 362).

Snyder and Spreitzer write about the types of sport women have been encouraged or discouraged from pursuing. 'The "appropriate-ness" of the type of sport continues to reflect the tenets of the Victorian ideal of femininity' (1983: 156). They go on to identify three types. The *categorically unacceptable* includes combat sports, some field events, and sports that involve attempts to subdue physically opponents by body contact, direct application of force to a heavy object, and face-to-face opposition where body contact may occur. *Generally not acceptable* forms of opposition include most field events, sprints, and long jump; these strength-related events are acceptable, the authors believe, only for the 'minority group' women, particularly, we presume, ethnic minorities. Sports that involve the projection of the body through space in aesthetic-ally pleasing patterns or the use of a light implement are *generally acceptable* for all women; no body contact is possible in sports such as swimming, gymnastics, figure skating, and tennis.

The long-standing beliefs about why some sports only are appropriate for women are almost certainly changing, as the inclusion of marathons and 10,000-metre races in the Olympics indicates. Women also competed in taekwondo, an exhibition event, at the 1988 games. Power lifting and body building, both of which necessitate intense resistance training, are now established events for women. Women have recently shown themselves as aggressive, robust, and resilient competitors capable of achieving levels of sporting performance comparable to those of men – when given the opportunity. Black women, especially, have achieved excellence, in relation to blacks generally, presumably for the reasons we outlined earlier and not because of any innate ability. The justification for denying women the opportunity to compete on equal terms with men combines biology with politics and commonsense with illogicality. Women have been regarded as biologically incapable of the same physical feats as men; it has been seen as impolitic even to let them try. One result is that, over the years, they haven't achieved as much as men and that is obvious; yet the conclusion that women *can't* achieve the same levels doesn't follow logically from the original premiss that they are biologically different. In fact, it could be argued that, if women had been regarded as equally capable as men physically, then they would perform at similar standards, and that the only reason they don't is because they've been regarded as biologically incapable for so long.

It barely needs stating that the experience of women in sport virtually replicates their more general experience. They have been perceived and treated as not only different to men – which they manifestly are, of course – but also inferior in many respects. Modern-day feminists have argued plausibly that, historically, women's position has been subordinate to that of men. They have been systematically excluded from high ranking, prestigious jobs, made to organize their lives around domestic or private priorities, while men have busied themselves in the public spheres of industry and commerce. Being the breadwinner, the male has occupied a central position in the family and has tended to use women for supplementary incomes only, or, more importantly, as unpaid homeworkers, making their contribution appear peripheral. Traditionally, females have been encouraged to seek work, but only in the short-term: women's strivings should be towards getting married, bearing children, and raising a family.

Since the late 1960s and the advent of legal abortion and convenient female contraception, women in the west have been able to exercise much more choice in their own fertility and this has been accompanied by feminist critiques of male dominance. Empirical studies showed wide discrepancies in earning power and this prompted legislation on both sides of the Atlantic designed to ensure equality in incomes for comparable jobs. One of the loudest cries of feminists was about the abuses of the female body: women, it was argued, have not had control over their own bodies; they have been appropriated by men, not only for working, but for display. 'Sex objects' were how many women described themselves, ogled at by men and utilized, often dispassionately. Against this, they recoiled. Even a 'respectable' magazine like *Sports Illustrated*, ostensibly interested in what women do, as opposed to what they look like, used to devote issues to photographs of women posing in swimwear.

Women are underrepresented in politics compared to their total number in the population. They consistently earn less than their equivalent males and are increasingly asked to work part-time. Despite recent changes in the number of places in higher education occupied by women, they tend to opt for subjects (like sociology and art) that won't necessarily guarantee them jobs in science and industry. When they do penetrate the barriers of the professions they find that having to compete in what is, to all intents and purposes, a man's world, has its hidden disadvantages.

Some argue that this state of affairs has been brought about by a capitalist economy geared to maximising profits and only too willing to exploit the relatively cheap labour of women who are willing to work for less than men, mainly because they've been taught to believe that their work is unimportant and subsidiary to that of men, and that their 'real' work is domestic not industrial. Others insist that women's subordination has a larger resonance that transcends any political or economic system and is derived from *patriarchy*, a state in which men have continually sought to maintain the grip they have had on society and have found the deception that 'a woman's place is in the home' a great convenience which they wish to perpetuate. Whatever the motivation behind the successful effort to keep women subordinate, its effects have been felt in sport, where women have for long been pushed into second place.

'Unladylike' is one of those words with a certain ring to it: the many activities to which it refers are to be avoided by any female who favours keeping her dignity. In a Victorian environment, the application of the term to behaviour that involved some degree of physical exertion was commonplace, unless the behaviour was performed by females out of necessity. Washing, cleaning, fetching coal, and emptying chambers were activities performed by working-class women, but they could have few pretensions to being ladies. These were typically the kind of women whose daily duties were so draining that they wouldn't have the inclination to add to their physical workload. Gentlewomen and the wives of the emergent bourgeoisie would have time for croquet, tennis and perhaps archery, but were self-consciously 'ladies'. The situation reinforced the social perception of women as delicate creatures in need of men's protection, which manifested itself in terms of the treatment afforded women. But, as the nineteenth century passed and women were made to play a vigorous role in the 1914–18 war effort, the flimsy illusion of delicacy was eroded. A vocal and effective suffragette movement was prising open new areas in politics and education for women. As more women entered formal education, so they began to participate more fully in sport, often demonstrating high proficiency. This led to another set of spurious reasons, this time based on medical evidence, as to why women shouldn't be permited to compete.

Perverting nature

It was for long suspected that women had less energy available than men, so engaging in sport might lead, it was supposed, to an atrophy of reproductive organs as they would be deprived of necessary energy. This was tin-pot theory, of course, but one which raised doubts in the mind of some: could exercise have a detrimental effect on a woman's fecundity? No one knew the answer, but it was thought wise to err on the side of caution, which meant that women should abstain from sport. Tony Mason, in his *Sport in Britain* mentions a bizarre conjecture. 'Hockey', he writes 'was said to inhibit breastfeeding'. He adds that this wasn't just a false idea invented by men to keep sport exclusive: 'Many women shared the idea that their role was primarily domestic, their natures inherently unsuitable for "manly" physical exertion' (Mason 1988: 7–8).

Even more intimidating was the folk belief that involvement in sport not only interfered with fertility, but actually affected a woman's endocrinal system, possibly leading to *virilism*, the development of secondary male characteristics. The idea here was based on the fact that testosterone, the hormone responsible for facial hair, deep voice, broad shoulders, muscle mass, and other typically male features and which is produced primarily in testes, is found in both sexes, though significantly less in females' adrenal glands. Women, on the other hand, carry proportionately higher levels of estrogen and progesterone. Prolonged exercise, it was speculated, induced an imbalance in women's hormones causing an overproduction of testosterone and so resulting in 'defeminization'. Among the advantages for a female competitor would be a reduction of subcutaneous fatty tissue and a proliferation of muscle cells. While this had no basis in scientific fact, scattered cases did seem to support this speculation. There was the mysterious gold medal winner at the 1936 Olympics, who, several years later, confessed that 'she' was actually a man who had been pressured into competing for the glory of the Third Reich. In 1952, two French female medallists were later exposed as males. Speculation over the invincible Press sisters, Irene and Tamara, circulated in athletics. Were they actually 'sisters' at all? They retired rather suddenly when sex testing was introduced in athletics in 1966 thus fuelling more suspicion about their gender. (In all, six female competitors missed the European championships at Budapest after it was announced there would be sex tests; and of the 243 tests, no one failed.) Had the Press sisters somehow trained themselves into men, had they experimented with anabolic steroids so much that they had induced permanent sex changes, or were they men in athletic drag? Whatever the answer, they were two of countless other Soviet bloc women who were thought to have undergone some sort of transformation or mutation.

Barr sex test
The test requires that a sample of cells be scraped from the inside of a woman's cheek and subjected to a laboratory test to determine whether a minimum number contain what are called 'Barr bodies' (collections of chromatins). Although the exact number of these chromatins varies from woman to woman and may change over time for any given woman, usually about 20 out of every 100 cells contain this characteristic. If the count drops below a minimum percentage, the competitor is disqualified.

Sex tests, such as the Barr Sex Test, which involve a microscopic examination of cells from the inside of the cheek or a hair follicle to identify a typical female chromosome pattern, could only determine effects, not causes. In 1967, the Polish sprinter, Eva Klobkowska, failed such a test because she showed an excess of male hormones; to her apparent surprise she was found to have internal testicles. This condition is not as uncommon as it may first sound, though in hindsight, the muscular bulk and power possessed by Soviet female athletes were the result of neither this nor excessive training, but anabolic steroids. Still, the 'natural successor' to the Press sisters, Jarmila Kratotchvilova, of Czechoslovakia, never tested positive for drugs. The mêlée of folk story and science that purported to explain what Linda Birke and Gail Vines (1987) call 'the perversion of women's true nature' as caused by too much exercise was inconclusive. What evidence we have today contradicts the earlier speculations: vigorous exercise is beneficial for women in a general sense and may have a reciprocally positive effect on their reproductive functions. For example, Evelyn Ashford, of USA, broke the 100-metre world record in 1984 and, 40 weeks later give birth; Ingrid Kristiansen, of Norway, did it in reverse order, first giving birth, then returning to the track to record the world's best times for 5,000 and 10,000 metres (presumably, heart and lung efficiency were improved during pregnancy). Virtually every argument about the physical and mental improvements that men derive from sporting activity of any order apply with equal force to women, who have, particularly in the 1980s, demonstrated no apparent deficiency or fragility even in the most exacting events. From the vantage point of the 1990s when women such as Portugal's Rosa Mota, regularly grind out sub 2:20 marathons, it seems staggering that Kathy Switzer was disqualified from the 1968 Boston marathon for no reason other than that she was a woman. Women were simply not meant to be able to run such distances; this myth held sway despite the 3:40 run, in London of a certain Violet Percy in 1926. It took until 1984 for the Olympics to allow a women's marathon: Joan Benoit, of USA, won and, incidentally, earned over $400,000 in the following year, thanks to her unique success.

The marathon is rather an instructive case-study. Between Switzer's 'illicit' run and 1989, the world record for women improved by 48 minutes; in the same period, the men's record was reduced by just 90 seconds. At the time of writing, the difference is less than 14 minutes (or about 9 per cent). Adrianne Blue, in *Grace Under Pressure* (1987), records how, in 1928, the first Olympic 800 metres for women was considered 'dangerous'! The moral of this would seem to be that, when women are allowed legally to compete in an event, they can perform at least on comparable terms with men. One wonders how great or small the marathon time differential would be had a women's event been allowed in the Olympics at the time of Violet Percy's run. 'The same as it is today', might be the sceptic's answer, marshalling the support of significant differences in all women's and men's track records. But marathons, though separate events in major international meets, regularly pitch men and women together. From the 1970s and the boom in popular marathons and fun runs, women have mixed with men, competed against them, and, on many occasions, beaten them. It is misleading comparing performances in male and female events which have developed separately. Tennis has for long been open to at least those women of resources sufficient to afford it. Only in the most playful mixed doubles have they been allowed to confront male adversaries. One-off exhibitions between the likes of an aged Bobby Riggs and Billie-Jean King (and, before her, Margaret Court) have produced inconclusive results after matches that owed more to pantomime than competitive sport. The question we asked of marathons stands with tennis: how would Steffi Graf fare in a head-to-head with Mats Wilander had women been playing competitively against men for the past sixty or fifty years? Again, the sceptic might argue that the results would be basically the same, the support this time coming from the copious amount of evidence on the physical differences between the sexes, that is differences which do not refer to social or cultural influences.

Not all physical differences between men and women have a bearing on sporting performance, so interest is here confined to those areas that may affect a person's ability to compete on equal terms. The areas are the skeletal and cardiovascular systems and body composition. Typically, women are shorter, with narrower shoulders, shorter limbs, a wider pelvis, and leg bones that are less bowed than men's. So, compared to males, women have a lighter body frame to carry, a lower centre of gravity, slightly less leg rotation (because of the pelvis) and shorter arm movements when running, and a marginally greater proneness to knee injury because of the less bowed lower leg bones (although this may possibly be because girls are not encouraged to exercise as much as young boys so their bones do not grow as strong and dense in maturity).

Generally, untrained women carry a greater percentage of body fat than untrained men (22 per cent to 14 per cent); they have less bone and less muscle. A female will have a greater concentration of subcutaneous adipose tissue, particularly in her buttocks, which are relatively inactive metabolically (making it hard to 'burn off' the fat, but helpful for buoyancy). In swimming this is an advantage, especially in distance or open-water events, where the insulating effects of fat are needed against cold water. Importantly, the smaller proportion of muscle in relation to body fat, gives a lower ratio of strength to weight than in men, but this ratio is significantly changed by resistance training. Training can also minimize differences in muscle strength as women power lifters demonstrate. Untrained women can be as much as 50 per cent less efficient than men, though at peak a woman's lifting strength can be within 5 per cent of a trained man's. Here is a key to equalizing: research shows that women's strength responds to training in much the same way as does men's. After training, when fitness levels are equalized, there are more differences in performance ability within sexes than between them. Women gain strength without corresponding muscle bulk. They have less muscle and bone to drive, so don't suffer from having smaller heart and respiratory volumes (which affect the amount of oxygen used).

During distance events, males sweat sooner and more profusely than females in response to increases in body temperature. This apparent advantage is balanced by a woman's ability to adjust her sweat rate more efficiently. Both sexes acclimatize to work or exercise in heat, but females do so without increasing sweat rates: before a woman sweats her body temperature will have to be 2 or 3 degrees higher than the equivalent male's. Because she has more active sweat glands than the male, her sweat is more evenly distributed over the body, for maximal cooling by evaporation, thus compensating for the smaller body surface. This is why women seem to go red while men pour with sweat.

As we've seen, myths about the detrimental effects of strenuous exercise on a woman's fertility reigned for many years but eventually died away. It's no longer believed that during menstruation women lose the all-important haemoglobin that combines with oxygen and travels to muscle. Women have reached peak performance during all phases of their menstrual cycle. There is no conclusive evidence to suggest that menstrual function affects sporting performance.

The point to remember when charting the physical differences between the sexes that may influence sporting performance is that there is also an equally important reverse effect: performance causes very serious physical changes that tend to compensate more than adequately for any disadvantage a female may have in terms of muscular strength or oxygen uptake. The body is extremely susceptible to change, even transformation in certain contexts. For example, strenuous physical training can boost levels of growth hormone in children, perhaps enhancing their growth; increases in the hormones prolactin (which regulates breast development and milk production) and androgens (the male sex hormone) may be promoted by strict training and specific diets. At a more obvious level, we know athletes develop stronger bones and larger hearts after prolonged training and muscles obviously grow as a response to demands made on them. As evidence, witness the many 8-year-old children in Darjeeling who regularly carry about 3 tons of bricks on their heads in the course of a day. Women in various parts of east Africa perform similar tasks. Making habitual demands on the body from an early age can induce physical changes in both men and women. The idea that biology is destiny in sport is nonsense. Extraordinarily strong Australian power lifter Gael Martin has done her very best to show that, though she has been known to augment her efforts with anabolic steroids.

There is, of course, the tried-and-trusted argument that, no matter how hard a woman may train or supplement her regime, she will forever be handicapped by her breasts; not just because they burden her with extra weight to carry, but because they're vulnerable to damage. Boxing has led a brigade of other sports which won't allow women competitors. But amateur boxing in particular equips fighters with headguards and all boxing, as well as many other sports, permits the use of protective cups, worn about the genitals. In taekwondo, where punching is confined to the upper body target area, women wear body pads which seem to provide adequate protection. There seems no reason to suppose that these would be any less effective in other combat sports. And there is interest from women in the west, as the number of active female kickboxers indicates.

The picture that emerges in the west is one in which women have not excelled in sports. Yet this is not because they are physically ill-equipped, but because 1) they haven't been encouraged to compete; and 2) when they have been allowed to compete, they have done so against themselves and not against trained men.

Soviet bloc countries, especially the GDR and Soviet Union, have shown what can happen when women are assisted in their development in a partially integrated programme that starts during school years. Since the mid-1950s, women have progressively made up more of official Soviet and GDR international teams (now about 40 per cent), the trend, according to James Riordan, being consistent with the general treatment of women. 'The Soviet authorities have used sport as a vehicle for that type of women's emancipation officially desired in the USSR', he writes in his book *Soviet Sport* (1980: 142). It's still interesting to note that women's participation in soccer and wrestling is disapproved of, on the grounds that they are open to 'commercialization' and may be turned into 'strength-and-beauty' contests.

If Riordan's point about 'emancipation' might be borrowed, we might suggest that women's involvement in sport in the west reflects their 'officially desired' position. They've been shut out of sport in a way that mirrors their shutting-out of society. Since the sea change of the late 1960s and 1970s, when legislation technically outlawed discrimination on the basis of sex, women have made much more of an impact in sports not traditionally associated with western women. Tessa Sanderson and Fatima Whitbread, both of the UK, perhaps exemplify this with their successes in the javelin. Despite sex discrimination, equal pay, equal opportunities laws, and Title IX, the general attitude western societies have towards women is ambiguous.

Title IX
Part of the USA's educational amendments, 1972, Title IX reads: 'No person in the United States shall, on the basis of sex, be excluded from participation in, be denied the benefits of, or be subjected to discrimination under any education program or activity receiving Federal financial assistance.' Educational institutions were made to accommodate females within their sports budgets. This was, at first, unpopular among the male-dominated sports officials of schools, colleges, and universities. In 1979, three women athletes from the University of Alaska sued their state for failing to comply with Title IX in providing better funding, equipment, and publicity compared to the male basketball team. This set in train more actions, so that, by the end of 1979, sixty-two colleges and universities were under investigation by the Office for Civil Rights. The resistance to offering equal opportunities to women has continued to the present day.

Whether this is because of the timeless, iron-clad oppression of patriarchy or the more time-limited, but equally iron-clad system of capitalism is open to debate. Either way, there is substantial evidence for both theories, all of which adds up to the fact that women have been subordinated and encouraged to play out their lives as private auxiliaries rather than public prime movers. Most of the women who have penetrated sport at the higher levels haven't exactly defied this publicly. Gymnast Mary-Lou Retton cut the image of a dainty playgirl; Florence Griffith Joyner, a glitzy, shock-haired glamour queen, equally at ease modelling running gear or camiknickers. These are more typical than the non-stereotype women who occasionally succeed. Most of the others who don't fit the mould are regarded as anomalies, the most famous being Martina Navratilova who was known to favour the company of other females. Black male sports stars also continue to be put into categories. Even in the UK, a placid US footballer like William 'Refrigerator' Perry, of the Chicago Bears, attracted more attention than London's world champion boxer, Lloyd

Honeyghàn, whose unpredictable posturings endeared him to few people.

Neither blacks nor women have entirely shrugged of their stereotypes: each group is in the process of redefining itself in a way that suggests they are much more capable than popular images have given them credit for. But old ideas die hard. Blacks have unwittingly contributed to the stereotype of a brawny and physically adept specimen but with little 'upstairs'. They've grasped the only opportunity they were offered for escaping deprivation and, in the process, have become so brilliant that their prowess appears natural. Women's experience has been one of denial: they simply haven't been allowed to enter sports, again on the basis of a mistaken belief in their natural predisposition. Because of this, the encouragement, facilities, and, importantly, competition available to males from an early age hasn't been extended to them. In the very few areas where the gates have been recently opened – marathon being the obvious example – women's progress has been extraordinary. Given open competition, women could achieve parity with men in virtually all events, apart from those very few that require the rawest of muscle power. The vast majority of events need fineness of judgement, quickness of reaction, balance, and anticipation; women have no disadvantages in these respects. Their only disadvantage is what men believe about them!

Biology has not held women back in sport any more than it has propelled blacks, male or female, to sporting excellence. Sexual and racial discrimination has been responsible for both trends. On the one hand, sexual discrimination has indirectly persuaded women that their proper place is at home where they can care for children and present no effective challenge to male dominance. On the other hand, racial discrimination has had a more direct effect on blacks and has worked to keep them pressed into subservience and offering them as a way out only the opportunity to entertain white audiences. The experience in sport of both groups has been shaped by these powerful social forces much more than putative biological ones.

Further reading

Broken Promises *by Richard Lapchick (St Martin's Press/Marek 1984) begins with an account of the author's own beating-up by racists because of his vocal opposition to a Davis Cup tennis competition between the USA and South Africa. Later, the scope of* the book broadens to include a general assessment of racism in American sport. Lapchick has edited a kind of companion volume, Fractured Focus *(Lexington Books, 1986) which contains a chapter on 'Racism in sports'.*

Black Sportsmen *by E. Cashmore (Routledge & Kegan Paul, 1982) is my own work on the rise of blacks in sport, principally in the UK, but with reference also to the USA. Based on research in the 1980s, it examines the reasons for the success of blacks in certain sports through the eyes of performers themselves.*

Women's Studies International Forum *(vol. 10, no. 4, 1987) is a special edition of a journal with the subtitle 'The gendering of sport, leisure and physical recreation' and contains thirteen feminist articles, as well as four reviews, all focusing on aspects of sexism in sport.*

Sport and the Physical Emancipation of English Women, 1870–1914 *by Kathleen McCrone (Routledge, 1988) looks at the entry of women into sport during the Victorian period. It was a crucial time in the development of sport and also one in which myths about women abounded. At public schools, the new sports with rules and time-scales were meant to instil character and decisiveness fitting for future purveyors of the empire. Women, having no need of such qualities, were largely pushed out of sport.*

Assignment

Construct a scenario, beginning at the turn of the century, in which women are allowed to compete with men in sport. Take three sports and describe the development of both sexes using projected performance indicators and times where necessary. Also, imagine yourself in the position of a black youth approaching school-leaving age and who has shown potential in a sport (of your choice). Weigh up some of the career choices available to you. (Write subjectively, in the first person.)

Chapter six

A question of drugs

The other athletic's revolution

Years hence, people will tell their children about the Olympic games of 1988. They may recall the sprint treble victory of Florence Griffith Joyner, Surinam's first-ever medallist, Anthony Nesty, or perhaps the upset Soviet defeat of the US basketball team which had won eighty-four out of eighty-eight previous games in six decades of Olympic play. But the event that will be stamped in people's memories will not be a sporting achievement, but rather, Ben Johnson's positive dope test and its aftermath. This included his being stripped of the gold medal he had won for his 100-metre sprint win, the expunging of his time from the record books, and the most exhaustive ever international media coverage of a sports story. The vast majority of the millions who watched Johnson stride imperiously to victory in 9.79 seconds on 24 September might have confused the name Stanozolol with others, like Shanavozov, the Soviet boxer, or Butuzova, the archer. By 26 September, only recluses wouldn't have realized that this was the brand name of the anabolic steroid detected in Johnson's urine sample.

Modern sport has taken on an almost Manichaean character in which good coexists with evil; the evil is represented increasingly by the spread of the use of drugs amongst athletes eager to improve their performance and willing to risk all manner of chemical side-effects, or even direct effects in the attempt to build muscle, steady the hand, flush out body fluid, speed up the metabolism, or spark more aggression. There are drugs available that can assist in all these, but woe for any athlete caught taking them. Johnson was quickly demythologized from the fastest man in the world, to the 'world's greatest cheat', cloven hoofs and horns virtually replacing his Diadora spikes and gold medal. While he was the thirty-first competitor to be disqualified for drug use since the International Olympic Committee (IOC) instituted full-scale testing in 1972, Johnson's stature in world sport ensured that his case would make news everywhere and that he as an individual would carry the sins of everybody. As well as his medal and record, he instantly lost at least $2 million in performance-related product endorsements.

Johnson was extraordinary in that he was discovered with traces of steroid in his system and roundly shamed because of it. The vast majority of the twenty-two athletes tested daily at the Olympic games yielded negative results. But the suspicion was, and is, that Johnson was quite ordinary in another respect: he was simply one of countless others who systematically used drugs to enhance performance and who either 'came off' them early enough to escape detection, or masked their presence with an additional drug, such as probenecid (sometimes used to treat gout), though this too was banned in 1988. In 1987 (not an Olympic year) IOC tests brought to light 521 infringements using anabolic steroids, 37 of them involving the use of stanozolol. but this almost certainly conceals the true extent of drug use among athletes. Prior to the Olympics of 1988, it was estimated that one in ten British athletes regularly used drugs, an estimate that contrasted markedly with that of former Olympic silver medallist and convicted trader in steroids, David Jenkins; he guessed that as many as 50 per cent of athletes had used drugs at some time. The discrepancy suggests a 'dark figure', the true proportions of which are destined to remain unknown.

Track and field events have no monopoly on drugs, of course, and scandals of lesser proportions have affected American football (stimulant use) and, to a much lesser extent, boxing (stimulants and narcotic analgesics; diuretics use is overlooked). Weightlifters and body builders compete in sports in which steroids confer obvious advantages. It's quite probable that drug use in sport dates back to ancient times. Greeks are said to have used hallucinogenic extracts from mushrooms to aid their performance. Chemically active derivatives of plants have had many applications. The opium extract morphine has been used extensively for the relief of pain, colchicine from the autumn crocus is a well-known treatment for gout, and the heart drug digitalis comes from foxglove. There are countless other examples in history and, today, natural derivatives are quite commonly used to treat ailments and often to enhance performance; the Asian root ginseng is thought to have all manner of beneficial properties. Natural stimulants to alter body functions have been used extensively, particularly as a prelude to fighting. In sport we know little of the systematic application of stimulants, though after 1879 when 6-day cycle races began in Europe, riders favoured ether and caffeine to delay the onset of fatigue sensations. Sprint cyclists used nitroglycerine, a chemical later used in conjunction with heroin, cocaine, strychnine, and others to make 'speedballs' which were given to race horses before races in the 1930s. The highly poisonous stimulant strychnine was also used by the winners of the 1904 Olympic marathon.

Cycling perhaps more than any other sport drew world attention in the 1960s to both the extent of drug taking in sport and its perils when two competitors actually died after taking doses of amphetamines. Knut Jensen collapsed and died at the 1960 Olympics after taking nonicol, a blood dilatory, and, seven years later, Tommy Simpson died during the Tour de France. In the same decade, stories escaped from American baseball and football clubs that told of the extensive use of amphetamines and narcotic analgesics. Paul Hoch, in *Rip Off the Big Game*, drew together a number of accounts from the 1960s to conclude 'that the biggest drug dealers in the sports world are none other than team trainers' (1972: 122). Coaches were administering aphetamines to 'pep' players up, and analgesics to help them play painlessly while carrying injuries before a game *and* 'tranquilized to get their eyeballs back in their head – to even get a night's sleep' after. Hoch cites two players who filed law suits against their clubs for administering drugs 'deceptively and without consent' (1972: 123), and which eventually proved detrimental to their health. Various exposees led to a California state legislative subcommittee on drug abuse and alcoholism to extend the tight regulations governing drug use in horse racing to human sport! The movie *North Dallas Forty* graphically shows football players trotting onto the field as virtual zombies after taking copious amounts of dope.

Law and drugs

Many of the drugs used by sports performers are available, often without prescription, in EC countries and the USA. But, in 1989, an amendment to the British Misuse of Drugs Act 1971, made the illegal possession of anabolic steroids a criminal offence. This was the first time that sport's own rules for banning the use of drugs were given the force of law, making sport's own sanctions (e.g. bans) largely irrelevant. Possession of drugs, which if used excessively can promote cancers, carried a maximum of a fine and a two-year gaol sentence. Producers, importers, and suppliers faced unlimited fines and gaol sentences of up to five years.

The drugs we now tend to associate with sport are anabolic steroids and cocaine. Sketchy evidence suggests that some NFL players were experimenting in the 1960s. Jack Scott in *The Athletic Revolution* (1971) reported that over a quarter of one college team had used steroids. In the same book, Scott covered the 1968 Olympics, at which competitors talked freely not about the morality of taking drugs but of the practicality: which drugs were most effective? While estimates about the extent of steroid use are always hopelessly flawed, it's at least suggestive that less than twenty years after Scott's information, an article in *Sports Illustrated* stated that NFL steroid users accounted for between 40 and 90 per cent of all players (13 May 1983). The Players' Association rejected this. In 1984, Robert Goldman, the director of sports medicine research at the Chicago Osteopathic Medicine Centre, attributed the death of six sports performers to steroid use. In the UK, body builder, Keith Singh, died with liver tumours after a period of using steroids. In 1987, the IOC recorded 521 cases which tested positive for steroid use; and this was sixteen years after the International Amateur Athletic Federation (IAAF) had introduced antidrug legislation.

Cocaine
This drug's striking effects on the CNS have made it appealing to many sports performers. The first site of action is the cortex and the effects of the stimulant can manifest themselves as exhilaration, euphoria, or laughter. There is some evidence that cocaine increases perceptual awareness and thinking abilities. It also reduces fatigue sensations. In low doses, there is no impairment in body movement co-ordination to offset the increase in activity levels. Higher doses may lead to excessive stimulation of the lower brain centres, prompting convulsive movements. Long-term effects are severely detrimental. Used topically, cocaine can work as a local anaesthetic. Contrary to popular belief, it has little in common with opiates such as heroin or morphine and is not physically addictive in the same way as these, though it often leads to a powerful psychological dependence.

While anabolic steroids have specific functions and are confined mainly to sports, cocaine is used recreationally by a variety of groups. In the 1980s, its status as a yuppie drug enhanced its appeal. Tales of cocaine use by football, baseball, and basketball players are legion. Richard Lapchick (1986) refers to an 'epidemic in American sport' and highlights some of the sports stars who are still either in gaol or fighting addictions. Seven New England Patriots were identified as having a 'serious drug problem' on the day following their appearance in the 1986 SuperBowl. In the same year, a pro footballer and a college basketball player died from cocaine poisoning, fifty-seven top senior collegiate prospects for the NFL draft tested positively, twenty-one major league baseball players were penalized, and Michael Ray Richardson was banned by the National Basketball Association after his fourth failed test for cocaine. Many world class boxers, including Hector Camacho and Gilberto Roman (former holders of world titles) were penalized in the 1980s. Atlanta Falcons' Dave Croudip was, at the time of writing, the most recent victim of a cocaine overdose.

Trying to quantify the amount of drug use in sport is as futile as trying to assess the extent of drug taking in society generally: the truth will never be known. Yet there is enough illustrative evidence, anecdotes, 'insider accounts', and publicized cases to infer that drug use in sport has been growing steadily since the 1940s and more rapidly since the crucial decade of the 1960s, when drug use generally became widespread. Questions arise out of this. What are the drugs and what are they supposed to do? Why are more and more sports performers prepared to use them? How do governing bodies react to drug use and how will this reaction affect sport?

Banned substances

The IOC's banned list includes 4,000 substances which are grouped into five categories of drugs. They are anabolic steroids, stimulants, narcotic analgesics, beta blockers, and diuretics. I will deal with them in that order.

Johnson's case led to a general awareness of the 'danger' of anabolic steroids, but little appreciation of the actual purpose they can serve in the human body. The idea behind using an anabolic steroid is to mirror the chemical action of the male hormone testosterone in the body and facilitate muscle growth; 'anabolic' means build up. The basic function of testosterone is to control the natural production of sperm cells and this, in turn, affects the male's masculine appearance. A feedback control system is at work involving the hypothalamus; this secretes a hormone called LHR which stimulates the pituitary gland to secrete luteinizing hormone (LH) and this, in turn, stimulates the testes to produce the testosterone. A high concentration of testosterone inhibits the secretion of LHR by the hypothalamus which causes a drop in the level of testosterone, triggering the hypothalamus to release more

LHR, LH, and ultimately testosterone in a smoothly regulated system.

Once in the bloodstream the molecules of the hormone discharged by the testes can affect other parts of the body. It is the task of endocrinology to study the processes and effects of molecules produced by glands and secreted directly into the blood. Experiments are complicated by the obvious fact that organs that are suspected of producing hormones always have important functions and their removal is followed by death. There are alternatives to surgical removal and combinations of methods have established what the main hormones are, the endocrine glands, or organs, that produce them, and their major effects. Other effects are less well established, but still strongly suspected and the muscle building spin-off of testosterone is one of them. Sceptics still harbour alternative suspicions and suggest a placebo might be at work; believers in the power of testosterone convince themselves even in the absence of physical change.

Placebo

A pharmacologically inert substance is given to patients usually to humour them rather than effect any cure. Yet the substance often works as effectively (if not more so) as an active substance because the patient believes it will. The substance is called a placebo and its result is known as the *placebo effect*. This has many applications outside the clinical setting. Weight lifters have been told they were receiving an anabolic steroid while, in fact, only some of them received it – the others were given a placebo. Both groups improved leg presses, the first group by 135 lbs, the other (receiving the placebo) by 132 lbs. The sheer expectation of benefit seems to have been the crucial factor. A similar process can work in reverse. For example, subjects may be given active drugs together with information that they will have no effect: consequently the drugs may not have any effect. In other words, the direct effect of drugs alone may not be any more powerful than the administrator's or experimenter's suggestions alone.

As long ago as the 1930s, a synthesized version of testosterone was produced and used to help castrated males. Its clinical use was seen as limited, being confined to individuals with rare blood disorders, including some anaemias (having too little haemoglobin) and for wasting conditions in the elderly. But this testosterone appeared to encourage the proliferation of cells in muscle and to induce more aggression in the user – known as 'roid rage'. This alerted coaches to the benefits: first, in rapid muscle faculty for more intense training; second, in encouraging a more positive and aggressive approach to both training and competition.

While anabolic steroids are the most widely used drug in track and field events, stimulants are the second most common and probably the most popular in sport as a whole. Amphetamine use has been widespread for at least three decades. The basic effect of stimulants is to get messages to a complex pathway of neurons in the brainstem called the arousal system, or reticular activating system (RAS). This system is ultimately responsible for maintaining consciousness and determining our state of awareness. So, if the RAS bombards the cerebral cortex with stimuli, we feel very alert and able to think clearly. Amphetamines are thought to cause chemical neurotransmitters, such as dopamine, to increase, so enhancing the flow of nervous impulses in the RAS and stimulating the entire CNS. The sympathetic nervous system is stimulated, speeding up heartrate, raising blood pressure, and dilating pupils. In sports terms, the performer is fired up and resistant to the sensation of fatigue, particularly the muscular pain associated with lactic acid.

One problem facing users active in sport, who need nutrition for the release of energy is that amphetamines depress appetites. They used to be prescribed to dieters, though less so nowadays because dieters became dependent on the drug. This came about because the body quickly develops a tolerance, probably through the readiness of the liver to break down the drug rapidly. An obvious temptation is to increase the dose to achieve the same effect. So, with increased use of the drug, the user becomes dependent. Weight loss and dependence are the more obvious effects; others include irritability (probably due to irregular sleep) and even a tendency towards paranoia. Cyclists Jensen and Simpson demonstrated that the effects can be terminal.

There is another class of stimulants called sympathomimetic amine drugs, such as ephedrine, which, as the name suggests, acts not on the brain but directly on the nerves affecting the organs. (This produces effects in the sympathetic part of the autonomic nervous system: it speeds up the action of the heart, and constricts the arteries and increases lung inflation). Ephedrine is used commonly as a decongestant and is often prescribed for asthma sufferers.

At the 1988 Olympics, a pentathlete, Alexander Watson, of Australia, was disqualified for having an excessive level of caffeine in his system. To have reached such a level he would have needed to have drunk forty regular-sized cups of coffee; other methods include the use of a suppository or the chewing of small nuts of caffeine.

Narcotic analgesics are used in all walks of life, but especially in sports where injuries are commonplace and a tolerance to pain is essential. Soccer and US football are examples of games involving the 'walking wounded'. Derivatives of the opium poppy were probably used by ancient Mesopotamians around 3000 BC; they left instructions for use on wax tablets. There are now methods of producing such derivatives synthetically. Opium, heroin, codeine, and morphine, along with the newer 'designer' drugs, are all classified as narcotics which relieve pain and depress the CNS, producing a state of stupor. Reflexes slow down, the skeleton is relaxed, and tension is reduced. The negative effects are much the same as those of amphetamines, with the additional one of specific neurons becoming dependent on the drug and so providing a basis for addiction.

The immediate effects of stimulants or narcotic analgesics would be of little or no service to sports performers who rely on fineness of judgement, sensitivity of touch, acuity of sight, and steadiness of hand. Success in sports like darts, archery, snooker, shooting, or show jumping is based on calmness and an imperviousness to 'pressure'. The Canadian snooker player Bill Werbeniuk was famed for his customary ten pints of beer to help him relax before a game. His CNS would become duller and tensions presumably disappeared. How he managed to co-ordinate hand and eye movements, stay awake, or even just stay upright is a mystery! Alcohol has serious drawbacks, which include nausea and impaired judgement.

Werbeniuk
While Vancouver-based professional snooker player Bill Werbeniuk was known for his consumption of large quantities of lager, he was also a habitual user of inderal, a beta blocker which helped counteract the effects of an hereditary nervous disorder. After criticism from the British Minister for Sport, the World Professional Billiards and Snooker Association (WPBSA) reviewed its drugs policy and included inderal on its list of banned substances. Unable to find an alternative, Werbeniuk admitted to the WPBSA that he intended to continue using the drug and was eventually banned from tournaments.

Beta blockers are a newer alternative. Originally used by patients with irregular heartbeats, these relieve anxiety by controlling the release of adrenaline and by lowering the heartrate; they are used by edgy showbusiness performers.

Weightlifters and other sports performers who compete in categories based on body weight have to calibrate their diet and preparation carefully. A couple of pounds, even ounces, over the limit can destroy months of conditioning if the performer is made to take off the excess at the weigh-in. Skipping, saunas, and other methods of instant weight reduction can be debilitating. Competitors in weight-controlled sports always check-weigh during the days preceding an event and, should their weight seem excessive, may take diuretics. These substances – widely used therapeutically for reducing fluid levels – excite the kidneys to produce more urea and, basically, speed up a perfectly natural waste disposal process. Diuretics are found in alcoholic drinks and coffee (in the caffeine), which explains why a visit to the toilet is necessary shortly after imbibing any of these liquids. Diuretics inhibit the secretion of the antidiuretic hormone which serves as a chemical messenger, carrying information from the pituitary gland at the base of the brain to parts of the kidneys, making them more permeable and allowing water to be reabsorbed into the body (thus conserving fluid). Hormones, of course, are carried in the blood. If the messages don't get through, the kidneys move the water out of the body. Continued use of diuretics can damage the kidneys. In recent years, the suspicion has grown that competitors have not only been using diuretics to reduce weight, but to flush out other substances, in particular the above-mentioned drugs. It follows that competitors found to have diuretics in their urine immediately have their motives questioned. Kerrith Brown, of Great Britain, lost his Olympic bronze medal for judo despite pleading that the diuretic, furosemide, found in his urine was introduced into his system by a medical officer who gave him an anti-inflammatory substance containing the chemical to reduce a knee swelling.

Another athlete to be disqualified, though at an earlier Olympics, was Martti Vainio who lost his silver medal for the 10,000 metres at Los Angeles after steroid traces were discovered in his urine. The Finn had been careful enough to cease using the drug well before competition to escape detention, but had blundered by having himself injected with blood that had been removed from his body early in 1984 when training at altitude. In chapter 2 we noted the importance of protein molecule haemoglobin, which is found in red blood cells. It has a remarkable ability to form loose associations with oxygen. As most oxygen in the blood is combined with haemoglobin rather than simply dissolved in plasma, the more haemoglobin present in a red blood cell, the more oxygen it can transport to the muscles. Obviously then, performers can benefit from having a plentiful supply of oxygen to react with glucose and release energy stored in food. The advantage of training at altitude, where the oxygen in the atmosphere is scarce, is that the body naturally compensates by producing more haemoglobin. The performer descends to sea level carrying with him or her a plentiful supply of haemoglobin in the blood, which gradually readjusts (over a period of weeks). Each day spent at lower altitudes diminishes the benefit of altitude training: proliferation of haemoglobin ceases in the presence of available atmospheric oxygen. One way to 'capture' the benefits is to remove a quantity of highly oxygenated blood during intense altitude training, store it, and reintroduce it into the circulatory system immediately prior to competition, which is what Vainio and probably many others did. He neglected to take account of the fact that he had been on steroids during the time spent at altitude and that the stored blood contained evidence of this.

The 'doping' in this process doesn't refer to the administration of drugs, but to the more correct use of the term, pertaining to a thick liquid used as a food or lubricant. There is, however, a synthetic drug that can achieve much the same effect. Erythropreotin (EPO) facilitates the production of extra red blood cells, which absorb oxygen, and leaves the user with no tell-tale needle tracks. As EPO does not show up in urinalysis, inspection is possibly only by blood tests, before and after competition, to take red blood cell counts. As well as being more convenient than a transfusion, EPO has the advantage of being undetectable in competitors who object to invasive techniques on religious or ethical grounds. 'Blood doping' or 'blood boosting' and EPO, in a sense, copy the body's natural processes and, at the moment, their long-term effects seem to be broadly the same as those of living at high altitudes.

Another, more controversial, method of mimicking nature is by extracting the naturally occurring growth hormone somatotropin, which is produced and released by the pituitary gland, as discussed in chapter 2. This hormone controls the human rate of growth by regulating the amount of nutrients taken into the body's cells and by stimulating protein synthesis. Overproduction of the hormone may cause a child to grow to giant proportions (a condition referred to as gigantism), whereas too little can lead to dwarfism. The growth hormone also affects fat and carbohydrate metabolism in adults, promoting a mobilization of fat which becomes available for use as fuel, and sparing the utilization of protein. The potential of this mechanism for promoting growth has not been lost on field athletes, weightlifters, body builders, and others requiring muscle build. Illicit markets in growth hormone extracted from foetuses have been uncovered, though a synthetically manufactured version, somatonorm, may make this redundant. Eventually, skeletal and muscular abnormalities may result. These outward physical signs are some of the few reliable ways of determining whether performers have been taking the hormone, in either form, or whether they have an abnormally high level. Nor would pure EPO be detectable through existing techniques. This has led some to believe that drug users can always stay one step ahead of those wishing to identify them: the line between what is 'natural' and 'unnatural' for the human body is not so clear-cut as testers would like and science finds ways of replicating nature. Others believe that drug-testing methods are keeping pace and hold up the Johnson case as an example of how not even the elite can escape detection, given a vigilant team of toxicologists and a sophisticated laboratory. The system at Seoul was a costly state-of-the-art set-up and easily the most effective drug detection centre to date. Before moving on, we should briefly take note of its apparatus and methods.

Hewlett-Packard, the multinational computer specialists, charged the IOC $3 million to set up the scientific testing equipment at the Korean Advanced Institute of Science and Technology. The system of gas chromatography and mass spectroscopy could, according to its makers, 'detect concentrations [of banned substances] as low as one part per billion; roughly the equivalent to detecting traces from a teaspoonful of sugar after it has been dissolved in an Olympic swimming pool'. A further claim was that it could check a compound found in urine against 70,000 held in a computer's database in 'less than a minute'.

117

The entire testing process has four phases. 1) Within an hour of the finish of an event, two samples of a performer's urine are taken, one is tested for acidity and specific gravity so that testers can get a broad indication of any illegal compounds. 2) The sample is then split into smaller batches to test for certain classes of drugs, such as anabolic steroids, stimulants, etc. Testers make the urine alkaline and mix it with solvents, like ether, causing any drugs to dissolve into the solvent layer, which is more easily analysed than urine itself. 3) This solvent is then passed through a tube (up to 25 metres long) of gas (or liquid chromatogram) and the molecules of the solvent separate and pass through at different rates, depending on their size and other properties (such as whether they are more likely to adhere to the material of the tube itself). More than 200 drugs are searched for in this period, which lasts about 15 minutes. 4) Any drugs found are then analysed with a mass spectrometer, which bombards them with high energy ions, or electrons, creating unique chemical fingerprints, which can be rapidly checked against the database. Should any banned substances show up, the second sample is tested in the presence of the performer. (Another method is radioimmunoassay, in which antibodies to known substances are used like keys that will only fit one lock; the lock is the banned substance which is found by the key that fits it.)

Encouraged by the Seoul experience, the IOC stated its intention to implement all-year-round testing and while it is by far the most stringent sports body, others have followed its example. Efforts to stamp out drugs are obviously related to the degree of drug use in sport and, as I indicated earlier, there seems to have been a fairly sharp increase over the past twenty to thirty years. The reasons for that increase are discussed below.

Bodies under control

Sport is a human enterprise, as are the many sciences and technologies that have assisted or augmented it. Readers of this book may be engaged in a scientific endeavour to explore the application of academic study to sport. Some explorations, especially in the field of medicine, have yielded striking results. Injuries are better tended, pains are anaesthetized, and recoveries are accelerated. Nutrition has aided both training and performance. Psychology has helped strengthen commitment and develop beneficial attitudes. Biomechanics has identified more efficient methods of locomotion.

Pharmacology's specific contribution is more ambiguous. Sports performers can legally benefit from some drugs, for example painkillers, but not from others, such as those that add speed and power to an athlete's performance. Despite this ambiguity, many sports competitors seem willing to assist their performances by using both prescribed and proscribed drugs. Changes over the past fifty years have ensured that drugs are now part of sport. To authorities, sport has a 'drug problem'; to competitors, drugs are simply available for use should they be required. The first point to remember when trying to uncover the reasons for the apparent rise in drug use is that sport is not a solitary endeavour. Romantic visions of lone trainers are rife, of course, but, in practice, the pursuit of excellence in sport is a team effort. And, over the decades, teams have grown larger and have been augmented with a widening network of 'back-ups', including medical personnel and the whole range of technologies they employ. The scientifically designed and assisted preparation of Balboa's Soviet opponent in *Rocky IV* was a fiction that strayed only marginally from fact. High-tech training equipment, monitoring systems, and specialized personnel all combine to assist a competitor and, ultimately, improve performance. In the process, the individual's body practically becomes the property of scientists. Drugs are but one element in an elaborate technology of control, which has led to the hysterical view that modern sport is contested by scientists more than actual performers.

As we saw in chapter 4, the historical trend that Norbert Elias calls the civilizing process has fostered a dual approach to the human being in which the physical body is subordinated to the rational mind. Scientific advances have made it possible to 'rescue' the body from its natural state and reshape it in accordance with the mind's imperatives. We find in works of literature diverse treatments of much the same theme. Shelley's *Frankenstein* and Stevenson's *Dr Jekyll and Mr Hyde* show attempts by scientists either to reconstruct or remould humans, in both cases with hideous, unanticipated consequences. Many found the Press sisters, Irine and Tamara, rather hideous products of Soviet sports science. They dominated their events (hurdling and pentathlon; shot and discus, respectively) in the 1960s and retired – fortuitously, perhaps – before sex testing was introduced in 1962. But their appearances were freakishly muscular; their flat chests and heavy jaws had the hallmarks of steroid users. Mutterings suggested the sisters' bodies had undergone fundamental chromosomal changes during their preparations.

All sport demands changes in the body and bodily processes. Even though physical input varies from sport to sport, all involve some degree of mastery over technique and this by extension means adjusting the body, whether it be adding strength or sensitivity of touch. The higher the level of achievement, the higher the level of bodily control required. Every activity demands physical control; sport demands an exaggerated level of control that only discipline and surveillance will achieve. Control over the body has always been integral to sport. Yet recently, the degree of control technically possible has been raised considerably by the whole panoply of sport-related science. The claim made in the preamble to the tv series, *The Six Million Dollar Man*, namely, that 'we have the technology . . .', had a little too much truth concealed inside it to be totally dismissed!

The civilizing process itself implicates individuals in some form of control over their bodies; Elias focuses mainly on the restraint in using physical violence, but notes the simultaneous trend for people to subdue spontaneous bodily functions and control their physical being. Sport, in this sense, is regarded as a cathartic release from the stressful tensions generated by the trend towards control. But, of course, sporting activity has also been controlled externally by governing organizations and internally by individual participants who needed to transform and canalize 'their drives and feelings' as Elias puts it, rather than remain in the 'grip' of their impulses. Success of any kind in a competitive activity means conforming and this, in turn, means internal disciplining – control. So, control over the functioning and even appearance of the human body has been important to all societies where, as Elias puts it, 'fairly high civilizing standards are safeguarded'.

In the late twentieth century the body is open for big business. Health foods, fitness clubs, sports goods, diets, rowing machines; all these and many more money-spinning goods and services cater for people eager to reproportion their bodies according to socially desirable standards. Consider also some of the traumatic experiences to which bodies are subject, such as Aids, smoking, pollution, rape, and child abuse. These form layers of a rich soil, or, as John Hargreaves would have it, 'the compost in which moral panic flourishes and on which the forces of law and order thrive' (1987: 141).

Not only have we been encouraged to take control over our bodies; we have become acutely aware of the power at our disposal for doing so. Drugs are one such source of power. We can alter the most basic of bodily functions, like eating, sleeping, and defecating with the appropriate drugs. Pain can be removed, rest can be restored, even moods can be heightened or depressed depending on the 'need'. Nothing is more rational than the desire to have consummate mastery over the body. Only a short step away is the irrational, of course, and dependence surrenders mastery to the drug itself, taking away responsibility, and eventually resolve, from the user and subverting the control once held over the body.

Sports performers are meant to stop short of the irrational. Success is contingent on organizing physical and mental facilities in accordance with structured rules and imperatives, so control over the body is absolutely necessary. Careful use of artifacts to attain such a control has been generously endorsed in sport, but drugs have acquired a notoriety that has not affected exercise equipment, from stop watches to multigyms, esoteric diets based on everything from vitamins to recycled urine and monitoring that can produce elaborate physical and psychological profiles. What were once take-them-or-leave-them facilities became essential equipment for some sports. It seems quite illogical to suggest that drugs would be ignored in a world awash with devices to keep the body under control. Medications to alleviate pain or accelerate healing processes became parts of performers' baggage to be carried in kitbags. Many experimented with the alleged benefits of hypnotherapy, autogenics and other 'positive thinking' techniques. Vitamin, phosphate, and cortisone (steroid) injections became commonplace. Sedatives calmed nerves.

Set in a wider context, trends in sport reflect what goes on in life generally. The past twenty odd years have witnessed the rise of new spirits. Young people have welcomed the use of stimulants, hallucinogens, and all manner of narcotics to alter behaviour and perception. But recent generations have edged towards drug dependence: tranquillizers have led a seemingly endless list of prescriptives to counter the stress-inducing effects of modern life. The 'drug culture' is worldwide and transgenerational, embracing those who wish to open new doors to perception, those who merely want to make it to the next day, and many more besides. Whether they like it or not, sports performers are part of a universal culture in which drugs of one form or another play an important role.

The science-assisted effort to pursue athletic excellence and the enveloping swirl of drug dependence: take the two together and one has a compelling mixture. Sport, if only because of its competitive nature, has urged its competitors to exploit the gifts of science, and our habits as a population have been transformed by the availability of drugs. Some might wish to add a further factor to this combination – an exaggeration of the importance of winning. Commercialism is the malefactor here; as sport has slid further from the corinthian ideal, its passage lubricated by business interests, so the joy of competing for its own sake has been superseded by an unprincipled win-at-all-costs approach; winning is what matters in modern sports. Exactly *how* one wins is largely irrelevant. Few people would doubt that victory in any sport is currently very important. Whether this is anything new or just a continuation of old traditions is open to question. Those to whom the cherishing and upholding of ideals are so important, often ignore the fact that sport, by definition, is competitive and competition is meaningless unless some individual or group is actually doing their level best to win. Commercialization has certainly increased the tangible rewards for winning. Olympic winners of ten years ago went home with a gold medal; today they take with them a portfolio of contracts worth six figure sums. A victorious world championship boxer can look forward to a purse worth dozens of thousands of dollars – if not millions – while his vanquished opponent may be relegated straight to low-budget promotions.

It was but a few years ago that snooker and darts were down-to-earth sports enjoyed by those who liked a drink at the local pub; quite unlike the modern players for whom a major professional title means a substantial premium on their earnings. Clearly, there is more at stake nowadays, in terms of both material gains and status. And this has fostered more aggressive competitors, prepared to train more and even risk more to realize their ambitions. If science can help the realization, then common sense dictates that sports performers use it; if drugs can assist, one can be sure many competitors will give only a sideways glance to moral signposts reading 'road to corruption'. Sport is too profound, too serious, and too lucrative for simplistic slogans. The crucial edge which drugs can provide may be the difference between a fortune and ignominy. Competition has come to occupy such a central place, not only in sport but in modern society, that it would be a virtual betrayal of sporting ideals to neglect the potential of drugs in maximizing performance. Three trends together help explain why sports performers have been prepared to use drugs: advances in science; growth of drug culture; and intensification of competitiveness. But, equally important as changes in actual use are the changes in reactions to drugs and, more pertinently, the reasons for the changes.

By accident or choice?

The reasons why the IOC and other sports' governing bodies are prepared to go to quite extraordinary lengths in their efforts to solve the supposed drug problem may be self-evident to many. But we will evaluate each reason on its own merits, beginning with the most obvious.

Drugs are not fair. They confer artificially induced advantages on the user and competing with such advantages is tantamount to cheating. Fairness is a rather troublesome concept to define, but we can assume, with Peter McIntosh, who wrote the book *Fair Play*, that: 'Fairness is related to justice' and 'breaking the rules with intent to avoid the penalties' as a definition of 'cheating' is too simple (1979: 2 and 182). He favours the definition of Gunther Lüschen who believes that the 'principle of chance beyond differences in skill and strategy are violated' when the conditions agreed upon for winning a contest 'are changed in favour of one side' (1976: 67). Drugs change the conditions for winning. But, then again, so do many other things.

Take the example of blood doping for which athletes may draw penalties, including bans. In a strict sense, this is cheating. But, how about athletes born in Kenya or Ethiopia, both several hundred feet above sea level? Such athletes may be fortunate enough to be brought up in an atmosphere that encourages haemoglobin production in the body and they may find the transition to sea level really quite comfortable as a result. Witness as evidence the dominance of Kenyan middle and long distance runners over the past twenty years. Equipped with naturally conferred advantages, Kenyans capitalized on the track and cross country circuits, leaving weary European and American athletes in their wake.

Another 'accident of birth' meant that the 5-year-old Boris Becker was given every available coaching and equipment facility to help him develop his tennis skills. His parents, being wealthy, could afford to indulge their child and, as things turned out, their money was a shrewd investment, for Becker became the youngest ever Wimbledon champion and, in so doing, unlocked a multi-million dollar treasure chest. Let's imagine that tennis produced its equivalent of former boxing champion, Mike Spinks, an archetypal ghetto child from St Louis, who had the added disadvantage of being black. Were this imaginary figure to play Becker, would it be a fair match? When they came face-to-face in matchup, the conditions may appear fair, but one would hardly say they were 'fair' in a deeper sense. One player has benefited from *social* advantages in a similar way to Kenyan runners, who have benefited *naturally* from being born at high altitudes. Sporting competition has inbuilt inequalities that militate against fairness. What fairness, for instance, is there when Zola Budd, a female runner of little athletic distinction and with only one major international title, can command £90,000 for a single race, while many of her competitors (some of whom beat her) run for expenses only? Budd's worth was based yet again on birthplace, in her case South Africa. It would be a naive person indeed who believed all is fair in sport in the modern world and that background, whether social or natural, is irrelevant to eventual success or failure.

Drugs are taken by choice. There is a difference between the advantages bestowed by social background or place of origin and those that are enjoyed by the taker of drugs. Sports performers can, as the slogan goes, 'say "no" to drugs' in much the same way as many say 'yes'. Swallowing tablets or allowing oneself to be injected are voluntary activities over which individuals have a high degree of control; one presumes – and only *presumes* – that they realize the potential costs as well as benefits and they exercise volition when doing or agreeing to the action. Obviously, the same performers have no say in where they were born or the state of their parents' bank account. By contrast, using drugs involves procuring an advantage quite voluntarily.

Yet there is more to this: first, because there are many other forms of advantage that are actively sought out and, second, because some are better placed than others either to seek out or eschew them. Were you a Briton following home John Nguge in a 5,000-metre race, you might wish you were born in Kenya. Impossible, of course, so you might think about going to high altitudes and engaging in a spot of blood doping. Quite possible, but illegal. Another possibility is just to train in some part of the world high enough to give you some advantage, or at least to neutralize Nguge's advantage. Perfectly possible and legal. The probable result is an advantage quite legitimately obtained through voluntary effort. But an advantage is gained all the same.

Not that everyone is able to exercise choice in such matters: a dedication to competition, a determination to win, and an un-flinching resolve to withstand pain are needed and these qualities are easier to come if the alternative is a one-way ticket back to the ghetto. If your alternatives look unpromisingly bleak, then choices can be rather illusory. Ben Johnson was born in Jamaica and migrated to Canada in 1980 at the age of 19, his ambition being the same as any migrant, namely, to improve his material life. Lacking education, but possessing naturally quick reflexes (which couldn't be changed) and fast ground speed (which could), he made the best of what he had, so that, within four years, he was in the Canadian Olympic team. Sport is full of stories like Johnson's: bad news – poor origins, little education, few occupational prospects;

good news – physical potential and the opportunity to realize it. There's no realistic choice, here. Countless young people with some form of sporting prowess when faced with the 'once-and-for-all' decision of whether or not to sink their entire efforts in the one area in which they just might achieve success don't want to contemplate the alternatives. Given the chance, they'll go for it. And this means maximizing every possible advantage in an intensely competitive world. It's doubtful whether any athlete with a similarly deprived childhood would have any compunction about gaining an edge by any means. The choices they have are often too stark to need much mulling over.

Asking whether choice was exercised in trying to determine whether cheating took place is not adequate. Even if we were to dismiss the claims of a performer (who tested positive for a given drug) that his or her drink was spiked (or similar), the question of whether that person *freely* exercised choice remains. Returning to Becker, let's suppose he was found guilty of something untoward; it's feasible to argue that his choice was less restricted than a Turkish migrant worker's son in West Germany whose one chance for some material success is through sport. All this isn't intended to exonerate those from deprived backgrounds who have sought an advantage through 'foul' means rather than 'fair'. It merely casts doubts on the hard-and-fast distinction between fair play and cheating. If we want to sustain the distinction, we have to ignore the manifold advantages or disadvantages that derive from a person's physical and social background and which are beyond his or her power to change. We can attempt to get round this by isolating the element of choice and defining cheating only when a person has consciously and deliberately taken some action to gain advantage. This works up to a point if we cast aside doubts about the circumstances in which the decision was made. Again, backgrounds are important in influencing the decision. So the pedestal on which sport stands when it tries to display itself as a model of fair play is not quite as secure as it might at first seem. Not only are advantages dispensed virtually at birth, but they operate either to limit or liberate a person's ability to make choices.

Drugs are harmful to health. Sport's central philosophical point seems to be that, whatever people's backgrounds, if they are given the chance to gain advantages over others, they may fairly do so as long as they stop short of knowingly using chemical substances (at least *some* chemical substances). Most drugs used to enable or assist performance rather than gain advantage by enhancement are acceptable. So it was perfectly possible for British runner Peter Elliott to earn his 800 metres silver medal while being treated with a painkilling drug to alleviate a groin strain, while ten other competitors at the same Olympics were disqualified, two for using the diuretic pseudofurosemide (which *may* have been used to conceal anabolic steroids).

Some might counter the argument that supports this by saying that the ability to achieve anything at all in sport is limited by the body's natural early warning system – pain – and interfering with this is artificial and unnatural. 'But unlikely to cause any long-term damage in the user of certain painkillers' might be the riposte. To which the answer might be that there are other types of conditioning that do not include drugs, but which are detrimental to a performer's health. A good example of this might be the former gymnast, Olga Korbut, who in her early teens was a lovable urchin who charmed the world's tv viewers by her spellbinding displays, but who in her twenties was a haggard, arthritic anorexic. The effect on health of a great many banned drugs is negligible by comparison. Intensive training, controlled dieting, hypnotherapy, and 'psyching' techniques, as well as many more practices used by modern competitors may yet prove to have long-term consequences. Looking at monstrously distorted wrestlers, weightlifters, and body builders, whose training includes massive protein ingestion, one wonders what state of health many will have twenty years from now.

This has led some observers to believe that the use of drugs is no better or worse than some other aids to performance. They are certainly no worse than many of the drugs commonly available outside the world of sport and, obviously, tobacco and alcohol come into the reckoning as major factors in cancer and heart disease. Most sports frown on smoking and drinking too, though some, like motor racing and cricket, have been grateful for sponsorship from tobacco companies while others, like soccer, have been uncertain what position to take towards alcohol. Even everyday drugs, such as aspirin and antihistamine, which we presume to be innocuous, are not completely without potentially harmful consequences. Caffeine found in coffee and tea is mildly harmful, but who would dream of banning its general use? The argument that some drugs are more harmful than others has an *Animal Farm* logic to it and, as such, is fraught with inconsistencies. Even if some drugs were found to be dangerous (and steroids in particular are thought to be responsible for cancers and deaths) it would be something of an intrusion into the lives of responsible individuals to tell them not to take them.

Medical bodies are not averse to doing this as the campaigns, or more properly, the crusades of the British and American Medical

Associations against boxing have shown. Prolonged involvement in boxing exposes the boxer to the risk of brain damage and many other less severe injuries, is the claim of the anti-boxing lobbyists. So boxers have to be protected, if necessary from themselves, in exactly the same way as any other sports competitors contemplating actions that may result in harm to their health. The effect on health of many banned drugs is small compared to that of boxing. But to make boxing illegal because of this presumes that all the young and physically healthy young men (and a few women in some parts of the world) are oblivious to the hazards of the sport when they enter. It assumes they are not rational, deliberating agents with some grasp of the implications of boxing – a grasp sufficient for them to do a cost-benefit calculation and weigh up the probable rewards against the probable losses.

Were information about the long-term consequences of boxing or drug use concealed, then the 'protectors' would have a very strong case. But the results of scientific tests are available and to assume that competitors are so witless as to know nothing of this is insulting and patronizing. If young people with a chance to capitalize on the sporting potential are informed of the dangers involved in their decision to pursue a line of action, then it is difficult to support a case for prohibiting this, at least in societies not prone to totalitarianism. Boxers may well judge the brain damage they risk in their sport preferable to the different kind of 'brain damage' they will almost certainly sustain in a repetitive industrial job over a 40-year period, or in an unbearably long spell out of work. Other sports performers with few prospects outside sport may evaluate their own positions similarly and, when the mephistophelean bargain presents itself, the decision of whether or not to box should be theirs. Unless, of course, one believes that superordinate moral agents should guide our thoughts and behaviour.

But the crudity and patronage of one argument doesn't license disingenuousness in the attack on it; which means that we should acknowledge that sports performers of whatever level do not reach decisions unaided. We have noted previously that all manner of influence bear on an individual's decision and, quite apart from those deriving from background, we have to isolate coaches and trainers. Bearing in mind the case of American football in the 1960s when coaches were assuming virtual medical status in dispensing drugs, we should remind ourselves of the important roles still played by these people in all sports. We must also realize that sport is populated by many 'Dr Feelgoods' who are only too happy to boost performance without necessarily informing the competitor of all the possible implications. It's quite probable that many competitors are doing things, taking things, even thinking things that may jeopardize their health. But do they know it? Perhaps sports authorities might attempt to satisfy themselves formally that all competitors in sports which do hold dangers are totally aware of them and comfortable about their involvement. This would remove the educational task from coaches and trainers and shift the onus onto governing organizations.

Drugs *are* harmful to health – as are many other things. Sports authorities quite properly communicate this, though the distinctions that are often made between harmful substances and activities and apparently innocuous ones are frequently arbitrary and difficult to support with compelling evidence. Further, the assumptions carried by governing bodies in their efforts to regulate the use of drugs can be seen in some lights as demeaning, suggesting that performers themselves are incapable of making assessments and decisions unassisted.

Sports performers are role models for the young. It follows that if athletes are known and seen to use drugs of any kind, then young people may be encouraged to follow. There is adequate evidence to support this and, while the substances which competitors use to enhance performance are often different to the ones that cause long-term distress at street-level, the very act of using drugs may work as a powerful example. But the argument can't be confined to sport: many rock musicians as well as writers and artists use drugs for relief or stimulus. Rock stars arguably wield more influence over young acolytes than the sports elite. The shaming of a sports performer found to have used drugs and the nullifying of his or her performance is a deterrent or a warning to the young: 'Do this and you will suffer the same fate.' But Bon Jovi isn't disgraced and the band's albums aren't taken from the charts if it's discovered that they recorded it while using coke. No one considers asking Rick Astley for a urine sample after one of his concerts. The music of Charlie Parker, a heroin addict, the acting of Cary Grant, who used LSD, the writing of Dylan Thomas, an alcoholic, all have not been obliterated; nor has the idolatry afforded them. Sports performers are different in the sense that they operate in and therefore symbolize a sphere where all is meant to be wholesome and pure. But this puts competitors under sometimes intolerable pressure to keep their haloes straight and maintain the pretence of being saints. Clearly, they are not, nor, given the competitive nature of sport, will they ever be. Gone are the days portrayed in *Chariots of Fire* when winners were heroes to be glorified and losers were 'good sports' for competing.

Nowadays, hard cash has spoiled the purity. A yearning for money has introduced a limitless capacity for compromise and previously 'amateur' or 'shamateur' sports organizations, including the IOC, have led the way by embracing commercialism rather than spurning it. Competitors too are creatures of a competitive world and probably more preoccupied with struggling to win than with keeping a clean image.

These then are the main reasons why governing bodies have sought to eliminate drugs from sport and discredit those found using them. Yet the opposing school of thought has advanced its argument quite simply on two grounds. The first ground is practical and involves recognizing that drugs are part of modern sport and whatever attempts are made to extirpate them, ways and means will be found. In a decade's time, it is possible that there will be no way of preventing competitors from taking drugs which does not involve prison-like supervision in training as well as competition: inspection, invigilation, regulation, and punishment would become features of sport.

The second ground is a moral one and involves bringing into the debate the people who are least frequently consulted – the performers. Peter Corrigan of *The Observer*, writing on the positive test of 1988 Tour de France winner, Pedro Delgado, observed that none of the other 180 competitors had protested at Delgado's infringement or showed any disinclination to continue to race with him. Corrigan suggested that the demands of the race itself were so great that drugs were essential and that cyclists should be allowed to make up their own minds on whether or not to use them. This harkens back to my previous point about the appropriate assumptions organizations hold about performers. Were they to be seen as able, reasoning, and aware humans equipped with up-to-date information on drugs, then it's possible that we could safely leave the big decisions to them, as Corrigan suggested.

It's quite possible that many would object to drugs, but it is also possible that many would object to those elite performers who can afford to employ a staff of doctors and nutritionists and use only permitted drugs. It's possible that some might object to the use of blatant pace-makers in track events, for they are only of service to specific athletes. Maybe they wouldn't see steroid-pumped sprinters as mere projectiles fuelled by drugs, but as athletes so utterly committed to pursuing excellence that they are prepared to rip apart the limits of their own frame to run faster than others. It would be useful to know what competitors thought. This is not an argument designed to satisfy purists, but it is certainly a cogent one and one wonders why sports organizations, in particular the IOC, haven't paused to consider it. Instead they have gone headlong down the road of regulation and punishment, spending millions of dollars on test centres all over the world in a campaign that borders on the obsessive. In the process, the mystique of drugs is enlarged, convincing sports performers that drugs do enhance performance, when, in fact they only *may*. Richard Nicholson, editor of the *Institute of Medical Ethics Bulletin*, has for a long time, through his journal, suggested that the main benefit of drugs is a placebo effect – that psychologically competitors expect an improvement in performance and produce it. In other words, inert substances can affect improvements if only the user believes in their efficacy. Banning drugs makes them appear more useful than they probably are and so makes them more attractive and ultimately more effective.

Why then has sport committed inordinate amounts of money to the control of drugs? We have considered the more conventional and predictable reasons for the hard line against drugs. We have also exposed some of the ambiguities and even contradictions in these. Against these reasons, there is what seems a practical and morally-sound case for legitimizing drugs in sport. It seems insufficient to argue that sport benefits from purging itself of drugs; this may be so in an ideal world, but in reality, the concept is vague and unspecific. Exactly who or what in sport benefits? Were we to approach the question cynically, we might cast eyes outside sport and isolate beneficiaries who have no formal position on drugs in sport, but stand to profit very handsomely from the current attack on drugs. The companies supplying the equipment used for testing clearly have vested interests in the attempts of the IOC and other organizations. They have the technology without which those attempts are worthless. For the campaign on drugs to be in any degree successful, detective technologies will have to keep pace with ingenious chemists. This is an expensive business. The 1988 laboratory cost the IOC $3 million from Hewlett-Packard. Future centres are to cost more. Drug testing in sport is set to become a virtual industry in itself. The cost of drug testing represents a multimillion dollars outflow from sport into private industry. Clearly, someone is profiting. Perhaps it is sport – if it can successfully instigate a return to its glorious past. This is unlikely. But while it tries, big business will stand by and applaud its stance, pausing only to prepare its next colossal invoice.

This is but one facet of an alliance between sport and business that has developed over the past several decades. Many nowadays go further than calling it an alliance: sport *is* big business, they would argue. Next, we'll consider the argument.

Further reading

Living with Drugs *by Michael Glossop (Temple Smith, 1982) is a calm and detached analysis of drugs and their misuse in modern society by a psychologist who is clearly not convinced that the effects of drugs are solely due to the substances themselves. In other words, Glossop looks at the influences on drug taking, not only the placebo effect, but the range of other factors that surround drugs and make them attractive.*

Drugs in Sport *edited by D. Mottram (E. & F. N. Spon, 1988) is, as its title suggests, a specialist text designed for those seeking a detailed account of drug use in sport. It is a useful source book.*

'Becoming a marijuana user' by Howard Becker (in American Journal of Sociology, *vol. 59, 1953) has become something of a classic article on drug use. In a sociological perspective, the article describes the cultural aspects of drug use: how one actually learns the methods of taking drugs, interprets their effects and generally experiences drug taking. Its relevance to sport is in highlighting how cultural contexts (e.g. in athletics) can commission drug taking and provide a frame of reference for understanding the results.*

'Sport and drugs' by Martyn Lucking (in Sport, Culture and Ideology, *edited by J. Hargreaves, Routledge & Kegan Paul, 1982) provides the recent background to drug use in sport and the effects of drugs on athletic performance. The article is useful on a factual level but concludes embarrassingly: 'I anticipate that the 1980s may well see a virtual elimination of the current widespread use'!*

Assignment

Imagine you are a researcher for a television documentary on drugs in sport. You have five telephone calls to make. Whom do you call? What are the first three questions you ask each? What answers do you get?

Chapter seven

The business

Vanishing amateurs

'It's not sport any more: it's business!' The argument's premiss is a popular one and, basically, it is that nothing is sacred. Well, nothing that can be profitably used to turn a penny, anyway. Sport has much utility in this respect. Being turned into a business, according to this argument, doesn't simply mean that commercial profits have been derived from sport. It means that filthy lucre has actually corrupted the ideals that were once integral. Moral qualities and principles associated with justice and fair play have been sacrificed on the altar of market forces. Now sport is bought and sold rather like any other service or commodity, but most like entertainment – showbusiness.

Business
An habitual activity in which commercial considerations take priority; this term embraces trades, professions, and virtually any field interested in financial return rather than artistry or aesthetic principles.

Part of this argument is undeniably true. Sport, or at least vast areas of it, have become the prey of commercial interests and these have transformed sheer competitive activity into high-yield business. Whether this has corrupted the central values of sport or merely taken sport in a new direction is open to question. Defenders of commercial interests would insist that they are only part of an inexorable movement. People enjoy watching and appreciating a contest and, in some circumstances, are willing to pay to do so. The trend has been that they are prepared to pay more and more. And where there is a demand and a raw supply there is rarely a shortage of enterprising people with ideas on how to connect the two – and appropriate a surplus.

In a sense, all sports that are watchable have such a potential. An after-dinner game of snooker played in private and with no pecuniary motive would not have this potential. Nor would a one-to-one basketball matchup in the privacy of a school gym. Make the snooker players Steve Davis and Jimmy White and transport them to Wembley Arena, or the ball players Michael Jordan and Magic Johnson and pitch them together in Madison Square Garden and they become spectator sports. If contests can draw crowds they qualify as spectator sports. This doesn't make them implicitly corrupt, of course: those who rue the commercialization of sport might insist that it's perfectly possible to have mass spectator sports, but without the taint of money. Proponents of this view harken back to the golden days of amateurism when sport was for, as the name implies, love (from the Latin *amatorious*, 'pertaining to love'). Fondness for the activity itself or the satisfaction drawn from winning were the motivating principles, though competition was, or should have been, regarded as more important than achievement.

Nowadays, 'amateur' is virtually a pejorative word implying unskilful and lack of refinement – the opposite of professional. In the eighteenth and nineteenth centuries, the reverse held sway. The amateur was the elevated symbol of all that was good in sport, while the professional was despised as someone who prostituted athletic exercises as a means of livelihood. 'Sports had as their ideal aim the production of pleasure', write Eric Dunning and Kenneth Sheard, 'an immediate emotional state rather than some ulterior end, whether of a material or other kind' (1979: 153–4). It was regarded as 'unsportsmanlike' and 'ungentlemanly' to show elation in victory and disappointment in defeat. Public schools and universities were the wellsprings of the amateur ethos and there was concern at the prospect of the 'dignified' ball games practised at Rugby, Harrow, and elsewhere being copied by 'lower classes' whose opportunism and desire to win amounted to a defilement. 'Subsidized' players who were reimbursed for work time lost when playing, or who accepted straight payment for their services were a particularly threatening development in rugby because amateurs could not devote so much time to their game as professionals and so would be hard-pressed to maintain their superiority. There was also the suspicion that dangling a carrot in front of players would encourage them not only to play harder and forget the joy of it all, but to raise their level of competence through training. This was unfair in the eyes of the amateur: it produced a competitive advantage for those who committed themselves to improvement. Sport was meant to be about enjoyment, whereas 'to train for sport and take it too seriously was', as Dunning and Sheard observe 'tantamount to transforming it into work and, hence, to destroying its essence' (1979: 148).

Alarming as it seemed to members of an upper class weaned on a conception of sport unspoiled by the intrusions of the working class, professional sport grew steadily, so that by the second half of the nineteenth century, cricket, ball games, prize fighting, and pedestrianism (the equivalent of competitive walking) were able to subsidize competitors for their efforts. Some sporting clubs, specifically golf and cricket clubs, were able to employ coaches, while other sports could pay expenses simply because they were popular enough to attract paying spectators. This actually caused the amateur gentlemen to confound the professional trend with even greater fervour. Mass gatherings of working-class spectators, some of them strongly partisan, posed what was seen as a threat to public order, so much so that such assemblies were outlawed in certain circumstances, as we have seen. Spectators didn't benefit from sport in the same way as participants; quite the contrary, they suffered by degenerating into an excitable amoral mass. The gentlemen amateurs' reaction to spectator sport presents us with a metaphor for changes that were occurring in society generally: the industrial working class was getting organized and showing signs of cohesion and solidarity in the face of employers clearly troubled by the prospect of having their absolute authority challenged from below.

Class antagonism or sheer prejudice manifested itself in several notable incidents, all designed to cocoon the exclusive elite of gentlemen from others. As well as the landowning aristocracy, gentlemen would have included *nouveux riches* merchants, physicians, solicitors, MPs, and others with prestige rather than inherited wealth. In 1846 at Lancaster, in the north-west of England, there was a dispute following a Manchester crew's victory in the Borough Cup rowing competition. Two of the crew, a cabinet maker and a bricklayer, were not, it was alleged, acceptable entrants on the grounds that 'they were not known as men of any property'. The debate continued until, in 1853, when the category of 'gentleman amateur' was distinguished from the pure amateur, for the Lancaster Rowing Club's purposes. Other clubs followed suit stipulating that those who worked as mechanics, artisans, or labourers would not be eligible for competition as their employment, being physical in nature, equipped them with advantages. This may have seemed a subterfuge to members of the working class, but it was perpetuated by the Amateur Athletic Association which, in 1866, officially defined an amateur as a person who had either never competed 1) in open competition; 2) for prize money; 3) for admission money; 4) with professionals; 5) never taught or assisted in the pursuit of athletics exercises as a means of a livelihood; or 6) was not a mechanic, artisan, or labourer. Condition 6) was removed in 1880, but the intent of this typical pronouncement was clear: to exclude working-class competitors by seeming to respond to the evils of professionalism. Redrawing the boundaries around amateurs effectively secured sport as an upper- and middle-class stronghold. But this was not so in all sports.

By the mid-1880s, rugby and soccer had become so popular, especially in the English north and the midlands that spectators, particularly those in the industrial cities, would pay to watch *en masse* thus making money available to induce good players to appear regularly. The Rugby Union was intractable in its opposition and by 1895 had effectively forced the formation of a professional union, which in 1922 became the Rugby League. Soccer prevaricated, but by 1885 had agreed to strictly controlled professionalism, with maximum wage and transfer stipulations. From this point, we see soccer becoming increasingly organized so as to offer entertainment to spectators, not fulfilment to players. We find success growing in importance; competitions spring up. Spectators watch winners so clubs encourage winning; competing for itself is fine, but appears slightly anachronistic by the 1920s.

Some sports, such as athletics and tennis, held out staunchly, refusing to permit those who had earned money from playing sport into the major events. Boxing, for long a pursuit of professionals at some level, whether in fairground shows or street fighting, evolved two coexisting organizations with amateurs often proceeding to professional ranks in their early twenties. In other sports, amateurs played with and against pros, though, as the example of English cricket demonstrates, they would not necessarily 'mix' and were provided with separate changing facilities. As hostility to professional players gradually dissipated, cricket desegregated, though some sports, Rugby Union included, continued their elitist policies. Tennis refused to allow professionals into its prestigious competitions until 1968 when it became 'open'. From that point, players like Rod Laver, who had previously changed to the status of pro, reintegrated with amateurs whom they dominated so overwhelming that amateurism vanished from top levels over the next several years. Athletics for long buried its head in spite of widespread knowledge of 'shamateurism' with performers accepting generous gifts and exaggerated expenses for their services. In 1983, the International Amateur Athletics Federation took a new approach, recognizing that competitors were being paid, but insisting that their monies should go directly via a subvention to a trust fund and dispensed later to cover 'expenses'. Prior to this, athletes who were either discovered to have accepted payment, or publicly transferred to a sport where professionalism was recognized were forbidden from track and field competition; though in the USA, strictures were often relaxed to reinstate such athletes as Dwight Stones and Renaldo Nehemiah, who, like many others before him, signed to play pro football. (He returned to athletics after it had gone 'open'.)

Athletics and some other sports, like soccer, now allow participation between professionals and those who, in official terms at least, wish to preserve amateur status. So that there is no compromise involved when Soviet football teams play western sides in European Cup competitions or Cuban athletes compete against pros in, for instance, the Pan-American games. The integration doesn't extend to boxing and top Soviet and Cuban boxers have not been permitted to fight pros unless they relinquish amateur status. Occasionally, this happens: Mate Parlov and Slobodan Kacir, both Yugoslavs, and some Soviets competed successfully as pros after amateur careers. The most celebrated refusal to do so was that of Teofilio Stevenson, Cuba's four-times heavyweight gold medallist, who resisted multimillion dollar offers to fight American professionals. It would be inaccurate to label Soviet sports as amateur, in the original sense at least. There is a pronounced emphasis on winning and the rewards of success are tangible. The state-assisted programmes enable performers to devote themselves to preparation with meticulous attention paid to every facet of training. It would be no contradiction to describe the approach as totally 'professional', business-like, thorough, and disciplined (as we will see in chapter eight.)

Even Rugby Union which has witnessed the professionalization of sport from a position of supreme detachment, has been known to condone some clubs' efforts in attracting players by offering employment packages – in other words, 'jobs for the boys', the idea being that a player signs for a club on the understanding that the club will arrange suitably undemanding but well-paid work. In 1988 the English Club, Bath, introduced the concept of an athletics-style trust fund system in which players would receive a lump sum at the end of their playing careers. Hockey too is poised to follow suit.

There are few current examples of amateurism left in modern sport. Gentlemanly pastimes and the noble spirits that guided them have ceded place to an industry with products, producers, and buyers and this has transformed the structure and, in some cases, the content of modern sport. A corruption of a misty ideal it may be, but the trend is undeniable and quite unstoppable. Sport has changed in nature over the past century; it hasn't so much been infiltrated by business, rather, it *is* business.

Promoters and owners

No one is officially credited with being the first sports promoter, but we can assume that, in some dark and distant age, an enterprising witness to a contest noticed a crowd react excitedly to the sight of competition and thought, 'Lo! the gathered masses act as if twas them joined in battle!' Inspired by this, the first promoter would have brought the same or similar contestants together and drawn the same crowd but this time charging a fee for watching – the assumption being that the pleasure taken in just observing the spectacle was worth a small amount. So the sports business started.

James Figg improved on the basic idea when he opened his 'Amphitheatre' in 1743. As we saw previously, Figg attracted large crowds to watch his combat events, which were arranged on a regular basis and supplied him with a successful business. His concept was adopted from that of the ancient Romans, except that his motive was merely to extract a profit from the enterprise. His patrons' motives were probably mixed; to identify with and support their favourite, to extract vicarious pleasure from watching, to wager, or just to meet other members of the 'fancy' (as patrons of prize fighting were collectively known). This reflects much the same mixture of impulses of fans today.

Early promoters (though not called by that name) would have been less interested in why spectators attended than with their actual presence, though the positive correlation between high calibre performers and large crowds would not have been lost on them. Figg's natural successors were the prize-fight organizers of America in the 1800s. Some states, like Massachusetts, outlawed prize fighting and this prompted the organizers to stage illicit contests 'behind locked doors' with a small but paying crowd. Jeffrey Sammons, in his history of American boxing, *Beyond the Ring*, writes that the first unofficial world heavyweight championship between Paddy Ryan and Joe Goss, in 1880, was 'fought in virtual secrecy at Colliers, West Virginia. Organizers chose the tiny Brooks County town for its proximity to the Ohio and Pennsylvania state lines: if raided by hostile law officers, participants and followers could scatter across the border to escape arrest' (Sammons 1988: 6).

In the same period, an Irish migrant named Richard Kyle Fox was scratching a living by writing about events such as oyster-opening and one-legged dancing and, occasionally, promoting the events which he could then cover for his newspaper. In 1881, he had a chance encounter with John L. Sullivan, a prize fighter, who, so folklore has it, spurned Fox's offer to promote him. Sullivan went on to become the most famous boxer of his day and Fox's determination either to secure his services or ruin him drove him to the position of American sport's first major promoter, offering either purses (fixed sums) or percentages of gate receipts to fighters. By the mid 1890s, top pugilists fought for what were then enormous purses of thousands of dollars. Sullivan is known to have charged in the region of $25,000 per championship fight.

The legalization of prize fighting in New York in 1920 opened up new commercial possibilities. Sammons notes that, in 1922 alone, gate receipts in New York State totalled $5 million, a sum that prompted some to contend that boxing was 'an industry, financed by banks, and licensed and supervised by state laws and officials just as banking and insurance' (quoted in Sammons 1988: 66). If this was so, then boxing was a prototype for other sports. Opportunistic entrepreneurs were key agents in the process of establishing the sport along business lines. Unquestionably, the most visionary was George 'Tex' Richard, who promoted all but one heavyweight title fight that resulted in a new champion from the reign of Jack Johnson to that of Gene Tunney and whose elaborate publicity stunts and gargantuan promotions (regularly attracting over 100,000 spectators, with receipts of nearly $1.9 million for one fight in 1926) established him as *the* sports promoter of his era and, probably, of any other. Allegations that many of Richard's contests were not only run as but actually were showbusiness events complete with scripts and stage directions were commonplace. But the controversy only added to his infamy and he was able to exploit the growing mass enthusiasm for 'live' sport, which featured not only contestants, but a sense of occasion – an atmosphere that drew together the working class and the plutocracy, the anonymous and the famous.

Massed audiences for sports events were not confined to boxing. For the English FA Cup Final in 1923, 200,000 people were squeezed into Wembley Stadium. By this time soccer had become totally professional, top clubs having charged admission since the 1870s – around the same time that race track events began imposing entrance fees. Rugby League football, which had split from Rugby Union in 1895, was committed to taking gate money and made no pretence to uphold the ideal of the unpaid gentleman of its amateur counterpart, which refused to turn rugby into a spectator-oriented sport.

American fans too showed a penchant for ball games, their favourite at the turn of the century being baseball. The game had eclipsed cricket as the sport of the wealthy, and the fact that an admission was charged at the games of teams from the National League, founded in 1876, ensured that it was beyond the reach of the poor. But the rival American Association halved admissions and even enhanced its appeal by selling cheap beer at the ball parks. The sport was well-patronized by Irish and Italian fans. By the 1920s and 1930s, baseball had developed into America's 'national game', attracting five-figure crowds. In the midst of economic depression, star players like Babe Ruth were able to command staggering sums of $80,000 p.a. They were able to do so, not because gate receipts were soaring, but because entrepreneurs had seen the commercial possibilities of having their products identified with a formidably popular sport. For example, in 1934, Henry Ford paid $100,000 for the rights to the World Series. The sport's most prestigious event effectively became a vehicle for advertising Ford's automobiles. Gillette and major brewers followed suit, setting in motion a trend that was to continue to the present day, as we will see later in this chapter.

Unlike British ball clubs, which are run by an elected committee, the chairman of which has executive, but not autocratic, power, baseball and football clubs in the United States are invariably under the control of an individual. The owner's influence is extensive; to have control of a ball club is to be able to make decisions on every facet of the operations. So owners have played a pivotal part in commercializing sport. As they are established in business before moving into sport, owners, according to Jonathan Brower's research, have been 'neither accustomed to nor comfortable with losing money in business ventures' (1976: 15). Not surprisingly, they have established and run sports organizations as if they were any other business, with a criterion of success in the form of a winning season (when wins outnumber defeats) being added to that of profit. While they're run on broadly similar lines, British clubs, particularly soccer clubs, have less success in yielding a profit, if only because they outstrip demand with supply, with a nine-month season featuring ninety-two league clubs in at least three consecutive competitions. But, while buying into a British football team may not seem a sound business investment, as Jay J. Coakley points out, 'To be an owner or part owner of a sport or a banker of a large sporting event is likely to enhance personal prestige more dramatically than any other form of business investment' (1978: 212–13). Whatever the motives of promoters, owners, chairs, or any other entrepreneur in sport, their impact has been to transform sport into a unique commercial enterprise. Why unique? Because sport may have veered towards, but has never become, pure entertainment. It's packaging is nowadays indistinguishable, but sport's abiding appeal has lain in its essential unpredictability. The outcome of competition is never known, at least, nearly never. During the 1950s, organized crime had such a stranglehold on American boxing that the outcome of a great many title fights was prescribed.

Audience effects

The very presence of one onlooker can affect a sporting performer. This observation has provided the premiss for a series of experiments designed to explain the exact psychological processes behind the relationship. Some theories indicate that drive-like motivational effects due to the presence of others facilitate enhanced muscular performance, though at the expense of skill. Zajonc (1965) proposed that the mere presence of another individual was sufficient condition for arousing a biologically-based innate drive. It was an influential idea, but too simplistic for more recent researchers, who have highlighted situational factors (summarized by Wankel 1982). One of the more interesting findings in recent research on this subject contradicts the common-sense view that champions, or ex-champions, who have experienced stressful and distracting championship events with their mass audiences, have an advantage over challengers who are not used to the 'big occasion' and are unfamiliar with performing in front of large audiences and so may be overawed. What research there is on this subject points to the opposite conclusion: having the experience of stress in front of an audience confers no advantage and lacking an awareness of this may give the inexperienced performers an edge.

Promoters of sports events and owners, or chairs of clubs are integral parts of a modern landscape filled with sponsors, agents, and hard-boiled marketing executives, all seeking to manipulate competitive sport to their own requirements. The early efforts of Rickard and others were to lay sport bare to the stern Mammon of market forces. But they, and the others who improved on their ideas, have not been simple conveyers of public demand. They have, in some cases, originated the demand, shaped it, managed it, occasionally destroyed it, and, even more occasionally, been stung by it – as the abortive North American soccer league of the 1970s demonstrates. Market forces being what they are, it's unlikely that sport would have secured the interest of the aspiring entrepreneurs who have dragged competition towards something resembling showbiz without too much assistance from the mass media. As things transpired, they did have such assistance and the media have implemented changes that have taken the commercial possibilities of sport into realms that would have been considered pure fantasy by any one of the 120,757 people who watched Dempsey and Tunney fight it out in Philadelphia in 1926.

Mass media

CBS, the US broadcasting group, spent $1.1 billion for the exclusive rights to show the jewels of major league baseball for a four-year period starting 1990. The cost was about 25 per cent more than the previous contract for the games, shared by ABC and NBC. The high price, coming after NBC had bid a comparatively paltry $400 million for the 1992 summer Olympic games, showed the lengths to which networks will go to wrench prestige programming from competitors, including the expanding cable systems. The irony of this deal was that advertisers, who are American tv's principal source of revenue, would be unlikely even to cover the outlay, as interest in baseball declined from about 1978, and this was reflected in viewing figures. But, in a business where a few rating points (the measurement of viewing audiences) means hundreds of millions of dollars in advertising revenue, CBS was prepared to absorb losses in the expectation that it could use the World Series to include October promotions for its prime-time shows in its crucial autumn schedule, from which ratings are extrapolated. CBS effectively wanted to use the sport as an instrument for generating interest in its future programmes. Not that baseball cared: the deal meant that each team would start the 1990 season with about $10 million in its coffers before a single ticket had been sold.

The contract reveals the extent of television's virtually symbiotic relationship with sport. Tv uses sport to boost its viewing figures and sport uses tv as an irreplaceable means of income. Most major sports today could simply not exist without the prop of tv. It would be unthinkable to stage a SuperBowl or an FA Cup Final without tv coverage. Quite apart from the outrage amongst consumers who now expect transmission as a right, the medium would lose out on valuable prestige as well as income.

Both television and sport have seen the mileage in a relationship that had its beginnings in the early nineteenth century when the news-sheet *Bell's Life in London* (founded 1822) found its circulation rising as it included more sports reports. It held a monopoly until 1865 when the *Sporting Life* issued what was to prove a successful challenge, with the result that *Bell's* eventually folded. The success of the *Sporting Life*, with its quick and detailed reporting and varied advertising, prompted newspapers to include sports sections. The US equivalent, *The American Farmer*, first appeared in 1819 and was followed by many others, including *The Spirit of the Times* (founded 1831). 'It was the press who first elevated a minority of sportsmen and women into national celebrities, whose names and faces were recognized by people uninterested in sport; performers whose mere presence on the pitch would tempt people to the event; the exceptional performer', writes Tony Mason on the beginnings of what we now call the 'Superstar' whose fame relies as much on the media as on performance (1988: 50). Nationally-recognized individuals were, and are, good news for newspapers and over the decades sports celebrities have been created by the media for matters quite unrelated to their technical capacities. The case of Eddie 'The Eagle' Edwards, an inept ski jumper at the 1988 Winter Olympics, proves the point – he made headlines around the world by being a gawky, but amiable, loser.

There was a clear symmetry of interests between those with an interest in exploiting the mass spectatorship potential of sport and those who could sell newspapers with stories about sport. Reporting in the press had the useful effect of raising public awareness, so enlarging the spectator market which had emerged by the 1920s. But radio didn't have such an advantage for promoters and organizers. It would relay information on any event, but any advantage it held in terms of boosting interest might be outweighed by its immediacy; that is, listeners might prefer to listen to 'live' firsthand accounts of events instead of physically attending. Big events such as the England–Wales Rugby Union internationals, the Oxford–Cambridge boat race and Wimbledon were all reported 'live' in 1927 and by the mid-1930s, the BBC had started its now standard magazine format, Saturday afternoon coverage.

Despite the possible drawbacks of radio, it did have one big factor in its favour: it paid – and sometimes very well. In 1935, the radio rights to the Joe Louis–Max Baer world heavyweight title fight drew a then record $27,500. What's more, the gate was 88,000, so fears that 'live' coverage would hurt the gate were unfounded. By this time, radio coverage was commonplace and, as this involved issues of proprietorship and copyright, it gave rise to an economic relationship between the mass media and sports organizers. It was a relationship that was to broaden with the coming of television.

Filmed news of sports events occupied a segment of newsreels shown in cinemas even before radio transmissions, but the films were at least a week after the event and couldn't compare with the excitement of a 'live' radio broadcast. In the United States, a ban from 1912 on showing fight films was under pressure from 1927 after an exhibition of the Tunney–Dempsey rematch. In 1939 Senate passed a bill to permit the transfer of boxing films from state to state, in spite of strong disapproval from the Women's Christian Temperance Union. By this time, a new medium had crept into the homes of a select few.

In 1937, a few hundred Londoners were the first to *see* the first outside broadcast coverage of British sport, when 25 minutes of a men's single match was televised from Wimbledon. It was strictly an experimental service from the BBC which had improved on an earlier, unsatisfactory, attempt by CBS to broadcast a fight by 'sight and sound'. The main technical shortcoming of televising events was that cameras were fixed and were fitted with lenses that made the performers appear as tiny figures. Boxing, whose action takes part in a small, finite territory seemed reasonably suitable for the new medium and, in 1939, BBC and NBC both broadcast fights, BBC being fortunate enough to capture the British light-weight title fight between Eric Boon and Arthur Danahar, which is regarded as amongst the best-ever fights on British soil. In the same year, the BBC, still in its infancy, showed its first FA Cup Final and NBC telecast baseball, at first with one camera and, later, with two, which was a significant innovation as it permitted close-ups not even visible to audiences watching the game live.

Television was still only a futuristic luxury of the rich, with just 5,000 sets being sold in the USA in 1946. Within ten dramatic years, 75 per cent of the country's households had a set. John Goldlust, in his book on sport and the media argues that 'The significance of sports for this phenomenal rate of penetration should not be underestimated' and that the televising of major events was 'a key element in launching the television industry' (1988: 8).

Goldlust cites the transmission of the Melbourne Olympics in 1956 as a key event that greatly assisted the sale of television receivers. After this, the television industry of continental Europe and Latin America developed within the framework of either the BBC, which considered the televising of sport one of its statutory obligations in order to provide as many aspects as possible of the 'national culture', or the American companies, which geared their schedules so as to maximize demand from advertisers. If manufacturers had products to sell and wanted exposure for their products, then placing commercials in the 'natural breaks' of a high profile event was rational and effective. The basic formula has been followed ever since with tv networks paying huge fees for the rights to telecast events and charging advertisers proportionately huge fees for advertising slots. So, a 60-second commercial during a SuperBowl broadcast might cost an advertiser over $0.5 million. The network will calculate on accumulating enough of them to exceed the cost of buying the rights to the game from the NFL. Hence, market forces once more determine how much revenue sport takes from the media.

Such an accommodating relationship has its pitfalls, however, and television's evolution from a relaying device to, at first, an alternative and then a preferred alternative to actual attendance caused sport some serious misgivings. As television improved its technology and techniques, it was able to combine documentary accuracy with a fast tension worthy of the most thrill-packed sports occasions. The high-gloss presentations had analyses of slow-motion replays and frozen moments, knowledgeable commentaries-cum-evaluations, and detailed close-ups that captured facial – and sometimes verbal – expressions that the attending fans could never pick up. Around the event, tv learned to edit events down to lean action and pad events with previews, postscripts, and all manner of factual information, all designed to make viewing from home a more enriching experience. In contrast to the swirl of tv coverage, attendance seemed quite pedestrian. The freshness and appeal of tv sport were undeniable and sport had no magic strong enough to resist it.

Boxing was the first to suffer. In 1952, televised fights reached an average of 5 million homes in the USA; that is, 31 per cent of the then available audience. By 1955, the figure was up to 8.5 million, with the International Boxing Club (IBC) taking in the region of $1.5 million p.a. from telecasts. Advertisers were lining up for space. IBC was itself under investigation for running a monopoly and being run by organized criminals. (Between 1949 and 1959 the IBC staged 99 per cent of all championship fights, according to Sammons 1988: 164.) It may be that it sacrificed quality in the second half of the decade, or simply that tv viewers were saturated with the sport. Whatever the cause of the decline, by 1959, boxing commanded only 10.6 per cent of the viewing audience (which sounds more impressive nowadays than it did when the market was less intense and uncluttered by cable channels).

NBC was the first to cut boxing from its schedules in 1960. The other networks followed suit. The reaction from boxing, which had become reliant on tv as its 'live' gates had declined – no doubt because of television's coverage – was that tv had 'destroyed' and taken 'the personality out of boxing', as the New York State Athletic Commission put it (quoted in Sammons 1988: 174–5). In fairness, both the sport and the medium had merely followed the logic of the market. But the signs were clear: much of sport was deeply implicated in a cosy and highly profitable relationship, but it was also baring its throat. By exposing itself so completely to television it was risking either ruining itself if tv decided to pull out, or becoming totally dependent for its existence on tv networks.

It would be mistaken to think that television reports sport. Its presence in sport is so invasive that it actually determines the organization and administration of certain sports. And it's for this reason that some analysts, like Goldlust, argue that tv nowadays has an 'overpowering sporting autonomy' and that its calculated intervention in sport has been a 'critical and possibly decisive factor' affecting the overall development of sport (1988: 164). He cites the crisis of cricket in the mid-1970s as an example. In 1976, one of Australia's major commercial broadcasting organizations, chaired by Kerry Packer, offered the Australian Cricket Board (ACB) a deal for the exclusive rights to screen Australian cricket for five years. The offer was refused, so Packer decided to run his own cricket tournament called World Series Cricket, for which he secured the services of thirty-five international players. The 'rebel' tournament was networked by Packer's own Nine channel, but in a way that was offensive to traditionalists. It wasn't simply that players were asked to wear brightly coloured uniforms (as opposed to 'whites') and play under floodlights with a yellow ball, but the monitoring techniques intruded so as to make each match both observable (eight different cameras were employed) and audible (microphones picked up players' often blasphemous comments as well as general sound effects). Its one-day format was, as Goldlust puts it, 'unabashedly spectator oriented, geared towards providing entertainment, tight finishes, big hitting and aggressive play . . . ideally suited for television' (1988: 163).

The cricket that Packer promoted was barely recognizable as the nineteenth-century pursuit of gentlemen, but people watched it. After a nervous first season, viewing figures and, interestingly, attendances rose, enabling the Nine network to attract more advertisers. While the established cricket organizations, including England's MCC opposed the wanton commercialization, they capitulated after legal pressure from Packer, whose marketing subsidiary PBL Sports in 1979 secured a ten-year contract to organize the sponsorship of official cricket. Packer's attempt to capture exclusive broadcasting rights succeeded and he had virtually taken control of Australian cricket by the mid-1980s. Crowds continued to attend and, more importantly, more viewers watched tv cricket. The players themselves earned more money, the organizing bodies took a substantial fee for the rights and the network increased its advertising revenue by selling more commercial time in the traditionally quiet summer season. The arrangement satisfied all except those who wished to see cricket as having more than a faint resemblance to the game that was once played with a straight bat and stiff upper lip. To those traditionalists, cricket *à la* Packer was short, violent, and battered into distortion. To Packer and his patrons, including his sponsors, this was simply cricket moving with the times.

Television's interference in the organization of sport is not always so obvious. Some argued that the decision of boxing's three main governing bodies to reduce championship contests from the traditional fifteen to twelve rounds was motivated not so much by safety reasons as by commercial demands. There was little conclusive evidence that the serious injuries associated with boxing were incurred in the final three rounds, but in the mid-1980s, the World Boxing Council, World Boxing Association, and International Boxing Federation all changed their rules. Fifteen three-minute rounds, as well as fourteen one-minute intervals, preamble and post-fight interviews amounted to an awkward seventy to seventy five minutes. Twelve rounds yielded forty-seven minutes, as well as, say, thirteen for padding, which fitted perfectly into a one-hour time slot.

The influence extends beyond the match itself and into the ambience: tv caught up with darts, a late nineteenth-century British pub parlour game, which was virtually tailor-made for the small screen in all but one respect. Potential advertisers and sponsors didn't like the look of the habitual smoking and drinking in the crowd. Tv approached the British Darts Organization, which instructed spectators and players to refrain from smoking and drinking in front of the cameras. Considering that the game's origins lie in pubs, the move was a major break with tradition.

In monetary terms, some sports have profited as a direct result of tv's quite recent involvement. Darts, for instance, took shape in 1896 in Lancashire and remained a pub activity until the 1980s when tv took an interest. In 1989, the sport's top earner, Eric Bristow, picked up the equivalent of £45,000 for one tournament alone and his earnings in the 1980s are estimated at over £2 million. This has been made possible solely by television. The case of snooker runs parallel to that of darts: traditionally identified as a pastime for unemployed males, top players, like Steve Davis, earn an average of £250,000 p.a. And, as players earn more, governing bodies take a larger slice. Not surprisingly, they rarely challenge publicly a system that has rewarded them well. Television, for its part, continues to exploit to the full the relationship with sport taking up to 20 per cent of its total air time with sport in the USA, somewhat less in the UK, and not less than 5 per cent in other parts of Europe.

But, the penalty is often a heavy one and sports must be prepared to bend or change rules, allow intrusions into previously private domains, and generally jump when tv shouts, 'frog!' Commercial considerations come before those intrinsic to the sport itself and we need to investigate another aspect of this in the next section.

The business

Sponsors

In sport, *nothing* is for nothing. Look at it this way: television fans may sit in the comfort of their own homes, taking in the 'live' tv coverage of the Olympic games and enjoying every second of it. The cost is a miniscule fraction of the tv licence fee, or cable-satellite subscription, or – if you wanted to push it – the mild discomfort of having to sit through the commercials that punctuate the action. The viewer may or may not buy a roll of scotchtape made by 3M or a CD player by Panasonic, or a can of coke, but whoever does will probably have to pay a few extra pence for their products as a result of the Olympic games. 3M, Panasonic, and Coca Cola were three of nine companies who sponsored the Seoul Olympics to the tune of $100 million. It's unlikely that the room in which you're now sitting does not contain at least one item made by either of these or the other sponsoring companies who bought into The Olympic Movement (TOP): Visa, Brother, Philips, Federal Express, Kodak, and Times Inc. Such companies do not donate money to sport out of the goodness of their hearts. They do it to increase their share of the world market and so make more profit. The mechanism is quite simple: the telecast of the games and the attendant previews and post-mortems give sponsors a potential vehicle for promoting their product, not in an intrusive way, but by association, by linking their logo (the distinctive style of lettering, or initials, used as a badge) with an event as pristine and 'clean' as Olympic sport. While companies can't include obvious messages, the actual exposure helps elevate their image and persuades viewers to identify their products with something exciting and enjoyable.

Since 1976, the Olympics, like most other sports, have grown increasingly dependent on television money. ABC paid 45 per cent of the cost of staging the 1984 games in Los Angeles. NBC contributed marginally less than the South Korean government to Seoul. Compared to these, sponsors provide only a little more than 5 per cent of the costs. But the IOC's Juan Samaranch has made it clear that, under his presidency, the Olympics will try to extricate itself financially from governments and become economically independent.

Prior to Seoul, Samaranch had a problem, for the IOC had no power to licence its five-rings symbol on a world-wide basis as, under Rule 53 of the Olympic Charter, exclusive rights to use all Olympic names and symbols is held by individual member countries, who may do so only in their own territory. Basically, the problem was solved by buying the rights from 150 member countries over 18 months. Negotiations were smoothed by the involvement of Horst Dassler who had interests in a sports marketing group called ISL and in Adidas, the sportswear manufacturers which held contracts with many IOC member countries. ISL worked the oracle with most members, then approached forty-four commercial companies with project TOP. The lure was the chance of exposure in 167 markets, though the Olympic-rings logo could be used commercially only in the 150 countries which had sold out. So, for example, Belgium refused and a company like Kodak, which incorporated the rings in special packages, had to create alternative packaging for the Belgian market, omitting the rings and the instant recognition they carried. The question of whether the exercise was cost-effective to the sponsors will presumably be answered in the lead-up to the 1992 games when ISL will invite applications for TOP once again. The biggest sponsor paid $14 million, which will take quite a lot of justifying in terms of increased sales. In a slightly different sense, the Olympic games themselves, are being sold and the indications are that a bigger piece of the games will be sold than the 5 per cent at Seoul.

The IOC is able to sell the games in this way because of tv's continuing interest. Take away the international coverage and sponsors will take away their millions. Similar principles operate in other major sports that can offer comparable market penetration through mass media. Soccer's World Cup finals offer another vehicle for potential advertisers to reach international markets. Advertising boards surrounding pitches have FIFA's approval and are sold off in metres to commercial organizations eager to have their product name or logo form a backdrop to the players who stampede across the world's tv screens every four years. The same mode is employed at domestic levels with major sponsors enhancing their exposure by having players' shirts bear their logo. The more often the players appear on tv, the more valuable the sponsorship grows. For example, Candy electrical appliances can enjoy ninety virtually uninterrupted minutes of exposure every time a Liverpool game is screened; a photograph of the game appearing in a newspaper is also valuable.

The concept of associating a commercial product with a sports phenomenon with which it has no natural connection is not a particularly new one. 'The first sponsor of sport was probably a Roman patrician currying favour with his Emperor by underwriting a day of blood-letting at the Colosseum', writes Neil Wilson in *The Sports Business*. 'Since he was seeking a return on his investment, he was being no more philanthropic than any of today's commercial sponsors' (1988: 157). Wilson goes on to quote one-time British sports minister, Denis Howell: 'Sponsorship is the support of sport, sports event, sports organization or competitor by an outside body or person for the mutual benefit of both parties' (1988: 157).

There are isolated examples of commercial companies financing events and tours in the late ninteenth century, but the significant factor in alerting commerce to the possibilities of exposure via sport was, of course, the mass media. In the USA, commercial companies had realized the potential of radio in the 1930s, Buick in particular paying the then astronomical amount of $27,500 for the radio rights to the second Dempsey-Tunney encounter. Parts of the media, specifically the press, sponsored athletics, billiards, and snooker in Britain between the wars. Newspapers had a clear and fairly direct interest in events, which they would cover extensively and hope to boost circulation as a result. Companies such as Dunlop and Penfold supplied golf equipment and were ideally suited as sponsors for the sport.

After the war and the burgeoning of television all manner of sponsors sought to help raise the market profile by associating themselves with sporting events. Breweries were particularly eager to have their beverages associated with sport and the macho tendencies it implied. Pabst Riband was actively involved in the United States and, in the UK, Whitbreads sponsored a horse racing cup in 1957. The events were televised. The Gillette razor company was an interested party on both sides of the Atlantic. The beginning of its sponsorship of one-day cricket in 1963 also marked the beginning of an era, for since then, as Tony Mason observes, 'sports sponsorship has become an industry in itself. In the last fifteen years or so, in particular, its growth has been phenomenal' (1988: 4). In 1971, the British Sports Council calculated that the sponsorship of sport was worth only £2.5 million. By 1982, this figure had grown to £84.7 million. This rose to £200 million in 1988, with more than 2,000 companies involved. The figures for the USA are $1.4 billion spent by 3,400 companies.

The money is dispensed in a variety of ways, by using logos, as in the Olympics, or by advertising on boardings, as soccer's World Cup. Product endorsement is another way: individual sports performers are contracted to declare publicly their approval of a product or service. Middlesex cricketer, Denis Compton, became known as the 'Brylcreem Boy' after his endorsement of the hair preparation in the late 1940s. More recently, William 'Refrigerator' Perry has endorsed hamburgers and Ian Botham beer. This can result in a clash of interests if individual players endorse particular products. The endorsement lacks some plausibility if, say, a footballer's shirt is emblazoned with JVC while the individual player endorses Sony!

But, if this tends to diminish the purity of some sports, they still stand unsullied when compared to motor racing, a big-budget sport which has consumed the billions of commercial sponsors as voraciously as it has fuel. Motor sport has long since seen the end of days when a willing enthusiast with a few thousand dollars or pounds would buy an off-the-peg car and race it with the assistance of a few mechanics and courtesy oil and tyres.

In 1985, the French car company, Renault, pulled out of the sport because of the punishing costs; it had dropped £1 billion in 1984 and estimated that £60–80 million would be needed over the next four years from sponsorship. Honda's engine development programme for the Frank Williams' racing team cost £21 million. For such sums, the car companies have their vehicles displayed on every meet of the Grand Prix circuit, all sixteen of which are televised internationally. They also gain the prestige associated with winning, a feat they include in their direct advertising. The car firm has to share space with any number of other companies, the logos of which are plastered over every square millimetre of the car's bodywork and the driver's uniforms. (Most drivers take 30 per cent of prize monies, as well as expenses and a retainer; Ayrton Senna's retainer from the Lotus team was $5.4 million in 1988.) In motor racing, the chief sponsors virtually own the sport and sublet pieces of the cars to affiliates. Canon, for instance, in 1987, bought the rights to prefix its name to Williams' Honda team and adorned the sides and rear wings in its colours, red and white. The cockpit and engine cover were sprayed yellow for ICI, the front wing and plates being sublet to products as diverse as after-shaves and tyres.

Sponsors in other sports insist on exclusivity. Barclays Bank, in 1987, took over from Canon as the sole sponsors of the English Football League, which then became 'Barclays League' (though clubs were allowed to negotiate with their own sponsors independently). Potential sponsors were scared off by the Football Association's prohibitive price for the rights to the FA Cup and to date, the competition, surprisingly, has no sponsor. It's unlikely that any major British sports competition will avoid having its name prefixed or appended with that of a commercial product over the next decade. In the United States, the situation is different, with the cardinal leagues operating franchise deals, which means that, for a fee, they authorize commercial companies to manufacture and sell goods bearing their name, or logo, within a particular area. Official NFL jackets, coffee mugs, even underpants are commonplace. It obviates the problem of having brand names appearing on telecasts for which tv companies have paid huge fees and need to recoup funds through advertising. Miller beer may find it uncomfortable to have its ads appearing in the breaks of a game in the 'Budweiser League', for instance.

Beer companies have been consistent sponsors of sport. While sports organizations may have reservations about being identified with an alcoholic product that has no health benefits, apart from working as a vasodilator, breweries have targeted energetic and healthy pursuits. So there has been an accommodation of sorts, though some individual soccer clubs have refused brewers' sponsorship, pointing out that they can't credibly argue that alcohol is a contributory factor in crowd disorders if they actively promote it. Despite this, beer and sport have learned to live with each other. The advances of cigarettes, on the other hand, have been spurned, though not until quite recently. Tobacco clearly undermines the personal health and fitness that sport allegedly represents. Yet in the 1940s, the links between cigarettes and such conditions as heart disease and lung cancer weren't realized and sports personalities gladly had their pictures on cards distributed within cigarette packets.

Like other sponsors, tobacco companies, including Gallaghers and Philip Morris, were tempted by the possibility of mass exposure through television, especially after British tv banned the direct advertising of cigarettes. Sport, which occupied up to 20 per cent of a network's output, seemed an ideal way of having a cigarette's name and crest shown to millions throughout the year. John Player made incursions into various sports, most notably cricket with its Sunday John Player League. The Virginia Slims women's tennis circuit in the USA was also fashioned to meet the requirements of the tobacco company as much as the sport. Tobacco companies started their now considerable interest in motor racing in 1968 when Imperial Tobacco created the Gold Leaf team. Marlboro followed, signalling a strong trend for cigarettes to maintain their presence on television through racing cars flashing their logo across screens, or drivers wearing overalls with the appropriate appliqué, or even the words of a commentator announcing the 'Marlboro team'. The Philip Morris organization leads the way by spending a reputed $85 million on sports, an amount sufficient perhaps for individual sports to rearrange formats, timetables, and presentations to suit sponsors' requirements. As well as motor racing, the main beneficiaries of tobacco firms' sponsorship have been tennis, cricket, golf, show jumping, and snooker.

Every time a tobacco-sponsored event is televised, it represents a negation of tv's ban on advertising. It is also, arguably, a more cost-effective method of gaining exposure for tobacco firms. While none of them reveals the actual benefit it derives, it's instructive to know the estimates of the car makers Volvo. They sponsored an international tennis Grand Prix tournament in 1986 for $3 million and reckoned it was worth six times that amount in exposure. Television, in the same year, tightened up its restrictions on tobacco displays on hoardings at televised events: it began covering them, just as it had taped over players' badges at certain events. It has also promised to phase out the televising of tobacco-sponsored sport. This won't shut cigarettes out of sport; it will simply divert interest to sports attracting large numbers of spectators, but which do not receive TV coverage. Sponsorship, many will argue, is not only desirable to sport, it is as essential as spectators. Perhaps neither was essential at some stage in history, but, with Allen Guttmann, I would agree that sport as we understand it is *spectator* sport and this can be traced back to the ancient Greeks and beyond (as Guttman does in his book *Sports Spectators*). Where sport can engage spectators' attentions, there is scope for commercialism of some degree. The fact that the structure and administration of contemporary sport bears a close resemblance to that of most other business enterprises suggests how closely the development of sport has shadowed business. Industrialism and urbanism, which made possible the large concentrations of people from which mass spectators were drawn, were components of large-scale changes in western society in the nineteenth century. Guided by the Protestant work ethic, the spirit of capitalism contributed to the creation of a unique culture in which profit-making enterprises were the rational response to market pressures. The mandate of capitalism was to organize resources so as to maximize the chances of exploiting the market to the full. Simple as the mandate seems, it was responsible for transformations not only of the environment, but of the mentality. People began to sense that they could control markets instead of being at their mercy.

Modern commercial sport was born from such an observation. The concept of staging sport and controlling the numbers of people wanting to watch may not have been totally original, but when combined with the principles of the business enterprise, it produced a type of sport that paralleled other capitalist ventures. Promoters and organizers adopted approaches similar to other entrepreneurs. Professional sport may have been a rogue when amateurs dominated, but its powerful simplicity made it an

153

unstoppable force, against which amateurism was ultimately no match.

Further reading

Playing for Keeps *by John Goldlust (Longman Cheshire, 1988) is an extremely valuable analysis of the media's manipulation of sport, which is, in itself, an analysis of modern sport* per se. *Rich in detail, this is staple reading for the student of sport and the media.*

The Sports Business *by Neil Wilson (Judy Piatkus, 1988) is a sport journalist's account of the various ways in which sport has become a commercial enterprise. Its chapters include for instance, 'The American agent', 'The promoter', 'The marketing man'. Other key personnel in the 'sports business' are discussed but the book lacks any theoretical way of linking them together and doesn't take a critical stance.*

Pay Up and Play the Game *by Wray Vamplew (Cambridge University Press, 1989) focuses on British sport between 1875 and 1914 and shows an odd and irregular pattern in which some sports (like soccer) become fully commercialized, while others (like cricket) strove only to break even. To illustrate the different approaches to commercialism, Vamplew quotes from* Wisden, *which virtually scorned the doubling of Warwickshire's gates in 1911 (when that county won the cricket county championship): 'Such sudden enthusiasm suggests rather too much the spirit of Association Football.'*

Sport in the Sociocultural Process, *3rd ed. edited by M. Hart and S. Birrell (Brown, 1981) devotes one of its sections (D) to 'Media, messages and sport' and has a selection of articles on this theme.*

Lester Piggott: Downfall of a Legend *by Roy David (Heinemann Kingwood, 1989) has more interest than a standard sports biography because it examines a successful sports performer who became an obsessive millionaire, spent little money on himself or others, had no tastes, hobbies, or possessions, save for trophies, and, eventually, was gaoled for failing to disclose to the Inland Revenue and VAT inspectors an income of more than £3 million. Though a* nonpareil *competitor, Piggott's commercial fixation overwhelmed all others in his life.*

Assignment

The year is 2010 and sport has come under the total control of the mass media. So much so, that it has dispensed with 'live' audiences and is viewed only via the screen. What were once mass open-air sports, like football and baseball, are now played behind locked doors. Indoor sports are performed in studios. How realistic is this? Support your argument with evidence from current trends.

Chapter eight

Political uses

Propaganda and boycott

This is the reason why sport and politics mix so well – because people think they shouldn't. So when political factions, or even whole nations, consciously manipulate events to make their points decisively and dramatically, they often opt for sport, knowing that the rest of the world will be so outraged that they'll take immediate notice. Hold a press conference in New York to announce that civil rights in the USA have amounted to nothing and that the majority of blacks are still struggling in poverty and the response of the media will be 'so what?' Announce the same message, this time silently and symbolically, with just two black people disdaining the US national anthem, and watch the press cameras' flashbulbs pop like a firework display. You have a political event on a near-epic scale. The difference? In the latter example the two people in focus are Olympic medallists and the moment they choose to make their gesture is after being awarded their medals on the victory rostrum. In the event – at the 1968 Olympic games in Mexico City – sport worked as an instantly effective vehicle for what was obviously a political statement. Sport *is* political if only because of its undoubted utility; it draws attention to particular issues, disseminates messages internationally and, occasionally, eases or exacerbates diplomatic relations.

In this chapter, we will see the diverse – and, to some, perverse – ways in which the development of sport has been and will continue to be influenced by political considerations and at certain points in history, *vice versa*. We will also see how sport is just too useful a tool not to be used politically. Denials of this come freely from the lips of those who have interests in presenting sport as an independent, transcendent force, one of the few jewels decorating a tarnished crown. 'Sport is completely free of politics', declared Avery Brundage in his capacity as president of the International Olympic Committee in 1956. Ironically, he was responding to an

156

event that actually undermined his central point – the withdrawal of six Olympic member countries from the Melbourne games in protest at the military conflicts in Hungary and Suez. The protests were part of a general pattern established before 1956 and which continue to the present day. Countries absenting themselves from Olympic games, either as a gesture of protest, or because of exclusion, have been a feature of Olympic history this century. They usually make headlines and attract the rhetoric of interested parties, who talk regretfully about how unfortunate the whole business of sport and politics has turned out to be.

The Olympics have bristled with political issues. They have been manipulated, often quite expertly, to spread messages to a mass audience; sometimes the messages have been quite doctrinal. Propaganda is the word used to describe the message and its dissemination. Sport has been a serviceable machine for propaganda because of the *naïveté* surrounding it. Comments like Brundage's give substance to the view that sport is politically neutral. So messages that do slip through are virtually subliminal, influencing opinion without being consciously perceived as such (hence sport's general appeal to advertisers, as we saw in the previous chapter).

Propaganda
This describes a body of political, religious, or even scientific information that is dogmatically taught; or it is the apparatus – 'the propaganda machine' – through which the information is diseminated to a large population. An agent responsible for the dissemination is known as a *propagandist*.

But, if a political message is given potency by dispensing it in the package of a major sporting event, it has just as much effect when administered in the form of *avoiding* an event. Instead of using sport actively, it is deliberately avoided when a boycott goes into motion. This isn't a passive withdrawal; it's the systematic refusal of a faction, or nation, to participate in an event or a series of events. It issues a political snub, the boycotters effectively saying, 'We're not opposed to sport. We just object to engaging in competition with people representing a regime we find politically and morally repugnant.'

The objects of scorn may themselves be part, or representative, of a political regime involved domestically in repression (South Africa being an outstanding case), or involved internationally in hostility (the Soviets' advance on Afghanistan being an example), or, the group may only have maintained contacts with such a regime (as New Zealand did with South Africa). Those instigating the boycott wish to minimize their contacts either to escape stigmatizing themselves, if only by association, or to isolate that regime. Either way, the message recorded is a resonant one: the boycotters are opposed to the political regime in question and want to place political distance between themselves and that regime.

In the course of this chapter, we will examine the various ways in which political messages have been stamped onto sport. Tensions are frequently catalysed when major events, such as the Olympic games are the focus and we will chronicle the political sub-plot of the games since the 1930s. As the games offer host nations the opportunity for some high profile media coverage and, thus, the chance to demonstrate how well their political systems must be working to stage such an extravagant event, propaganda of some degree is embodied in all Olympic games. But, many of the controversies of the games, especially in recent decades, have centred on the use of boycott to shame or embarrass nations and raise questions about their political operations.

Boycotts of Olympic games are often blows struck against particular nations because of their involvement in a specific event. Yet one boycott has gone on continuously so that it has now achieved the status of a permanent fixture in sport. It concerns South Africa and its relevance has gone far beyond the Olympics. So much so, in fact, that the South African issue deserves attention in its own right – which it gets in a later section.

Talk of sport and politics invariably leads to discussion of propaganda and boycott, but the chief area in which the two elements fuse is in state. Sport has been used by states, ancient and modern, for a variety of purposes. Soviet systems are often seen as the ultimate expression of state involvement in sport: an extensive programme of centralized control and direction has ensured a persistently high level of excellence in Soviet countries and in many systems following their example. Westerners may admire the achievements but often deplore the bureaucratic system that facilitates them and the ideology that underpins them. Yet, the state has tended to penetrate sport in the west too. There is nothing novel in this; even in the heartland of modern sport, England, where the amateur gentleman was an ideal to be revered, the state has for long been a force in the development of sport. The final section of this chapter will compare the state's involvement in sport in the two systems, with a view to assessing the overall 'politicization' of sport in the modern world.

The Olympic weapon

'Sport is a latently political issue in any society, since the cultural themes which inhere in a sport culture are potentially ideological in a political sense.' So writes John Hoberman in *Sport and Political Ideology* (1984: 20). If anyone doubts the point, they need look no further into history than 1936, the year of the 'Nazi Olympics'. The Berlin games were an occasion for Nazis to flex their Ayrian muscles and demonstrate the physical supremacy of the master race. Hitler had expressed his doctrine of the racial supremacy of the Ayrians and sought an international stage on which to reveal tangible evidence of this. The neutral arena of sport was such a stage.

Coubertin, in his original conception, saw the Olympics as having bridge-building potential. He wanted to bring nations of various political hues together in a spirit of healthy competition, always stressing that participation was to be considered before winning. Hitler's visions were as ambitious, but less noble. The political ideology he sought to propagate at the Berlin games concerned the superiority of one nation over all others and the essential disunity, rather than oneness of humanity. While the blatant use of sport as a propagandist tool at Berlin was roundly denounced, subsequent hosts were to sense the potential and turn the games into jingoistic extravaganzas. This was illustrated at the Los Angeles Olympics of 1984, an event popularly regarded as the crudest and most shamelessly nationalistic Olympics in the post-war period, but, as Rick Gruneau argues, 'in no way a significant departure from practices established in earlier Olympics' (1984: 2). Still, it seems fair to suggest that the particular utility Nazism found in sport warrants special attention, if only as a benchmark against which to gauge later expressions of nationalism.

Turner
This was the name of exponents of a system of gymnastics and physical exercises devised by Friedrich Jahn (1778–1852). During the 1870s and 1880s, the Turner movement staged regular exhibitions in Germany. The concept behind the movement was to use physical performance to enhance political unity and, as such, it avoided what it regarded as 'vulgar' competitive elements.

Friedrich Jahn's gymnastics *Turner* movement of the nineteenth century was partly designed to prepare German youth to wage war against Napoleon. Jahn was a significant figure in fostering the 'volkish' thought, which eventually gained political expression in Nazism, with its *leitmotif* of an overarching German essence. This was to be made visible through displays of physical control and strength, 'a spectacle of masculine power'. Hitler had no interest in sport other than this: to express national superiority and internal unity. His ally Mussolini, by contrast, was greatly enthusiastic about sport and promoted its pursuit at all levels from the 1920s. The Weimar Republic had assisted the growth of sport in Germany as part of the general morale restoration after World War I. But, under Hitler's National Socialism, it came to mean much more. 'Fitness was declared a patriotic obligation', writes historian Richard Mandell, author of *The Nazi Olympics* (1971).

The anti-semitism that characterized Nazism affected sport; in 1933, when the boycott of Jewish businesses came into effect, sports' organizing bodies excluded Jewish performers and officials. Two years later there was complete segregation in German sport, something that clearly contradicted Olympic ideals. In the USA, an abortive boycott campaign targeting the proposed 1936 Olympics failed to command support. Avery Brundage, the then president of the American Olympic Committee, warned that: 'Certain Jews must now understand that they cannot use these Games as a weapon in their boycott against the Nazis' (quoted in Hain 1982: 233). Germany reassured the world that the extent of anti-semitism and segregation had been exaggerated and, to underline this, included the fencer, Helene Mayer, who was half-Jewish, in the national team.

Reservations went beyond the Olympic movement. In December 1935, a soccer international between England and Germany in London was opposed by Jewish organizations supported by the Trades Union Congress and the Communist Party. In the event, the match went ahead. In a subsequent international in 1938, this time in Germany, the England team was instructed to give the Nazi salute as the German national anthem was played before the match. Thanks to newsreel, the moment will live on as one of English sport's most embarrassing moments, coming as it did so close to the outbreak of World War II.

Newsreel also depicts the Berlin games as a *faux pas* for Hitler, showing him leaving the stadium in apparent disgust as black American athlete Jesse Owens shook the ramparts of the Nazi's ideological platform by winning four gold medals. Doctrines of racial supremacy looked oddly out of place. Yet Hitler's departure was but one uncomfortable moment in what was in other respects a satisfactory and rewarding Nazi spectacle. Not only did Germans lead the medal table, they 'demonstrated to the whole world that the new Germans were administratively capable, generous, respectable, and peace loving', as Mandell puts it (1984: 244). 'Hitler, particularly, was greatly emboldened by the generally acknowledged, domestically and internationally, triumph of this festival grounded on the pagan (though very new) rituals of modern sport' (1984: 245). In terms of propaganda, the entire Olympic essay was of value to the Nazis: as the world exulted, Germany stepped up its rearmament programme and stamped down on Jews.

Only in the retrospect was the full resonance of the 'Nazi Olympics' realized. No single games since has approached it in terms of ideological pitch. Its sheer scale deserved the posterity afforded it by the openly propagandist film directed by Leni Riefenstahl, *Olympia*, which idealized German sportsmen as *übermenschen*, or supermen.

Yet no Olympic meeting since has escaped political incident. The defeated nations of Germany, Italy, and Japan were excluded from the first games after the war in London in 1948. Holland, Egypt, Iraq, and Spain boycotted the 1956 games in protest at the British and French invasion of Suez. In 1964, South Africa was suspended and subsequently expelled from the Olympic movement (in 1970). Zimbabwe, then Rhodesia, a country which adopted a similar system of stratification to apartheid, was barred in 1972, having made a Unilateral Declaration of Independence from the Commonwealth. New Zealand maintained sporting links with South Africa in the face of world opinion and the fact that it too wasn't expelled from the Olympics spurred twenty African nations to boycott the 1976 games in Montreal. Boycotts have since proliferated. Taiwan also withdrew after it was refused permission to compete as 'China'. The USA team pulled out of the Moscow games in 1980 after the Soviet invasion of Afghanistan. British Prime Minister Margaret Thatcher exhorted British athletes not to go, but the British Olympic Association went ahead. Soviet bloc countries (except Romania) and their allies replied by steering clear of Los Angeles in 1984. And, in 1988, Cuba stayed away from Seoul after the South Korean government refused to share events with North Korea (which itself pulled out). In short, every Olympics has been associated with some form of political issue, which has often prompted boycotts.

Incidents internal to the games sometimes led commentators to suggest that the Olympics themselves were haemorrhaging so badly that they would have to be either stopped, or scaled-down drastically. If any single event can be said to have provoked this,

161

it was that at Munich in 1972 when eight Palestinians occupied the Israeli team's quarters and demanded the release of 200 Palestinian prisoners in Israel. Negotiations proved fruitless and gunfire opened up. Ten athletes were killed. There followed a day's mourning before the competition resumed. Avery Brundage, by this stage notorious for his blundering efforts to separate sport and politics, drew parallels between the politically-charged incident with the equally political but quite different attempt to force the IOC into squeezing out racist Rhodesia.

The games immediately preceding this, in Mexico in 1968, had underscored the point made so strongly by Berlin's 'Nazi Olympics': that sport, given its world prominence, can be an effective stage on which to make a political point. The point in question was made by two black US track athletes, Thommie Smith and John Carlos. As occupants of the first and second places in the 400 metres, they stood on the victory rostrum to receive their medals. After receiving them, they bowed their heads and extended their black-gloved hands into the air to symbolize their detachment from America and American ideals. Throughout the victory ceremony, Smith and Carlos wore black berets, *de rigueur* headgear of members of the black power movement, which was at that stage sweeping across the United States. Frustrated at the lack of material improvement in the lives of blacks, despite the alleged progress of liberal civil rights movements, black power followers formulated a radical alternative to careful negotiation. They took violently to the streets, issuing messages of 'burn, baby, burn!' and argued for a radical type of separation. The gestures on the rostrum were not spontaneous responses; they were planned parts of a much wider campaign to bring to the attention of the world the specific grievances of blacks in the USA. And the strategy worked wonderfully. Not only did the demonstration supersede the 400-metre race itself but the runners were martyred by the US athletic bodies and barred from future competition. The most evocative image of the games was that of Smith and Carlos, their fists clenched as if punching a hole in the American dream.

The Olympic games have the kind of generic relevance that makes them a perfect theatre in which to play out political dramas. Ostensibly sporting occasions, the games have continually managed to capture grandly tensions, protests, and sometimes atrocities that circle the world. By celebrating the alleged unity, at least in spirit, of the world's population, Olympic games have sought temporarily to suspend terrorism, racism, imperialism, and other 'worldly' matters that are the bane of our age. But instead, they have been hijacked by them. The setting and imagery of the games have been used to dramatize events seemingly unconnected with sport. We opened this section with the observation that many of the themes inherent in sport have political and ideological potential: nationalism, competition, the pursuit of supremacy, the heroism of victory; all have a wider application. Differences between the contrived competition of the track and field events and the real conflict in the streets have often melted in the spectacle of the Olympics.

An Olympic games attended by all member nations is unlikely in the future. Issues that cleave loyalties are sure to precipitate boycotts of some order. These will be, as in the past, boycotts over specific issues, rather than a more general anathematization, in which a political regime or its doctrine is denounced. The outstanding example of this process is South Africa and we move on to this next.

South Africa's short delivery

In 1968, Basil D'Oliveira, a black cricketer from South Africa's Cape who had settled in England in 1960, reached the peak of his form. Selected for the MCC, he scored a triumphal century against Australia at London's Oval and was, almost without question, the most effective batsman in the country at the time. Yet when the national team for the winter tour of South Africa was announced, D'Oliveira's name was missing. The events that unfolded after the announcement presaged one of the longest-standing political controversies in the history of sport.

David Sheppard, a former England captain, later to become Bishop of Liverpool, led a protest, accusing selectors of submitting to the requirements of apartheid, which included the strict separation of those deemed to belong to different 'races'. D'Oliveira, having relatively pale brown skin, was officially classed by South Africans as 'coloured' and so had no legal right to share facilities with whites. Needless to say, the South African team comprised only white players. Several MCC members threatened to resign as the protest gathered momentum, prompting the selectors to slip D'Oliveira into the squad as a replacement for an injured bowler, Tom Cartwright. It was an act of unheard-of nerve as far as South Africa's premier John Vorster was concerned: he smartly denounced the squad as 'not the team of the MCC but the team of the Anti-Apartheid Movement, the team of SANROC [the South African Non-Racial Olympic Committee]'.

Wounded by the accusation, the MCC called off the tour. Vorster's intransigence and the MCC's pull-out were crucial: the

> **Apartheid**
> This word is Afrikaans – the South African language derived
> from Dutch – and means 'apartness'. It was first used by the
> ascendant National Party as an election slogan. But in the
> preceding 300 years, South Africa had developed a pattern of
> segregation of 'races' that was spasmodically enforced by law.
> This type of segregation was common to many imperial situa-
> tions. What's peculiar about apartheid is that it was brought
> forward at a time when imperial rule was receding and the
> enforcement of segregation was being relaxed. South Africa
> went against the world trend by strengthening barriers between
> blacks and whites and attempting to rationalize this by refer-
> ence to ideas about racial purity.

former in hardening South Africa's policy in the face of suspicions
that Vorster himself was beginning to soften; the latter in showing
the rest of the world's sports governing bodies how they might in
future react to South African policies.

The effects weren't immediate and in the following January, the
MCC actually countenanced a projected tour by the South African
cricket team in 1970. This was met with a 'Stop the Seventy Tour'
campaign and a series of disruptions of the Springbok's rugby tour
of the UK, which served as a reminder of what would happen to
any attempted cricket tour by the South Africans. Progressively,
more sports minimized or cut contacts with South Africa, effectively ostracizing that country's sport and creating a problem
that has resisted a decisive resolution in the decades since the
D'Oliveira affair.

The episode itself was by no means the first to surface: it simply
captured the elements more dramatically with a victim-cum-hero,
ex cathedra statements from South Africa, and the refusal of the
MCC to be dictated to by a regime that had been widely condemned. By grabbing the attention of the world's media, the
D'Oliveira case made the sport–South Africa link a significant
political as well as sporting topic and one which would press
governments into action.

The political significance of South Africa in sport had been
realized for at least ten years before D'Oliveira forced it into the
open. South Africa had, in 1956, made a formal declaration of its
sports policy programme, which, it insisted, should stay within the
boundaries of its general policy of apartheid. The physical segregation embodied in apartheid was instituted in 1948 and encouraged
by pass laws, police brutality, and a repressive state that dealt
unsympathetically with any attempt to challenge its authority – as

the slayings at Sharpeville in 1960 illustrated. Sports performers and teams visiting South Africa were, said the statement, expected to 'respect South Africa's customs as she respected theirs' (quoted in Horrell 1968: 9). Justifications, unnecessary as they were in a country utterly controlled and dominated by the numerically small white population, included the arguments that blacks had no 'aptitude' for sport and the alleged potential for conflict in 'mixed' teams and crowds of spectators. On the second point: blacks, who constitute over 70 per cent of South Africa's total population, were barred from a new rugby stadium in Bloemfontein in 1955. In the following year, Bishop Trevor Huddleston, who was to become a prominent member of the anti-apartheid movement, observed that sport may be South Africa's Achilles' heel, in the sense that its national teams were so obviously good in certain sports, particularly Rugby Union. To deny South Africa the opportunity to demonstrate its excellence would, as Huddleston put it in his *Naught for Your Comfort*, 'shake its self-assurance very severely' (1956: 202).

Sharpeville

A black township in South Africa that, in March 1960, was the scene of a conflict that ended in 69 deaths (all black) and 180 wounded. It signalled the first organized black resistance to white political rule in South Africa. The Pan-African Congress (PAC) had asked blacks to leave their pass books at home and go to police stations to be arrested. They did so voluntarily, but refused to be dispersed by the police who, eventually, opened fire. Sharpeville triggered nationwide demonstrations. The reaction of the government was to arrest leaders of PAC and the other main black organization, the African National Congress (ANC), and ban both movements.

Another world power in rugby, New Zealand, had traditionally selected Maoris in its national team, but capitulated to South Africa by picking only white players to tour. This opened up a national controversy in 1960, especially when a New Zealand tour went ahead despite the atrocities at Sharpeville. This event crystallized many fears about South Africa and a cricket tour in Britain in its aftermath prompted demonstrations. Cries that 'sport and politics should be kept separate' sounded pathetically weak in the context of 1960 and, in fact, the whole decade that followed was to be filled with examples of the inseparability of the two.

Sporadic protests continued, both at street level and at official levels. The integration-oriented South African Non-Racial Olympic Committee (SANROC) was launched in 1962 with the intention that it should apply for recognition from the International Olympic Committee and officially replace the whites-only Olympic and National Games Association. The government pre-empted matters by banning SANROC. As the 1964 games drew near, the IOC, whose charter forbids racial dicsrimination, demanded large concessions from South Africa before its entry could be approved. Some concessions were made in the trials, but the South African government maintained its insistence that sport comply with 'custom' so South Africa was denied entry to the Tokyo games.

New Zealand continued to send touring rugby sides to South Africa amidst negotiations aimed at allowing the entry of Maoris. But, in a key speech in 1965, the then premier Hendrik F. Verwoerd reaffirmed that no Maori players would be allowed to enter South Africa. Coming from the country's leader, the message was filled with political significance. In 1966, New Zealand finally declined an invitation to tour, but accepted another extended in 1968 under a new South African premier, John Vorster. In the interim, newly-independent African states had begun to recognize South Africa's vulnerability to sporting boycotts and were strenuously trying to convince the rest of the world's sports organizations to expel South Africa. The Supreme Council for Sport in Africa, as the alliance was called, reminded the world that, while sport may conventionally have been regarded as trivial or unrelated to politics, 'South Africans do not consider it minor' (quoted in Guelke 1986: 128). Outbursts from Verwoerd and Vorster confirmed this. They left no doubt that what was at first glance a sports issue was also one on which premiers were obliged to dispense judgements.

At a different time in history Vorster's conclusion that the MCC's selection of D'Oliveira was designed, as he expressed it, 'to gain certain political objectives', may have passed virtually unnoticed by all those cricket devotees and anti-apartheid campaigners. In 1968, an *annus mirabilis* in which conflicting forces of protest gathered and collided all over the world, its effects were more far-reaching. The IOC had already withdrawn its invitation to South Africa to attend the Mexico Olympics. A threat of boycott from about fifty member countries and protests from the black members of the American team were factors in the decision.

British Rugby Union, a sport reluctant to dissolve its relationship with South Africa, entertained a Springbok touring team in 1969–70 and every match was seriously disrupted by mass demonstrations. The message from the tour was that any future visit by

South Africans was likely to be met with a show of force. In May 1970, a planned cricket tour of South Africans to the UK was aborted quickly after the threat of uproar on the 1969–70 scale in the lead-up to a General Election. The same year saw the severance of more links with South Africa: expulsion from the IOC; elimination from the Davis Cup tennis competition; suspension from athletics; and a bar from gymnastics.

Isolation stirred Vorster into action and, in 1971, he announced what he called a 'multinational' sports programme in which 'whites', 'Africans', 'coloureds', and 'Asians' could compete against each other as 'nations', but only in international competitions. This rather devious move effectively allowed black sports performers to compete, provided they were affiliated to one of the government's 'national' federations. As such it served to divide blacks: some wishing to compete felt compelled to affiliate; others rejected the racist premiss of the divisions and refused to affiliate. With international links receding, the government permitted domestic contests between 'nations', and later club-level competitions between 'nations'.

Rugby Union resisted the international trend and, in particular, New Zealand set itself against world opinion by wilfully maintaining contacts. During a tour of South Africa in 1976, the near-cataclysmic Soweto uprising (official figures: 575 dead, 2,389 wounded) prompted ever-more searching questions. As New Zealand seemed intent on prosecuting links regardless of the upheavals, should it too be isolated? The answer from the black African Olympic member countries was affirmative and New Zealand's admission to the Montreal Olympics in 1976 caused a mass boycott. Thus the crisis deepened.

Soweto

On 16 June 1976, South African police opened fire on protesting students in Soweto, a large African township near Johannesburg, killing two and injuring many. The students retaliated by attacking government property and officials. Police countered and soon violence spread to every part of the republic, except Natal. For months, schools were closed. Students forced workers to stay away from their factories and offices in a series of one-day strikes. Some migrant workers refused and a battle between workers and students resulted in seventy deaths. The total number killed as a result of the conflict which began in Soweto was officially reported as 575 with 2,309 wounded – almost certainly an underestimate.

Commonwealth heads of governments met at Gleneagles in Scotland in 1977 to formulate a now-famous agreement 'vigorously to combat the evil of apartheid by withholding any form of support for, and by taking every practical step to discourage contact or competition by their nationals with sporting organizations, teams or sportsmen from South Africa'. The agreement was between governments not sports organizing bodies and, as subsequent events were to show, the ability of governments to overrule individual organizations was often tested. Rugby's robust stance against governments gave rise to several anomalies. In 1979, Britain entertained a 'mixed' Barbarians side (eight whites, eight 'coloureds', and eight blacks). Critics dismissed the team, which was said to reflect the tripartite structure of South African society, as window-dressing. The British Lions' subsequent tours in which they competed with similarly-composed teams, met with much the same scepticism. It was, so the argument went, a case of South Africa using sport to project a distortedly liberal image of itself while preserving its essential tyranny and oppression. The majority of black players belonged to the South African Rugby Union (SARU), which remained outside the aegis of the organization from which sides selected for international competition were drawn. Hence the sides were hardly representative.

Gleneagles' Agreement
The issue of sporting links with South Africa prompted government involvement at high levels and, in 1977, at Gleneagles, Scotland, Commonwealth heads of government unanimously accepted to override the autonomy of sporting bodies and 'take every practical step to discourage contact or competition by their nationals with sporting organizations, teams or sportsmen from South Africa or from any other country where sports are organized on the basis of race, colour and ethnic origin'. Sanctions were to be applied to those ignoring the agreement. The full agreement was published by the Commonwealth Secretariat, London.

It was a period of public relations initiated by Pretorian officials bent on convincing the world that every measure was being taken to desegregate sport – though not education, employment, and housing. For all its promises, South Africa fell short on delivery. Invitations went out to individual players of international repute who were drawn by moolah to South Africa to engage in what were known as rebel tours. Cricketers, buoyant after the triumph of the individual over governing bodies, courtesy of Kerry Packer, went to South Africa in their scores, both to play and to coach, usually in contexts that were notionally 'multiracial'. British soccer players took short-term contracts to coach, some, like Stanley Matthews working exclusively with blacks. American boxing champions, like Bob Foster and Mike Weaver, both black, defended their titles in South Africa against whites. South Africa made no secret of the fact that it had an embarrassment of riches with which to lure top sports performers.

There were prices to pay, however. In 1981, the United Nations special committee against apartheid published its first 'blacklist' (an embarrassing misnomer) of sports performers who had worked in South Africa. This served as an effective prohibition and ostracized South Africa further. Starved of decent quality opposition, promising South Africans, like Sidney Maree, a black athlete, and Zola Budd, who was white, left to campaign abroad. Maree took US citizenship, while Budd was rapidly granted British citizenship, a move that caused the anti-apartheid campaigners to roll up their sleeves and unfurl their banners once more. On this occasion, the campaigners may have missed one point, that is, that the isolation of South Africa was working so well that individuals with potential were forcibly leaving their country in order to realize it. The counterpoint was that, regardless of the citizenry, the performers were still, if only by accident of birth, South African, and their success would inevitably reflect on that country.

169

Controversies followed both those leaving South Africa and those who continued to flout the prohibition by going there. British cricketer Robin Jackman, who had played in South Africa, was deported from Guyana in 1981 just as a test match against the West Indies was about to begin. The match was abandoned. Others like Geoff Boycott and Graham Gooch, were banned for a number of years from test cricket as punishment for their 'sins'. It wasn't until 1989 that the International Cricket Conference (ICC) passed a resolution, in defiance of a crucial summons obtained by the right-wing Freedom Association, to formalize sanctions against players, coaches, or administrators who worked in South Africa. Automatic suspensions from test cricket were the penalty. It was the most unambiguous pronouncement on sport and apartheid since the Gleneagles' agreement. The decision was reached after the cancellation of England's scheduled winter tour of India, when Indians refused to play a team that included players with South African connections. 'A victory for sport over racism', was how the resolution was greeted by Sam Ramsamy, of SANROC. Norris McWhirter, the leader of the Freedom Association, described it as 'a crushing blow against cricketers' freedom to trade' and exhorted individual players to take out civil injunctions to prevent ICC carrying out its ban. It could be argued against this that the freedom of over 21 million black South Africans to trade – and not just in cricket – was of far greater significance than that of a relatively small number of cricketers.

The intrusion of the state

The traumas of the Olympic games and the issue of apartheid continue to raise big questions about sport and politics, the biggest being, 'how do we separate them?' There is no effective answer to this. What's more, we might add that sport is nowadays more political than ever in the sense that it's supported, assisted and, very occasionally, obstructed by political groups. The Soviet system and societies within its sphere of influence are held up as models of state-controlled sport. Yet, it could be argued that the state has had a deep penetration in sport in the west – and not, just in recent years.

The Soviet Union, in particular, has encouraged a vigorous role for the state in directing sport; it has integrated sport into its more general political programme. There are a number of reasons for this, one being the strategic military value of having a sports-oriented population, the other being the international prestige drawn from success in sport. Neither idea is new. A glance back into history tells us that activities that might now resemble competitive sport were once training manoeuvres for the military. Chapter three suggested that ancient versions of sport were retained as much for their strategic worth as their autotelic value. Sport has frequently had an instrumental element to it: geared to attaining military-level physical standards and the discipline that is important in combat. The physical well-being of individuals is a foundation for the nation's vitality: this is an abiding idea. For all his fine ideals, Pierre de Coubertin also had pragmatic goals when he revived the Olympic games in 1896. Distressed by France's poor military efforts, especially against Germany, Coubertin felt his country in need of a reminder of the importance of physical endeavour.

The Soviet Union communist party's 1925 resolution has influenced the entire Soviet approach to sport, in which 'physical culture must be an inseparable part of overall political and cultural education'. This passage is quoted by James Riordan in one of his publications on sport in communist societies (1982: 219). In his book *Soviet Sport*, Riordan writes that, in Soviet society where it had been decided that sport 'should be as free and natural as the air people breath, there has to be government intervention on a wide scale' (1980: 19). This makes sport political because, 'in a centrally planned state in which health and education and much else are administered centrally, it would seem natural to run physical culture on the same lines' (1982: 19).

Initial suspicions about the competitive element of sport being a reflection and relic of capitalism disappeared completely by the 1930s – a fact probably not unrelated to the military potential of sport training glimpsed in World War I. By the early 1950s, competition and record-breaking excellence had been given priority by Stalin's regime. Since then, sport has been used to fulfil a number of functions, none of them strikingly new, though the way in which the modern Soviet state co-ordinated them made them seem that way. For example, there's nothing unusual in a nation using sport as a means of obtaining the kind of physically fit and co-operative workforce that complements economic efficiency and military strength. The very origins of sport lie in this complementarity. In recent times, this function hasn't been fanfared in the west, although Stephen Jones, writing on British state intervention in sport, notices how, 'for wartime policy-makers, leisure was directly related to military aims and objectives' (1987: 164).

The Soviet system has consciously employed sport as a way of improving general standards of health and hygiene, by educating people about the benefits of exercise and nutrition. A healthy working population is more effective than a sick one. Similar uses of sport have been made by many industrial societies: sometimes the initiative has come from management, as in Japan where exercise sessions are integrated in the working day; and sometimes from workers' organizations, as in the endorsement of Britain's Trades Union Council of a National Fitness campaign in the 1930s.

Any society that is industrialized has had to negotiate the bumps and jolts that accompany a mass movement of population from rural areas into the cities. The transitions were accompanied by the growth of organized sport in western Europe and the USA. Team sport in particular helped smooth the passage, gathering people together and unifying them with the *esprit de corps* that competitive sport elicits. Team sports were made focal points during the USSR's industrialization; they encouraged the communal identification with representative teams that was ultimately crucial to internal stability. One further function of sport in the longer term was a buffing up of the image of the Soviet system abroad. Tony Mason sums up by writing that, by the 1950s, 'sport in the Soviet Union had come to have a similar function to that which it had in the capitalist West: to improve physical fitness, provide mass entertainment, gain support for the regime and build international prestige' (1988: 101).

In employing sport to fulfil these three basic functions, the Soviet system has not deviated from western patterns, though the depth of state penetration has meant that the functions have been much more centrally controlled and promoted. This is manifest in state-initiated policies and active programmes, like GTO, or *Gotov k trudu i oborne* (ready for labour and defence) which began in the 1930s and which was aimed at involving young people and, later, children in some form of disciplined sport. Sport, or physical culture was integrated in educational curricula and institutes of physical education were established for those showing aptitude and needing to specialize in order to develop it. A whole structure of establishments was built to accommodate a range of interests and capabilities. Institutes of physical culture laid special emphasis not only on practical elements, but on the theoretical foundations of sport and the scientific analysis of sport, and sporting performance became an accepted scholarly pursuit – some years before its acceptance in the west. Institutes of higher learning, while not specializing in sport, demanded of their students some mastery of a sport, in the same way as they would demand a qualification in chemistry and languages. This suggests the significance attached to sports, which, according to Riordan, 'has been regarded as too important to be left to the whim of private clubs with restricted entrance, commercial promoters, circus entrepreneurs and foreigners' (1982: 226). His observation is a general one relevant to all communist countries. States have decided that sport is of strategic value and deserving of political attention, assistance, and planning.

One almost inevitable consequence of this has been a bureaucratization of sport. There is no chance of some penniless youngster making his way to the local park, borrowing a pair of football boots and turning on a display that has a scout reaching into his briefcase for professional signing-on forms. One-off 'discoveries' just don't happen in the Soviet system: sporting prowess is cultivated through an ever-specializing series of academic and vocational establishments, each stage being carefully controlled and monitored by state agencies that have the latest developments in sports science and technology at their fingertips. The reason they have it at their fingertips is that sport-related research is continually funded and highly concentrated. Physical and psychological profiles are matched with apposite events at an early age. And the fruits of all this are obvious.

The athletic pre-eminence of the USSR is unquestioned, but the German Democratic Republic's progress in international terms has also been impressive, especially so in the light of its lack of natural resources and small population compared to its fellow Soviet partner. Basically, the reasons for sport's importance in the USSR hold good for the GDR. Although, lacking in military strength, the GDR opted for a mighty sport's programme as an *alternative* way of commanding international respect rather than as an adjunct. As we have seen, a vigorous sporting tradition was already well-established in Germany thanks to the Weimar government and, before this, the nineteenth-century *Turner* movement. From the 1950s, sport was incorporated into education up to university level, where participation in some event was made compulsory. But education was only one area: trade unions, the police, and the military were all made to develop sports divisions, again not as adjuncts, but as integral parts of their structures.

The flagship of the GDR programme was the University of Physical Culture, opened in Leipzig in 1950. By 1975, it had attracted 2,000 students. Some measure of the effect of this was gauged one year later at the Montreal Olympics of 1976, when the GDR's medal haul suggested its arrival as an international power to compare to the USA and USSR. A study around the same time attempted to quantify this: it divided countries according to size of population and measured the per capita output of world class sports performers. John Bale, the study's author, concluded that

Finland edged the GDR out of first place with the USSR way down in fifteenth place, one spot above the UK (1982). Tempering this is the fact that excellence has been achieved by the GDR in a relatively narrow range of sports: world class competitors tend to specialize in gymnastics, soccer, track and field events, and particularly swimming. The military emphasis of sport is reflected in the GDR's redoubtable record in shooting and riding.

Some critics have argued that children are tramlined into very narrow and specific areas and given little chance to develop imaginative skills and capacities in other aspects of sport. Related to this is the problem – if, indeed, it *is* a problem – of compulsion. This is applicable not only to the GDR, but to all communist countries, Cuba included, that place onerous pressures on children to reach proficiency in sport. Inevitably, many will fail and fall by the wayside; those who succeed will train more intensely. Westerners might find the high level of participation in sport artificial because it is compulsory. Those brought up to accept a more voluntary conception of sport, in which the individual freely chooses whether or not to participate, find the Soviet method unacceptable as sport – at least in the corinthian sense of the word.

But the corinthian ideal is not applicable in the Soviet context: sport does not have connotations of free will, individual expression, and conscious choice. It is approached very much as westerners might approach physics or geography; it is an integral part of the curriculum which children must study. If children show aptitude, then they will be favoured to attend specialist establishments where potential can be developed and exploited. Their position in society will be as sports performers: not people who are good at certain sports, but people who are state-financed as specialists in a valued occupation and whose successes will reflect favourably on the entire system.

Soviet sport has had no need to wrestle with the problem of amateurism, or shamateurism. Physical culture has not been conceived as a 'fun' pursuit distinct from work or education. As a central part of social and political life, it is approached with a seriousness that would have been abhorrent to westerners until quite recently. Contrasts with western sport, which is ostensibly meant to be enjoyed rather than assiduously worked-at or even bred-for, have given rise to pejorative stereotypes. David Triesman captures one typical image of Soviet female athletes: 'Drug-soaked, electrically-stimulated, manly women, who've been white-slaved into sport from the cradle' (1984: 26–7). This is a ludicrous exaggeration, but one with perhaps some truth concealed in it.

Athletes haven't been 'slaved' into sport; but they have been selected at an early age and ushered towards specialist training on the basis of formative physiological and psychological analyses.

Valery Borzov, the Ukrainian sprinter who reigned supreme for a period in the 1970s, is usually cited as the computerized athlete par excellence because he was screened as a child and given the benefit of every scientific training facility in his progress. His entire career was supported by continuous state assistance; as is that of any top Soviet sports performer. Such programmes have been criticized as dehumanizing and tyrannical; a state-centralized control of sport means no room for individual choice or freedom of expression. The fact that there has been little dissent from Borzov *et al.* is dismissed as the product of fear.

The voluntary conception seems to be isolated by the Soviet methods of selection and planning. There's no evidence one way or the other to indicate whether the child or youth has much autonomous choice within the parameters set by the state. But how realistic is it to view the typical western youth as unrestricted in choice, given the kind of social and historical constraints considered in chapter five? Questions of loyalty, commitment, and obligation enter into the equation when we try to identify factors in the typical Soviet performer's motivation. The prospect of status or prestige may loom larger than material rewards. For many western youth the prospect of material and status success in sport is often the only one they have. They certainly exercise choice, but often within very limited frameworks of opportunities.

This in itself is ultimately a political issue of sports, but of more immediate relevance is the intrusion of the state. Those who oppose the large-scale assistance of athletes by the state usually lapse into a *laissez-faire* idealism in which state interference is minimized. They would cite the USSR as an example of the monstrous consequences of *dirigisme*, a policy in which the state plans and directs all social and economic matters – a total politicization of sport.

But, even in the birthplace of organized sport, the idea of state involvement is not so odd. Stephen Jones' study traces the origins of state involvement to the nineteenth century. By the early twentieth century, the principle was well-established in Britain. Jones argues that 'state intervention took two forms: first, covert legislative control; and second, overt governmental manipulation for political purposes' (1987: 176).

He gives details of the national and local level legislation covering sport and the more general area of leisure, from the 1920s onwards, adding that 'such an official framework necessitated state intervention'. The 'most direct piece of interventionist legislation was the Physical Training and Recreation Act of 1937'. This was by no means the first legislation aimed at achieving 'a better standard of physical development in adults', but it was certainly the most ambitious to date, providing more facilities and offering more opportunities. Recent memories of the war would not have taken much reawakening and the fear of repetition was clearly a motivating factor behind the Act. Money was spent encouraging the population to exercise more, especially in the swimming pool: between 1937 and 1939, the government approved local authority plans to spend £3 million on public pools. Tennis courts, football pitches, and bowling greens were also subject to government initiatives. The central state was involved not only in funding, but in elevating the position of physical education in school's curricula. PE, which later became synonymous with sport, was established as part of a proper, balanced educational programme.

The most significant development in modern times has been the Sports Council which was granted its Royal Charter in 1971 with the remit to build bridges between the various voluntary organizations handling particular sports and the more general bodies like the British Olympic Association and the Central Council of Physical Recreation, the bureaucracy of which was eventually taken over by the Sports Council. Financed by the Department of the Environment, the Sports Council was a quasi-governmental organization ('quango'), with sufficient autonomy to make strategic decisions affecting both commercial and public sectors. It continues to formulate policy, nationally and regionally, and gives advice and financial support to all manner of organizations whether amateur or professional. Its original wide focus, which included promoting sport as a family activity, narrowed after the urban disorders of the early 1980s and, in recent years, its cardinal concern has been with working-class inner city youths.

As well as targeting groups and involving them in sport, the Sports Council is charged with responsibility for centres of excellence geared to the needs of top-flight sports performers who require specialist coaching and training. It also gives assistance to specific sports governing bodies to create and support national representative teams, an arrangement which has enhanced its own power and reduced that of individual sports organizations. Many sports are virtually dependent on continuous aid from the Sports Council. It has become the state's main vehicle for financing and affecting the overall development of sport in the UK.

Returning to Jones, whose interest is specific to the interwar years, we find other forms of state intervention, 'political manipulation', in a number of areas. Earlier in this chapter, we identified some issues in which governments were prepared to become involved, sometimes quite deeply. The English soccer team's matches against Germany in the mid-1930s were alive with political interest. Slightly earlier, in 1933, England's returning cricketers were summoned to the prime minister after their notorious 'bodyline' tour of Australia. Their punishing tactics had bruised not only Australian batsmen, but also politicians, who ventured to call diplomatic relations into question. In the 1980s, the government's attempt to abort Britain's entry to the Moscow Olympics was a major political interference set against a background of diplomatic strains. The South Africa affair has been covered in detail.

Yet the main form of manipulation has come about not so much as a result of international tension, but of domestic disorder – or, more precisely, the prospect of it. There has been no hesitation by governments to overrule sporting bodies and make pronouncements such as in 1922, when a heavyweight boxing contest between the white Joe Beckett and black Battling Siki was prohibited because of the dangers of the 'colour issue'. Football matches were forbidden for periods on the ground that they threatened public order, though the imprisonment of seven boys who were playing street football in Glasgow in 1933 seemed an over-reaction! Successive governments to the present day have directly intervened in sports affairs, often in defiance of sports governing organizations and public opinion; the implementation of an identity card system for English soccer in 1989 presents a modern illustration.

Control and manipulation: these two terms describe the methods of state intervention and reflect the political nature of sport, certainly in the UK, and most probably in the western world generally. Critics of the Soviet system of state-planning control and co-ordination of activities too often ignore the true extent of political involvement in sport in the west in the futile effort to establish its autonomy, an autonomy that is, as we have seen, largely mythical. The western world still can't see a mirror image of itself when it faces the Soviets. What it can see are trends, tendencies, and instances that might appear to contradict traditional notions of sport, but which have been incorporated *mutatis mutandis* in western systems.

It is too glib a generalization to say that the Soviet system of sport is something of a model which western systems will emulate. Gross ideological asymmetries will ensure separate paths of development. Professionalism of the order experienced in the west is clearly at variance with Soviet ideals, though state sponsorship and the material advantages that accrue from sporting success suggest that the Soviets lack professionalism only in a notional sense. Both systems have accommodated the idea of sports performers training and competing on a full-time basis with a reimbursement for their time and effort. Whereas the state is wholly responsible for making this possible in the Soviet system, a combination of public funding, perhaps the equivalent of the Sports Council, and private sponsorship operates in the west.

All the other features that make the Soviet system appear distinct and, to some, a type of 'white slavery' including its integration of sport into formal education curricula, have counterparts in the west. The USA has prestigious sports scholarships which attract specialist sports performers. In the UK, sports academies are being established for that elite group of pupils who warrant the label sporting prodigy. The Football Association's National School and the International Sports College are two examples. The west might have taken a while to cotton on to the idea that plucking raw talent and shaping it isn't necessarily as harsh and pitiless as some might have supposed after viewing the emaciated Olga Korbut in her early twenties, only a few years after her Olympic triumphs. But in the 1980s, the system of early selection was adopted by many western nations.

This leads directly to questions about the future of sport. Is the convergence between the Soviet and western systems set to continue? The final part of this chapter has shown that the development of sport in east and west has not had widely dissimilar trajectories, despite fundamentally different ideologies, which have been reflected in the organization of sport. Sport has been afforded importance and has been addressed by the state accordingly. We can safely assume that its development in communist societies will continue along broadly the same lines. But will state involvement in the west intensify and with what consequences?

These are the kinds of questions that discussions of sport and politics inevitably throw up. Questions about whether or not they can be kept separate are non-starters when we consider the intertwining of politics and sport. The big issues like South Africa and boycotts seize the headlines, but political influence in sport is pervasive and usually not worthy of sustained media coverage – which is presumably the reason why many assume sport, for the most part, remains unaffected by politics, when the opposite is true. For the final chapter, we will return to questions about state intervention when we speculate on the future of sport.

Further reading

The Politics of Sport *edited by Lincoln Allison (Manchester University Press, 1986) collects individual contributions from academics on various aspects of sport and politics. There is no underlying theme to the volume, as the writers (as the editor puts it) argue 'from different bases' and make 'assertions which occasionally contradict one another'. But the book at least shows how all sport is, in some sense, political.*

The Revolt of the Black Athlete *by Harry Edwards (Free Press, 1970) documents the build-up to the Smith–Carlos gesture at Mexico. What might have seemed to be a piece of rash judgement was actually a carefully-prepared and executed operation against a background of civil unrest in the USA.*

'The politics of sport and apartheid' *by Peter Hain (in* Sport, Culture and Ideology *edited by J. Hargreaves, Routledge & Kegan Paul, 1982) gives a view by the author who was actively engaged in the 'stop the tour' campaigns and should be read in tandem with* 'Apartheid, boycotts and the games' *by Sam Ramsamy (in* Five Ring Circus *edited by A. Tomlinson and G. Whannel, Pluto Press, 1984) which is written by the chair of the South African Non-Racial Olympic Committee (SANROC), who campaigned for a boycott of the Mexico games if South Africa was allowed to participate.*

Sport, Politics and the Working Class *by Stephen J. Jones (Manchester University Press, 1989) is concerned with the ways in which the working class has 'colonised' (as Jones calls it) commercial sport; one of the reasons for this is because sport assimilated pastimes such as gambling, drinking, and violence.*

Assignment

You are a national volleyball manager-coach in the final stages of your squad's preparation for a major international tournament to be attended by the world's volleyball powers. In a newspaper feature profiling one of the squad's outstanding attacking players, he/she reveals that he/she is a member of the *Order*, a group opposed to what it calls ZOG (Zionist Occupation Government) and which, as the newspaper journalist uncovers, has links or sympathies with the Ku Klux Klan, the Posse Comitatus, the Nazi Parties of Britain and the USA, and other anti-semitic and racist groups. What is the likely fallout and how will you, as manager-coach, deal with it?

Chapter nine

Future

Why ... ?

'The why of a fan' is the title of an article published in 1929 in which A. A. Brill argued that 'life organised too well becomes monotonous; too much peace and security breed boredom; and old instincts, bred into the very cells of the body ... still move the masses of normal men' (1929: 431). Brill wrote in terms of the 'restrictions of modern life' depriving people of their 'activity and scope, the triumphs and *réclame*' which were achievable through physical prowess under 'more primitive conditions'. In explaining the fans' attraction to sport, Brill exposed what he took to be a dark truth about human nature: 'an animal formed for battle and conquest, for blows and strokes and swiftness, for triumph and applause' (1929: 434). As the necessity for physical struggle was removed and modern organized society brought stability and security, so the nasty and brutish qualities were made redundant – but not irrelevant. They were of great use in sport. Here was a group of activities that required physical prowess. Not everyone had the star power to be able to exhibit their attributes; but they could at least identify with those who did. In the process, they would recover something of their natural state; they would 'achieve exaltation, vicarious but real' and be 'a better individual, better citizen'.

Improbable as Brill's argument might have been as a total theory of sport, it offered a timeless insight about the drabness and formality of much in the modern world and the security it holds for most of us. Security is something we seek, yet do not want. Probing this paradox of security has led novelists to some ingenious alternatives, such as running one's life as if a Vegas crap game, in Rinehart's *The Dice Man*, or discovering Pirsig's *Zen and the Art of Motorcycle Maintenance*; both best-selling novels and both in their own way tracts against the uniformity of bureaucracy.

> **Bureaucracy**
> A highly organized system of administration in which individual-
> ism and imagination is minimized and official rules, regulations,
> and practices are of paramount importance.

Bureaucracies proliferate in every major area of society. The ever-widening latticework of bureaucratic administrations has produced what the social theorist Max Weber called 'calculability'; meaning that the workings of bureaucracy are, as far as posible, protected against the personal emotions and whims of those who administer its policies. As a result, the performance of a bureaucracy is highly predictable. Once the applicable regulations and procedures are known, it's possible to calculate exactly how a bureaucracy is going to deal with a matter and what are the chances of a certain type of outcome. So, bureaucracy stabilizes a society, orders it, regulates it, and renders it entirely predictable. All this makes for a rational and smooth-running society. It also affects the mentalities of people who live in such a society. Calculability is an organizing principle in the overall personality. Spontaneity and randomness may be pleasant diversions but, in large doses, they can prove severely disruptive and threaten an individual's sense of security. Still, there is a residual attraction in the unplanned, surprise happening; a pleasant intrigue as to what its consequences might be. Were this to invade our working, or public lives, it would lead to serious disorientation. So, in the main, we confine the fascination for the unpredictable to our private lives. Office workers can approach their daily tasks with a strangulating regard for rationality and precision. Once out of the office, they might retreat to the tumult of a home resembling a Fellini movie – everywhere cluttered with formless confusion. Workers might have one set of rules for the office, but another for the home.

The separation of life into public and private spheres is itself a product of modern industrial society. It has the advantage of allowing the individual to compensate in one sphere for the tensions or frustrations that build up in the other. Office workers may quietly boil in rage at the meaningless or sheer prolixity of their employment. They might keep a lid on themselves at work, but wreak havoc at home. Most of us experience bureaucracies, if only indirectly and, equally, most of us have been irritated or angered by them. But we don't usually scream or assault others. We find outlets for these emotions elsewhere. Sport can be seen as one attempt to compensate for bureaucracy and the discontents it brings. Kicking or throwing balls, riding horses in a circle, or inflicting pointless damage on others may be irrational pursuits. But that is their beauty; whether watched or performed, they guide the participant well clear of the formal limits of bureaucracies and into an area where the outcomes of situations are wholly unpredictable and, therefore, in total contrast to those of bureaucracies.

For all its institutionalization and officialdom, sport has retained its fascinating nucleus: indeterminacy. Wrap it in red tape and smother it with a bureaucracy to rival that of the Kremlin, but you can never quite fix the outcome of a contest (unless by foul means, of course; in which case it ceases to be sport). The doubtfulness of sport, the way in which it resists predictability and the order it usually brings, makes sport a constant challenge to security. A result can never be ascertained in advance, even when odds overwhelmingly favour one party over another. It's one area where fairytale endings occasionally do come true: the underdog has a chance, however remote.

Perhaps this tells us something about the resilience of sport, its continuing popularity, and even its future. In a world where certainty has become a virtual norm, uncertainty is a prized commodity, especially if it is packaged in a visually moving and colourful display that excites the senses. Sport offers this uncertainty. It could be argued that it does so artificially, pitting contestants against each other in mock rivalry and in circumstances not of their own making. Then again, it could also be argued that, in this respect, it reflects much of life anyway.

Sport has accumulated its own bureaucracy in recent years, especially as modern states have intruded progressively into areas once thought to be relatively autonomous. Yet, indeterminacy can never be removed, or 'sport' simply ceases to be sport and is transformed into mere spectacle or drama. Sport has the same kind of job specialization, production, deadlines, and monotonous training regimes of industrial work. Computerization in both spheres has enhanced the similarity. Much of sport is routine and reasonably predictable. But not all: the uncertainty that hangs over the actual competitive match can be reduced but never eliminated; nor, therefore, can the inspirational freedom, self-controlled skill, independent vision, and innovative originality that emerge in the competitive encounter. No amount of bureaucratization can flush these out of sport and the facility to innovate creatively becomes a useful, if rather hopeless, counterpoint against the cube-headedness implied by bureaucratization.

Bureaucracy predominates in most countries where there is

organized sport and the shift from goods-producing to service-producing economies promises no significant reduction in formal organization and standardization. Sport itself has been and will continue to be affected in much the same way as all other institutions, such as religion, education, and science, have been subject to bureaucratic imperatives. At the same time, it will continue to prosper as, in some senses, an antithesis to bureaucracy; a virtual opposition in its reliance on an essential doubt over outcomes.

How come ... ?

With bureaucracy virtually guaranteeing sport a future, the matter of possible changes within sport needs attention. What will be the shape of sport in the years to come? The first point to bear in mind is that changes in the shape of sport, that is, its content and administration, will be initiated from without. Sources of change will be diverse and lie outside the formal sphere of sport.

The distinction between amateurs and professionals has become meaningless in most sports and there seems to be a growing recognition that it has impeded the development of sport, especially in Europe. The British, as we saw, invented the concept of amateur and regarded it as central to organized sport. In the 1990s, the term shamateur, semi-professional, and even state-amateur have complicated the old distinction. Some sports are choking on anomalies, such as that of the millionaire amateur, a creature which prowls the athletic tracks of North America and Europe. Or the university student supported by a sports scholarship, and whose college timetable is virtually filled by training sessions. In the USA, the National Collegiate Athletic Association has 547 colleges offering soccer scholarships alone, 577 offering golf, and 589 offering tennis – and these are relatively minor sports. The UK has little to compare: eleven only sports scholarships and thirty-four bursaries financed in the main by private sponsors. But there is bound to be more interest from commercial organizations which want to associate their corporate images with the nurturing of sporting prowess to a high level.

The various mutations of the amateur have effectively left the prototype extinct. Or rather, will leave it extinct; possibly within the next decade. Very few sports have maintained their pure amateur status. Rugby Union held out defiantly, but eventually allowed the introduction of trust funds in 1988, a landmark decision totally opposed by some members of the Rugby Football

Union, including secretary Dudley Wood, who denounced the trust fund concept as 'quasi-professionalism'.

The same idea could be applied to amateur boxing. The British Amateur Boxing Association, unlike its US counterpart, has strictly discouraged links with professional sport. Like Rugby Union and Rugby League, amateur and professional boxing are run by different governing organizations, have different rules, and different methods of evaluation. The majority of pros have campaigned as amateurs before discarding their vests and head-guards. In the UK, the professional British Boxing Board of Control have traditionally used a prospective pro boxer's amateur career as a form guide as to how he might weather in the paid ranks. But this is subject to change and it seems likely that the Board will at least entertain more licence applications from those without amateur experience. In other words, boxers will be able to short-circuit amateur boxing and fight for money rather than trophies. If this happens, it will ring the knell for amateur boxing. Already forced to accept substantial sponsorship monies from commercial organizations, the sport will be reduced to a rather insignificant minority sport with a slavish dependency if not on commercial firms, then on the British Sports Council.

The benevolence of the Sports Council and its continental European equivalents is greeted joyously by those wishing to see the state play a more active role in encouraging, promoting, and fostering sport – but with caution by those fearful of a Soviet-style state-amateurism. Old utilitarian ideas die hard and, even when they do, are troublesome to bury; there is bound to be some resistance to the progressive intrusion of the state into what were previously private domains. Yet the move is inexorable and agencies such as the Sports Council will eventually become not so much a source of assistance, but a crutch for many sports, whose appeal may not be sufficiently wide to attract commercial interest. Only in these sports will a residual amateurism – if indeed one wishes to retain the term – survive and, even then, on a state life-support system.

For the most part, western sport will continue on its current big business trajectory. As we've seen before, sport as a spectacle, in its literal sense (an object of public attention) has always had the potential for exploitation. There is nothing too evil or corrosive about this; some people will pay to watch sport and other people will make money from it. The important indeterminacy of sport will always prevent it from becoming just another branch of showbusiness, even if the methods of its marketing suggest very close similarities. Some traditional sports, wrestling being the obvious example, have been transformed into sheer theatre. But there the theatrical element has replaced the indeterminacy and modern wrestling has long ceased to be a legitimate competitive sport, despite the protestations of some of its followers. Competitive Graeco-Roman wrestling still exists, but as a very minor Olympic event; Sumo has begun to enjoy cult status outside its native Japan.

Other pursuits, not certifiable sports, are worried by the possibility of the opposite process once television takes an interest. Mountaineering, a practice that pitches co-operative teamwork and intricate human craft against obdurate natural forces, is presently being reminted for the screen. The painstakingly long and studious negotiation of rock faces do not make for dramatic watching, so a more febrile competitive event is promised with individuals or small teams asked to race each other to given destinations.

Like it or not, the media in general and cable-satellite tv in particular will become more integral to the development of sport. The symbiosis that has grown since the 1920s is volubly loathed by some critics, but it is a comfortable arrangement in which the media attracts punters and the sport revenue. Sport also gains the ambiguous benefit of mass exposure; like amphetamines, stimulating in moderate doses, but possibly deadly in large amounts.

Broadcast tv in the United States has been under some pressure from the cable networks, whose subscriptions enable them to stage sports events on the grandest of scales. I use 'stage' because tv has become a prime mover in many events, approaching sports promoters and making money available to them. Many sports events would be inconceivable without the active interest of television companies and the cables have pursued their interest aggressively. Home Box Office (HBO) has landed many coups, often to the chagrin of the big broadcast networks – and the non-cabled viewing population. In addition to its *table d'hôte* fare at a fixed price it offers its subscribers *à la carte* choices of sumptuous events, not only major sports contests, but new films. In return, it asks the viewers to pay extra money for the particular event. If you watch the latest Tyson fight, you order it and have an extra $25 on your monthly subscription. The system is called pay-per-view and the chance of a UK equivalent emerging as a force in British television is quite strong. Satellite-cable tv, although available regionally, was launched nationally in 1989 and its overall impact will not become evident for some years. There are grounds for believing that some of the big sports events could be annexed from the terrestrial networks' possession; which could lead to a pay-per-view delivery of events to the screens of subscribers only.

Home Box Office (HBO)
Home Box Office was founded in November 1972 when it broadcast a hockey match from Madison Square Garden in New York to 365 cable tv subscribers. It now has 16 million subscribers across 50 American states and screens 24 hours a day (this is still relatively small numbers compared to broadcast tv which reaches 90.4 million viewers). Besides being a major screener of international sports events in the USA, it actually promotes events, which, apart from 'live' audiences, are available exclusively to its subscribers.

This is a more specific subtrend in what is already a major movement; tv taking control of sport. The trend has been discussed in previous chapters and speculation on the future can only project more-of-the-same. Money from the media is no longer a welcome supplement to most sports' coffers: it is the main source of revenue. It requires little analysis to conclude that the arrangement will lead to a greater asymmetry of power in which 'he who pays the piper . . .'

These then are the broader changes that will affect sport and they concern sport's relations with agencies which ostensibly have no part in the actual content or performance of sport. But by changing the structure, you also change the content and the repackaging of events for tv will necessarily alter what actually happens. The mountaineering case is illustrative as it will compress a slow and exacting process into a relatively short competitive burst. One-day cricket, twelve-round boxing, and squash *sans* the server-only-scores rule are instances of how television has tampered with rules so as to make events shorter and more exciting. Others will follow.

We can also look to more specific changes of accent in sports. In the 1960s, many people hit upon the idea that sporting action would grow more violent. They mistakenly looked to a tv 'sport' called roller derby, which was really a contrived piece of mayhem more akin to tv wrestling than competitive sport and which was violent enough to make ice hockey look like a game of croquet. The thrilling blur of roller derby sped to the big screen in the form of the movie *Rollerball* in which the majority of the players left the rink on stretchers (some in bodybags). 'I've seen the future of sport and it looks like this!' crowed critics leaving the cinema. One of the subtexts of the movie was the message that sport functions as a substitute for war by providing a relatively safe outlet for aggression. A sustained spell of relative world peace meant more violence in sport. Implicitly, the thesis tied in with that of ethologists, like Desmond Morris whom we considered in chapter four and his mentor Konrad Lorenz who believed all humans are innately aggressive creatures. Sport serves as a safety valve – it is better that people discharge their aggression on the sports field than in the street or on the battlefields.

But, if Norbet Elias, whom we also met in chapter four, is to be believed, violence isn't such a permanent and finite quality. In fact, violence in sport decreases as the level of acceptable violence in society generally declines. The civilizing process involves an appropriation of the legitimate use of violence by the state and this process is mirrored in sport. As we saw, gouging, maiming, and a miscellany of physical brutality were acceptable in folk sports of the eighteenth and nineteenth centuries. But as the 'thresholds of repugnance' descended, so we stopped enjoying and grew disgusted at the sight of excessive damage being inflicted on humans and animals.

Despite this taking place within what Elias calls a 'civilizing spurt', the actual changes appear gradual to those who live through them and only when we draw back and look at history, do we realize the extent to which violence has been reduced in sport. This realization gives no real foundation for the view that it will suddenly increase. Since the release of *Rollerball* in the mid-1970s there has been a continuation of the civilizing trend in sport; referees in soccer and American football vigorously enforce rules to protect players, jockeys have been sternly warned against 'whip abuse' – lashing the racehorse too much in the final stretch – and another kind of abuse, that of the tennis racket, has been an official offence and players prone to tantrums are deducted points and fined.

These are but small modifications, yet they reflect a refusal to tolerate overt and gratuitous violence in sport. Having recognized this, we should also acknowledge that many, probably the majority, of sports entail an aggressive approach and a violent disposition on behalf of the competitors. Aggression is talked of in a very positive sense in most sports: defence may be admirable on occasion, but too much of it is downright boring. Even outright violence is encouraged in some combat sports, though always in a controlled setting – witness the admonishments of boxing authorities at the first hint of extracurricular fisticuffs. Sport is rather like an over-packed suitcase bulging with violence, but prevented from bursting open by authorities sitting on it. Its shape might be irregular and bits of its contents may escape here and there, but it stays shut and, every so often, a belt gets tied around its girth to make it secure.

Aggression–Performance

The effect aggression has on sporting performance has led many psychologists to conduct experiments, though their results are rather contradictory. Many favour a positive link; competitors who exhibit an aggressive behavioural state and hold positive attitudes towards committing violent acts are generally more successful than those who don't, in individual and team sports. Another research finding is that there is a curvilinear relationship; successful performers were either highly aggressive, or extremely non-aggressive; and moderately aggressive performers were usually mediocre. Another interesting finding is that aggression is effective when used early in a contest, but not later. An article by W. Neil Widmeyer (1984) provides a valuable summary of the research.

Sport is violent, but, as Michael Smith in his study *Violence and Sport* points out: 'The fact is, sports violence has never been viewed as "real" violence' and the public 'give standing ovations to performers for acts that in other contexts would be instantly condemned as criminal' (1983: 9). Despite this, audiences are getting very slightly queasier; we just don't notice it. Two hundred years ago, people would give standing ovations to executioners; now they'd find it repulsive. Elias, in his theory, allows for regressive spurts, but it's difficult to envisage one in the near future. Much more likely is an ever-tightening control over the permissible amount and level of open physical violence in sports and a corresponding adjustment of public taste.

What next ... ?

The intrusions of commercial interests and the decreases in violence describe what we might call morphological shifts in sport; changes in the form or shape sport is likely to take. There will also be demographic changes because the composition of the population of sports performers isn't likely to remain static. In chapter five, we identified two groups, one of which (blacks) has been severely overrepresented in sport, the other of which (women) has been underrepresented. One doesn't need to be a blithe and blind optimist to imagine a gradual tailing off of the enormous participation of blacks in sport. It's a virtual equation of our times that fewer blacks in sport equals less racism in society at large. So, if you're going to predict a decline in racism, then you're going to have to take account of a few less Michael Jordans and Carl Lewises. But is this strictly true? Racism and equal opportunities are related but not invariably correlated in the sense that a decrease in one always implies an increase in the other. It's possible to see the erection of equal opportunities (EO) apparatuses and a proliferation of EO policies – as we have in both Europe and the USA – without necessarily seeing an end to racism. As I disclosed in my book *The Logic of Racism* (1987), the same poison comes in assorted shaped bottles. In other words, people can harbour racist views and values but may not allow these to affect their day-to-day lives, nor the routines of the organizations in which they operate.

I don't necessarily foresee racism being ground down by EO policies. I do see an opening up of choices for ethnic minorities. The obstacles to progress in education and especially work will come down as if hit by an inept hurdler. As more blacks find their way into careers and climb to senior positions, one of the necessary conditions for their entry into sport will go, that of blocked opportunities. One of the many consequences of this will be a loss in the mesmeric power of sport. It will cease to attract black youths seeking a stable career simply because it isn't stable and, for the overwhelming majority, it isn't a career either. To use Jack Olsen again, it's a meaningless dream. Over the next several years it will be recognized as precisely that.

The position of women is almost the reverse in that they have been forcibly prevented from competing in sport at the highest level. Now we're firmly in the post-feminist era, the archaic images of gentle femininity which were essential to women's subordination have been well-and-truly eroded, though not destroyed – they've demonstrated a tough resilience. Still, women in sport have contributed appreciably to the onslaught, clocking great times on track and field events, posting significant victories in many individual sports, and showing impressive form in team games like soccer and basketball, which were once utterly dominated by men. Chances are they won't achieve the same standards as men without the stimulus of open competition, but their progress will be accelerated by the greater number of women entering competitive sport on a serious basis.

Again, one doesn't have to draw any conclusions about society at large from this. Women are chipping away at myths about their biological status and are proving the equals of their male counterparts in significant areas of employment as well as sport. This won't translate automatically into a drop in sexism or sexual discrimination. But it will open a few more doors for what was once regarded as the 'weaker sex'.

Women still haven't achieved parity in terms of salaries and wages. But they're getting there slowly. Equally slowly, they're pushing their way into hallowed areas. One of the most prominent bastions of male supremacy in British sport, namely the MCC, may yet be overhauled. Marylebone Cricket Club, whose doors were closed to women throughout its 200-odd-year existence, in 1989, circulated its 18,000 members with a newsletter, suggesting, albeit gently, that, as women now had voting rights and equal opportunities, they might also be allowed access to the club's venerated Long Room. England's 'ladies' team' was allowed in for two one-day internationals. Besides Lords, only Manchester's Old Trafford continued to bar women. With one half of the old guard considering the change, it could mean a very significant breakthrough for women in the 1990s.

Quite apart from the crumbling of male institutions, there is the cash incentive for women. Currently, not many sports offer women the chance of riches, nor perhaps even bread-and-butter. Successful careers in golf, tennis, or athletics are exceptions. Yet, as women's sport gains in popularity, as it surely will, the money will become available and this will enhance the attractiveness of sport. Equal opportunities will diminish the chances of young blacks going into sport, but in an entirely different manner it will pave the way for more young females, of all ethnic backgrounds, to sink their efforts into a sports career.

The unseen malefactor called Aids is no respecter of distinctions at all: blacks, women – all are targets in the same way as white males. In the 1980s, the HIV virus spread and mutated at a rate that simply left medical science stranded. No cure and only limited and expensive treatments were discovered. The only way to handle the prospect of Aids was to change lifestyles; forget the heady days of the 1960s and 1970s, when promiscuity was all but commended. In the late 1980s, the call was for 'safe sex' – stable, monogamous relationships or (possibly, and) condoms. Show-business has already had a number of Aids' victims, but the world of sport has so far escaped lightly. Yet there will almost certainly be deaths of sports stars from Aids in the 1990s.

Sport itself has to develop procedures for ensuring that the pandemic cannot spread through the physical contact that many events entail. In the UK, a professional African boxer Langton Tinago was prevented from fighting after he tested positive for HIV prior to a scheduled match. This is a sport in which facial cuts are frequent and close exchanges make it possible to ingest one's opponent's blood via the mouth, or possibly the eyes. Hence infection is very possible. Other sports don't carry such risks, but many involve personal contact and others, like swimming, involve the chance of absorbing others' body fluids. Mandatory Aids-testing procedures are bound to become as commomplace as drug-testing in a great many sports.

The sophistication of drug-testing and the rapidity with which they can provide results will prove a major disincentive to sports performers inclined towards performance enhancing dope, particularly steroids. Yet, I suggested in chapter six that drugs would continue to be used and their design or combination of use would proceed apace with improvements in testing procedures. There will also be a resort to drug-free performance enhancement. Neuromuscular electrical stimulation is one possibility: coupled with intense anaerobic exercise, the muscular gains from this technique are comparable with those from anabolic steroid use. At the moment, there are no manifest risks to health, nor known methods of detection.

Neuromuscular electrical stimulation (NMES)
This technique was developed by a medical research team headed by Anthony Delitto, at Washington University. Small amounts of electrical power were initially used to improve the recovery of knee surgery patients. The problem was to increase the power and stimulate the major muscle development without causing unbearable pain. Over a period of eight years before the 1988 Olympics, the research team became aware of the potential application to sport and chose as a subject Derrick Crass, a weightlifter, whose lifts improved by 45 lbs in the first two weeks of treatment and, eventually, by 85 lbs. Delitto claimed treatment with anabolic steroids over a similar period would lead to an improvement of only 20 lbs. NMES was effective only when coupled with exercise. Delitto suspects Soviet sport scientists have used NMES for some time. Crass was troubled by a shoulder injury in the games and managed only eleventh place.

This is another illustration of how medicine and sport have become joined over the past several decades. The initial collaboration over the treatment of sports-related injuries branched into several different areas. Soviet societies were quick to appreciate the potential contribution of medicine, not only for the treatment of injuries but for the maximization of performance. Medicine has made an immense input in terms of treatment, diet, monitoring, and, of course, specific training techniques. Ironically, the best known medical practitioner in sports is notorious rather than famous. Dr Jamie Astaphan's reputation grew with the revelations about the Ben Johnson case. It was he who played the role of the evil alchemist in the drugs melodrama. Retained by members of the Canadian national athletics team, Astaphan designed anabolic steroid programmes to enhance performances. The hearings of the case, in 1989, revealed that Johnson himself was by no means in a minority. It also added substance to beliefs that sport was rapidly reaching the stage where the performers themselves were bit-part players and the major roles were filled by the near-anonymous medics who prescribed their training as well as their dope. 'Scientist vs scientist' was how the future of sport was imagined; like clashing Svengalis, medics wielded almost total control over their subjects.

The image is deliciously amusing rather than sinister. Medics will continue to assist sports performers; in fact, they will probably be absolutely indispensable. But they will not produce performances, rather they will be one factor in an ever-elaborating

---

Sport for the disabled

In its original conception, competitive sport for the disabled was intended as an unconventional form of rehabilitation. Its inspirator, Sir Ludwig Guttman, who set up the spinal injuries unit at Stoke Mandeville Hospital, England, in 1944, set up the first organized meeting involving patients from different rehabilitation centres in 1948. At first, the meets were informal, but international teams were soon attracted by the idea and regular competition led to more organization. The British Sports Association for the Disabled (BSAD) was formed in 1961 and began co-ordinating with what became known as the Paralympic movement. Olympiads specifically for the disabled were held to coincide with Olympic meetings and, on all but two occasions after 1960 (Mexico 1966; Moscow 1980) countries hosting Olympic Games also hosted an international event for the disabled. The 1976 games in Canada included events for the blind and partially-sighted, paraplegics, tetraplegics, and amputees. Later, they were joined by those with cerebral palsy and les autres. From its original idea sport for the disabled turned into genuine competition rather than a method of rehabilitation.

---

production line. I'm not romantic and ingenuous enough to say the performer is the most important factor, if only because the whole of this book is filled with analyses of factors lying outside the individual which have crucial effects on the end-product – the performance. The performer him or herself is but one element amid countless others.

Progress as reflected in improvements in performances isn't the result of new breeds of supersportsmen and women. They come about because of better nutrition, more sophisticated training, effective recuperative and recovery treatment, and, of course, intense competition. Athletics and swimming have had demonstrable improvements which can be accurately measured. There's no reason to suppose that other sports haven't progressed in a similar fashion. Pub arguments about 'who was best?' invite false comparisons. 'The Wolverhampton Wanderers of the 1950s would have beaten the Liverpool of the 1980s.' 'Fred Perry would have run rings around Andre Agassi.' 'The heavyweights of today would be no match for those of the 1930s.' None of these can be proven. No one says, 'Roger Bannister would have burnt off Said Aouita', probably because it can be so easily disproved. Aouita consistently clocks times about 15 seconds faster than Bannister's best for 1,500 metres or a mile. By the same reasoning, we should have accepted that all other sports, including those that rely

Progress
Progress in sport is a uniquely human phenomenon, based more on intellectual abilities than physical ones. For example, over 1,500 metres, Said Aouita is about 40 seconds faster than his counterpart of 130 years ago. Yet if we compare the Grand National winners over a similar period, modern horses run only about 10 seconds faster. The reason for the difference is that a trained race horse will maintain between 85–95 per cent of its maximum speed, metabolizing anaerobic energy, which is, as we have seen, counterproductive in the long term as it produces lactic acid and retards muscle contraction. Humans have improved their performances through advances in techniques and training, including muscle-building. They will run at between 65–70 per cent of maximum speed for most of a middle distance race, kicking over the final phase. This requires timing, anticipation, and a tactical awareness as well as improved capacities to assimilate stress and discomfort – features that are built into modern training. There is also incentive: a horse has only a whipped flank to motivate it in the final stretch, whereas a human has plentiful rewards and for these he or she may be prepared to suffer. Apart from intellectual stimulus, we should note that humans are physically inefficient at running compared to horses, whose capacity for running is an evolutionary adaptation, probably resulting from their relative defencelessness. Humans' desire to run fast over distances is more a product of self-induced challenge; the machine itself has only modest locomotion capacities.

more on technique and strategy than sheer fitness, improve their standards at roughly the same pace. The old Wolves team probably wouldn't have survived in the English third division nowadays. Agassi would dispose of Perry, most likely in straight sets. Few of the relatively small (Joe Louis weighed just over 14 stones, or about 200 lbs) and immobile heavies would last the distance with today's 16 stone behemoths.

If the actual performers of previous eras enjoyed the benefits of better diet, training, and strategy as well as better social conditions, then the story might be different. Conditions change and these yield improvements. There will continue to be improvements, though at a slowing pace. Sebastian Coe's father and coach, Peter, once captured the logic of this when responding to the question of how fast the mile could be run. I paraphrase him: 'It's like taking a straight line, dividing it in two, splitting it again, then again and again and again and so on *ad infinitum*. The lines get smaller and smaller, but you're always left with something.'

This means that, every time an improvement of standard in any sport is made, the relative size of the next improvement is likely to be smaller. Quantitatively big improvements, such as Bob Beamon's long jump and Butch Reynold's 400-metre records are aberrant performances explicable only in terms of freak atmospheric conditions or exceptionally fierce competition.

One possible change in sport that we should finally mention is that it will be taken even more seriously as a proper subject for academic and scientific study. A book such as this would not have been written ten years ago; maybe not even five years ago. But recently, we have seen a proliferation of sports science, sports studies, and many related degrees and programmes of studies, all based on the view that sport deserves considered attention, that is, the kind of attention normally reserved for 'obvious relevant' phenomena such as crime, education, technology, employment, and any number of other subjects that have been the topic of textbooks. Sport hasn't achieved a comparable status, but there is certainly a greater recognition that it is a key area in society and one that has been too neglected in the past. Its association with frivolity, recreation, and play is virtually over. If there is one abiding theme spread through these pages it is that sport is now a serious business. No one doubted that it was business; more and more are realizing that it's serious enough to merit scholarly study.

There are still areas of bewilderment over the apparent irrationality of some aspects of sport, the near-manic following it commands, the almost suicidal tendencies of some of its participants, and the inexplicable political controversies it occasionally provokes. But, after nine chapters of analytical scuba-diving, in the depths as well as shallow waters, we are hopefully in a better position to comprehend these. For all its supposed lack of reason, we have at least been making sense of sport.

Further reading

'The why of a fan' by A. A. Brill (in North American Review *pt 228, 1929) sounds a very odd and old reference for a chapter speculating on the future of sport, but Brill's arguments are surprisingly relevant and well worth scrutiny.*
Violence and Sport *by Michael D. Smith (Butterworth, 1983) is not so much about the future of sport as about violence related to sport and, as such, overlaps one of the most important issues discussed in this chapter. Smith's book is the best on violence in sport and*

provides many pointers as to the possible future direction of this relationship.

Blowing the Whistle: the Politics of Sport *by Garry Whannel (Pluto Press, 1983) concentrates on the politics* of *(as opposed to in) sport, or as the author puts it, 'the social organization of sport, the institutions that govern it and the values invested in it'. So, Whannel covers many of the areas and themes in this chapter and gives useful grounds for speculating on the future.*

Sport, Leisure and Social Relations *edited by J. Horne, D. Jary and A. Tomlinson (Routledge & Kegan Paul, 1987) has ten essays written by different authors, each devoted to an aspect of current sport.*

Assignment

Describe what role, if any, sport would play in the world as depicted in one of the following futuristic (and, in some cases, fantastic) movies/videos: Terry Gilliam's *Brazil*, in which the world has become a vast bureaucratic labyrinth; Ridley Scott's *Blade Runner*, where androids coexist with human beings; and Stanley Kubrick's *A Clockwork Orange*, in which sadistic violence has become commonplace.

References

Alexander, R. M. (1975) *Biomechanics*, New York: Chapman and Hall.

Allison, L. (ed.) (1986) *The Politics of Sport*, Manchester: Manchester University Press.

Bale, J. (1982) *Sport and Place*, London: C. Hurst.

Bauman, Z. (1979) 'The phenomenon of Norbert Elias', *Sociology* 13: 117–35.

Becker, H. (1953) 'Becoming a marijuana user', *American Journal of Sociology* 59: 235–42.

Beecher, H. K. (1955) 'The powerful placebo', *Journal of the American Medical Association* 159: 1602–6.

Birke, L. and Vines, G. (1987) 'A sporting chance', *Women's International Studies Forum* 10, no. 4: 337–47.

Birtley, J. (1976) *The Tragedy of Randolph Turpin*, London; NEL.

Blue, A. (1987) *Grace Under Pressure*, London: Sidgwick & Jackson.

Brill, A. A. (1929) 'The why of a fan', *North American Review*, pt 228: 429–34.

Brohm, J. M. (1978) *Sport: a Prison of Measured Time*, London: Ink Links.

Brower, J. (1976) 'Professional sports team ownership', *Journal of Sport Sociology* 1, no. 1: 16–51.

Cashmore, E. (1982) *Black Sportsmen*, London: Routledge & Kegan Paul.

Cashmore, E. (1987) *The Logic of Racism*, London: Allen & Unwin.

Coakley, J. J. (1978) *Sport in Society*, St Louis, Mississippi: Mosby.

Curtis, J. and Loy, J. (1978) 'Race/ethnicity and relative centrality of playing positions in team sport', *Exercise and Sport Sciences Review* 6: 285–313.

David, R. (1989) *Lester Piggott: Downfall of a Legend*, London: Heinemann Kingwood.

Davis, P. W. and Solomon, E. P. (1974) *The World of Biology*, 2nd edn New York: McGraw-Hill.

Dunning, E. and Sheard, K. (1979) *Barbarians, Gentlemen and Players*, Oxford: Martin Robertson.

Dunning, E., Murphy, P. and Williams, J. (1988) *The Roots of Football Hooliganism*, London: Routledge & Kegan Paul.

Edwards, H. (1970) *The Revolt of the Black Athlete*, New York: Free Press.

197

References

Edwards, H. (1973) *Sociology of Sport*, Homewood, Illinois: Dorsey Press.

Elias, N. (1982) *The Civilizing Process*, 2 vols, New York: Pantheon.

Elias, N. (1986a) 'Introduction', in N. Elias and E. Dunning (eds) *Quest for Excitement*, Oxford: Blackwell.

Elias, N. (1986b) 'An essay on sport and violence', in N. Elias and E. Dunning (eds) *Quest for Excitement*, Oxford: Blackwell.

Elias, N. and Dunning, E. (eds) (1986) *Quest for Excitement*, Oxford: Blackwell.

Eitzen, D. and Sanford, D. (1975) 'The segregation of blacks by playing position in football', *Social Science Quarterly* 5, no. 4: 948–59.

Eitzen, D. and Yetman, N. (1977) 'Immune from racism?' *Civil Rights Digest* 9, no. 2: 3–13.

Fasting, K. (1987) 'Sports and women's culture', *Women's Studies International Forum* 10, no. 4: 361–8.

Glossop, M. (1982) *Living with Drugs*, London: Temple Smith.

Goldlust, J. (1988) *Playing for Keeps*, Melbourne: Longman Cheshire.

Gruneau, R. (1983) *Class, Sports and Social Development*, Amherst, Massachusetts: University of Massachusetts Press.

Gruneau, R. (1984) 'Commercialism and the modern Olympics', in A. Tomlinson and G. Whannel (eds) *Five Ring Circus*, London: Pluto Press.

Guelke, A. (1986) 'The politicisation of South African sport', in L. Allison (ed.) *The Politics of Sport*, Manchester: University of Manchester Press.

Guttmann, A. (1978) *From Ritual to Record*, New York: Columbia University Press.

Guttmann, A. (1986) *Sports Spectators*, New York: Columbia University Press.

Hain, P. (1982) 'The politics of sport and apartheid', in J. Hargreaves (ed.) *Sport, Culture and Ideology*, London: Routledge & Kegan Paul.

Hardin, G. and Bejema, C. (1978) *Biology: its Principles and Implications*, 3rd edn, San Francisco: W. H. Freeman.

Hare, N. (1973) 'The occupational culture of the black fighter', in J. Talamini and C. Page (eds) *Sport and Society*, Boston, Massachusetts: Little, Brown.

Hargreaves, J. (1982) 'Sport, culture and ideology', in J. Hargreaves (ed.) *Sport, Culture and Ideology*, London: Routledge & Kegan Paul.

Hargreaves, J. (1986) *Sport, Power and Culture*, Oxford: Polity Press.

Hargreaves, J. (1987) 'The body, sport and power relations', in J. Horne, D. Jary, and A. Tomlinson (eds) *Sport, Leisure and Social Relations*, London: Routledge & Kegan Paul.

Harris, M. (1988) *Culture, People, Nature*, 5th edn, New York: Harper & Row.

Hart, M. and Birrell, S. (eds) (1981) *Sport in the Sociocultural Process*, 3rd edn, Dubuque, Iowa: Brown.

Henderson, E. (1949) *The Negro in Sports*, Washington, DC: Associated Publishers.

Hoberman, J. (1984) *Sport and Political Ideology*, Austin, Texas: University of Texas Press.

Hoch, P. (1972) *Rip Off the Big Game*, New York: Anchor Doubleday.

Hoggett, P. (1986) 'The taming of violence', *New Society* (17 October): 36.

Holt, R. (1979) *Sport and the British*, Oxford: Oxford University Press.

Horne, J., Jary, D., and Tomlinson, A. (eds) (1987) *Sport, Leisure and Social Relations*, London: Routledge & Kegan Paul.

Horrell, M. (1968) *South Africa and the Olympic Games*, Johannesburg: Institute of Race Relations.

Huddleston, T. (1956) *Naught for Your Comfort*, London: Collins.

Jiobu, R. (1988) 'Racial inequality in a public arena', *Social Forces* 67, no. 2: 524–34.

Jones, S. J. (1987) 'State intervention in sport and leisure in Britain between the wars', *Journal of Contemporary History* 22: 163–82.

Jones, S. J. (1989) *Sport, Politics and the Working Class*, Manchester: Manchester University Press.

Kane, M. (1971) 'An assessment of black is best', *Sports Illustrated* 34, no. 3: 78–83.

Lapchick, R. (1984) *Broken Promises*, New York: St Martin's Press/Marek.

Lapchick, R. (1986) *Fractured Focus*, Lexington, Massachusetts: Heath.

Levine, L. (1977) *Black Culture and Black Consciousness*, New York: Oxford University Press.

Levins, R. and Lewontin, R. (1985) *The Dialectical Biologist*, Cambridge, Massachusetts: Harvard University Press.

Lorenz, K. (1966) *On Aggression*, New York: Harcourt, Brace and World.

Loy, J. and McElvogue, J. (1970) 'Racial segregation in American sport', *International Review of Sport Sociology* 5: 5–23.

Lucking, M. (1982) 'Sport and drugs', in J. Hargreaves (ed.) *Sport, Culture and Ideology*, London: Routledge & Kegan Paul.

Lukas, G. (1969) *Die Körperkultur in frühen Epochen der Menschenentwicklung*, East Berlin: Sportverlag.

Lüschen, G. (1976) 'Cheating', in D. Landers (ed.) *Social Problems in Athletics*, Illinois: University of Illinois Press.

McCrone, K. (1988) *Sport and the Physical Emancipation of English Women, 1870–1914*, London: Routledge.

McIntosh, P. (1979) *Fair Play*, London: Heinemann Educational. ✳

Mandell, R. (1971) *The Nazi Olympics*, New York: Macmillan.

Mandell, R. (1984) *Sport: a Cultural History*, New York: Columbia University Press.

Marsh, P., Rosser, E., and Harre, R. (1978) *The Rules of Disorder*, London: Routledge & Kegan Paul.

Mason, T. (1988) *Sport in Britain*, London: Faber & Faber.

Mason, W. H. and Marshall, N. L. (1983) *The Human Side of Biology*, New York: Harper & Row.

Michener, J. (1976) *Sports in America*, New York: Random House.

References

Midgley, M. (1979) *Beast and Man: the Roots of Human Nature*, London: Methuen.

Morris, D. (1981) *The Soccer Tribe*, London: Cape.

Mottram, D. (ed.) (1988) *Drugs in Sport*, London: E. & F. N. Spon.

Novak, M. (1976) *The Joy of Sport*, New York: Basic Books.

Olsen, J. (1968) *The Black Athlete*, New York: Time Life.

Poliakoff, M. (1987) *Combat Sports in the Ancient World*, New Haven: Yale University Press.

Ramsamy, S. (1984) 'Apartheid, boycotts and the games' in A. Tomlinson and G. Whannel (eds) *Five Ring Circus*, London: Pluto Press.

Richards, G. (1987) *Human Evolution*, London: Routledge & Kegan Paul.

Rigauer, B. (1981) *Sport and Work*, New York: Columbia University Press.

Riordan, J. (1980) *Soviet Sport*, Oxford: Blackwell.

Riordan, J. (1982) 'Sport and communism – on the example of the USSR', in J. Hargreaves (ed.) *Sport, Culture and Ideology*, London: Routledge & Kegan Paul.

Robins, D. (1982) 'Sport and youth culture', in J. Hargreaves (ed.) *Sport, Culture and Ideology*, London: Routledge & Kegan Paul.

Sammons, J. (1988) *Beyond the Ring*, Camden, New Jersey: University of Illinois.

Scott, J. (1971) *The Athletic Revolution*, New York: Free Press.

Silva, J. and Weinberg, R. (eds) (1984) *Psychological Foundations of Sport*, Champaign, Illinois: Human Kinetics.

Smith, M. D. (1983) *Violence and Sport*, Toronto: Butterworth.

Snyder, E. and Spreitzer, E. (1983) *Social Aspects of Sport*, 2nd edn, Englewood Cliffs, New Jersey: Prentice-Hall.

Stoddart, B. (1988) 'Sport, cultural imperialism and colonial response in the British empire', *Comparative Studies in Society and History*, part 30 (October): 649–73.

Triesman, D. (1984) 'The Olympic games as a political forum', in A. Tomlinson and G. Whannel (eds) *Five Ring Circus*, London: Pluto Press.

Villee, C. A. (1977) *Biology*, 7th edn, London: W. B. Saunders.

Wankel, L. (1982) 'Audience effects in sport', in J. Silva and R. Weinberg (eds) *Psychological Foundations in Sport*, Champaign, Illinois: Human Kinetics.

Whannel, G. (1983) *Blowing the Whistle: the Politics of Sport*, London: Pluto Press.

Widmeyer, W. N. (1984) 'Aggression–performance relationships in sport', in J. Silva and R. Weinberg (eds), *Psychological Foundations of Sport*, Champaign, Illinois: Human Kinetics.

Wilson, E. O. (1975) *Sociobiology: the New Synthesis*, Cambridge, Massachusetts: Harvard University Press.

Wilson, N. (1988) *The Sports Business*, London: Piatkus.

Vamplew, W. (1989) *Pay Up and Play the Game*, London: Cambridge University Press.

Vinnai, G. (1973) *Football Mania*, London: Ocean Books.
Zajonc, R. (1965) 'Social facilitation', *Science* 149: 269–74.
Zolberg, V. (1987) 'Elias and Dunning's theory of sport and excitement', *Theory, Culture and Society* 4: 571–5.

Name and subject index

Name and subject index

Title index